THE CHEFS GUIDE

TO AMERICA'S BEST RESTAURANTS

Visit us on the World Wide Web at
www.chefsguide.com

For more information, call us at
1-888-311-CHEF (2433)

Copyright ©1999
Publication date March 1999

THE CHEFS' GUIDE, INC.
Post Office Box 4001
Aspen, Colorado 81612

ACKNOWLEDGMENTS

We would like to thank the following people for their support: Bland Nesbit for her dedication to excellence, her literacy, and her layout expertise; Michael Bonds of Studio MB, for his great taste, artistry, and coordination skills; Scott Hankinson at Snowmass Tech for his digital wizardry and logical mind; Jessica Lorber for a beautiful web site; and all the chefs who took time out from their busy days in order to help us realize this book...

Charles and Aimée Dale
October, 1998

THE 10 MOST MENTIONED RESTAURANTS IN AMERICA

Ten restaurants stand out as "The Most Mentioned Restaurants in America." We determined this completely impartially by tallying the total number of times they were selected as a favorite by different chefs, at no prompting from us. Please join us in congratulating them as the most popular and respected restaurant chefs among their peers.

1. **Restaurant Daniel, N.Y.C., NY**
   Chef: Daniel Boulud

2. **The French Laundry, Yountville, CA**
   Chef: Thomas Keller

3. **Gramercy Tavern, N.Y.C., NY**
   Chef: Tom Colicchio

4. **Charlie Trotter's, Chicago, IL**
   Chef: Charlie Trotter

5. **Jean-Georges, N.Y.C., NY**
   Chef: Jean-Georges Vongerichten

6. **Nobu, N.Y.C., NY**
   Chef: Nobu Matsuhisa

   Spago Beverly Hills, L.A., CA
   Chef: Wolfgang Puck, Lee Hefter

7. **Chez Panisse, San Francisco, CA**
   Chef: Alice Waters

8. **Aureole, N.Y.C., NY**
   Chef: Charles Palmer

   Gotham Bar and Grill, N.Y.C., NY
   Chef: Alfred Portale

   Lespinasse, N.Y.C., NY
   Chef: Christian Delouvrier

9. **Patria, N.Y.C., NY**
   Chef: Douglas Rodriguez

   Zuni, San Francisco, CA
   Chef: Judy Rodgers

10. **Mary Elaine's, Phoenix, AZ**
    Chef: George Mahaffey

    Union Pacific, N.Y.C., NY
    Chef: Rocco DiSpirito

Note: all the groupings indicate tied scores.

TABLE OF CONTENTS

TABLE OF CONTENTS

INTRODUCTION

Does the world really need another dining guide? I guess that depends on who's doing the guiding...When we began the *Chefs' Guide*, it was in response to frequent questions from customers and friends who would ask us for a dining recommendation during their travels. People just sort of assume that chefs know the best places to eat. And they're probably right! I'm not going to waste a precious night off on an overpriced, under-flavored meal with perfunctory service, nor are my colleagues. Hence *The Chefs' Guide*, your ticket to the inside track on dining in America.

We polled one hundred and seventy-eight chefs from around the country, all recognized professionals who comprise our "chef contributors." A complete alphabetical list of the contributing chefs follows this introduction. Each chef was asked to choose three favorite restaurants in his or her home state, as well as three more from the U.S. as a whole. We asked them to comment on each of their "picks," and have printed their opinions in the form of quotes after each restaurant's information. We have kept all of the chefs' quotes anonymous, in order to protect the privacy and the integrity of our contributors.

The "chosen" restaurants were also asked to provide us with some amusing anecdotes about life in "the biz," and the chefs were asked for some cooking tips which we could share with our readers. We hope you find it amusing, entertaining, and educational reading, and that you might apply some of the pearls of wisdom you will find scattered within these pages…

Most chefs are not an affluent bunch, so you'll find that many of the restaurants featured in this book won't cause you to empty your savings account. Nevertheless, we do tend to go all-out on occasion, and there are plenty of opportunities in here to do that, too!

The Chefs' Guide does not claim to be a comprehensive guide to all the good restaurants in America, yet you can be certain that if a restaurant is in this book, no matter how humble it may appear, the food will be excellent. We think you will find *The Chefs' Guide to America's Best Restaurants* to be an extremely reliable resource when choosing a place to dine tonight.

And wherever you might find yourself, may you always live, love, and dine well!

LIST OF CONTRIBUTING CHEFS

Jody Adams
Rialto

David Adjey
Stonehouse Restaurant

Vince Alberici
The Marker

Claire Archibald
Café Azul

Angelo Auriana
Valentino

Daniele Baliani
Pignoli

Ben Barker
Magnolia Grill

Paul Bartolotta
Spiaggia

Mario Batali
Po

Rick Bayless
Frontera Grill

Rafih Benjelloun
*Imperial Fez
Moroccan Restaurant*

Jean-Michel Bergougnoux
*L'Absinthe Brasserie and
Restaurant*

Donia Bijan
L'Amie Donia

Kevin Bloodwin
Capitol Grill

Philippe Boulot
Heathman Restaurant

Daniel Boulud
Daniel

Terrance Brennan
Picholine

Albert Breuers
The Old Guard House Inn

Frank Brigtsen
Brigtsen's

Edward Brown
The Sea Grill

Scott Bryan
Indigo

David Burke
Park Avenue Café

Bruce Carey
Zefiro Restaurant & Bar

Mark Carter
*Restaurant 301
at The Hotel Carter*

Robert Carter
Peninsula Grill

Kathy Cary
Lilly's

Ann Cashion
Cashion's Eat Place

Joe Castro
The English Grill

Jack Chaplin
Daddy Jack's Lobster House

Danny Chevlair
*Nicholas Nickolas, The
Restaurant*

Michael Chiarello
Tra Vigne

Marshall Chin
Mon Jin Lau

Richard Cingolani
Café Arugula

Josiah Citrin
JiRaffe Restaurant

Ralph Conte
Raphael Bar-Risto

Jack Cory
Bexley's Monk

John Currence
City Grocery

Scott Martin Cutaneo
Le Petit Château

Sanford D'Amato
Sanford

Charles Dale
Renaissance and The R Bistro

Derek Davis
Kansas City Prime

Olivier De Saint Martin
*Dock Street Brewery and
Restaurant*

Jean-Robert de Cavel
Maisonette

Scott deLarme
LuLu Grille

Traci Des Jardins
Jardiniere Restaurant

Marcel Desaulniers
The Trellis Restaurant

James Didier
Vaqueros Restaurant

Christopher Dillon
Park Bistro

Rocco DiSpirito
Union Pacific

Eric DiStefano
Geronimo

Johnny Earles
Criolla's

Jonathan Eismann
Pacific Time

Mark Ellman
Avalon

Todd English
Olives

Odette Fada
San Domenico

Andrew Feinstein
Savona

John Folse
Lafitte's Landing Restaurant

Ted Fondulas
Hemingway's

Susanna Foo
Susanna Foo Chinese Cuisine

Diane Forley
Verbena Restaurant

Mark Franz
Farallon

Beverly Gannon
Haliimaile General Store

Thomas Gay
The Wildflower Inn

George Germon and
Johanne Killeen
Al Forno

Emilio Gervilla
Emilio's Tapas

Roland Gibert
72 Market Street
Oyster Bar & Grill

Debbie Gold
The American Restaurant

Mike Gray
Hanover Inn

Christopher Gross
Fermier Brasserie

Dale R. Gussett
L'Antibes

Philippe Haddad
The Abbey Restaurant

Gordon Hamersley
Hamersley's Bistro

Mark Haugen
Tejas

Maria Helm
Plumpjack Café

Gerald Hirigoyen
Pastis

Cameron Howard
Windham Hill Inn

Mark Jakobsen
The Fort Restaurant

Wally Joe
KC's

David Paul Johnson
David Paul's Lahaina Grill

Jean Joho
Brasserie Jo

Ephraim Kadish
China Grill

Stephen Kalt
Spartina

Donna Katzl
Café For All Seasons

Chrysa Kaufman
Rancho Pinot Grill

Anne Kearney
Peristyle

Katy Keck
New World Grill

Hubert Keller
Fleur de Lys

Loretta Keller
Bizou Restaurant & Bar

continued on following page

Thomas Keller
The French Laundry

Melissa Kelly
*Old Chatham
Sheepherding Co. Inn*

Matthew Kenney
Matthew's

Robert Kinkead
Kinkead's

DK Kodama
*Sansei Seafood Restaurant
& Sushi Bar*

Gray Kunz
Black Diamond of Provence

Emeril Lagasse
*Emeril's New Orleans
Fish House*

Roland Liccioni
Le Francais

Lisa Magadini
Club XIX

Steven Martorano
Café Martorano

Nobu Matsuhisa
Matsuhisa

**Lidia Matticchio
Bastianich**
Felidia

George Mavrothalassitis
Seasons

Thomas McEachern
1848 House

Robert McGrath
Roaring Fork

Jeff McMahon
Saucebox Café & Bar

Bruce McMillian
Tony's

**Mary Sue Milliken and
Susan Feniger**
Border Grill

Michael Mina
Aqua

Rob Mobilian
Piñons

Nick Morfogen
Nick & Max

Trish Morrissey
*Philadelphia Fish
and Company*

Carrie Nahabedian
Gardens Restaurant

Cary Neff
Cary Restaurant and Bar

Fortunato Nicotra
Felidia

Wayne Nish
March

Adam Odegard
Lexington Square Café

Toru Oga
Ginza Japanese Restaurant

Martin Oswald
Syzygy

Jeffrey Paige
The Creamery

Jean-Louis Palladin
Napa

Charlie Palmer
Aureole

**Mark Peel and Nancy
Silverton**
Campanile

Jacques Pepin
L'Ecole

Guillermo Pernot
Vega Grill

Georges Perrier
Le Bec-Fin

Harlan Peterson
Tapawingo

Don Pintabona
Tribeca Grill

Odessa Piper
L'Etoile

John Platt
*Q's Restaurant -
Boulderado Hotel*

Pierre Pollin
Le Titi de Paris

Monica Pope
*Monica Pope's
Boulevard Bistrot*

Alfred Portale
Gotham Bar and Grill

Nora Pouillon
Nora

Kevin Rathbun
Nava

Thierry Rautureau
Rover's

Roland and Sheila Richter
Pizza Etc.

Casey Riley and Eric Salnave
Agora Restaurant

David Robins
Spago Las Vegas

Hans Rockenwagner
Rockenwagner

Judy Rodgers
Zuni Café

Douglas Rodriguez
Patria

Michael Romano
Union Square Café

Luis Rubio
Vallones

Alain Sailhac
L'Ecole

Thomas Salamunovich
Sweet Basil

Oliver Saucy
Darrel & Oliver's Café Maxx

Jimmy Schmidt
The Rattlesnake Club

Cory Schreiber
Wildwood Restaurant

Pierre Schutz
Vong

Scott Schwartz
Carbo's Café

Bill Shapiro
BLT's Cobblefish

Lydia Shire
Biba

Jimmy Sneed
The Frog and The Redneck

Hiro Sone
Terra

Susan Spicer
Bayona

Tim Stephenson
Friends Lake Inn

Frank Stitt
Highlands Bar & Grill

Alessandro Stratta
Mirage Hotel

Allen Susser
Chef Allen's Restaurant

Jay Swift
South City Kitchen

Michael Symon
Lola

Mark Tarbell
Tarbell's Restaurant

Christian Thornton
Asia Nora

Matthew Tivy
La Cremaillère

Charlie Trotter
Charlie Trotter's

Anthony Uglesich
Uglesich's Restaurant

Ken Vedrinski
Dining Room at The Woodlands

David Walford
Splendido at The Château

Tyler Wiard
Mel's Bar & Grill

Robert Wiedmaier
Aquarelle at The Watergate Hotel

Michael Wild
Bay Wolf Restaurant

Janos Wilder
Janos Restaurant

Charles Wiley
The Latilla Restaurant-The Boulders

Brill Williams
The Inn at Sawmill Farms

Roy Yamaguchi
Roy's

Matthew Yohalem
Bistro 315

Joshua Young
Café Absinthe

ALABAMA

Bottega Restaurant and Café

2240 Highland Avenue South
Birmingham, AL 35205
(205) 939-1000 • Fax (205) 939-1165
Dinner Only M.-Sa.
Decor: A handsome restaurant in a Beaux-Arts,
limestone building with Italian tile floors and
walnut panels; also a bustling café with Pompeii-red
walls, a wood-burning pizza oven and a beautiful
courtyard for outdoor dining. 110 Seats,
Restaurant. 55 Seats, Café.

Frank Stitt   Dean Robb

Mediterranean

Parmesan Soufflé with Porcini and Prosciutto.
Italian Seafood Stew with Lobster, Tuna, Mussels,
Sweet Peppers, Tomatoes and Saffron Broth.

"Great pasta, pizza, and Mediterranean-Italian
food." "A beautiful setting!"

$$$ AMERICAN EXPRESS   VISA   MasterCard

Dreamland Bar-B-Que

1427 14th Avenue South
Birmingham, AL 35205
(205) 933-2133
Website www.dreamlandbbq.com/ribs
Lunch and Dinner 7 Days.
Decor: An eclectic restaurant with neon and lots of
memorabilia. 115 Seats.

Michael Stewart

Barbecue

Barbecued Ribs.

"Have the hickory-smoked ribs!"

$ AMERICAN EXPRESS   VISA   MasterCard   DISCOVER

ALABAMA

Birmingham

Highlands Bar & Grill

2011 11th Avenue South
Birmingham, AL 35205
(205) 939-1400 • Fax (205) 939-1405
Dinner Only Tu.-Sa.
Decor: An alluring, softly lit dining room with
French vintage posters, art deco lamps and rich
yellow walls. 74 Seats, Dining Room. 30 Seats, Bar.

Frank Stitt   Pardis Sooudi

Provençal

Grilled #1 Tuna with Pink-Eyed Pea Hoppin'
John and Tomato Chutney Aioli. Lamb Noisettes
au Pistou on Little Field Peas with Golden
Chanterelles and Tomato Confit.

"A cerebral approach to contemporary Southern."
"Very creative, elegant combinations." "The wine
list is extremely well chosen!"

$$$

Hot and Hot Fish Club

2180 11th Court South
Birmingham, AL 35205
(205) 933-5474 • Fax (205) 933-6243
Website www.hotandhotfishclub.com
Dinner Only Tu.-Sa.
Decor: A bustling room featuring a limestone
dining counter, open kitchen, wood-fired oven and
six-foot windows. 80 Seats, Dining. 20 Seats, Patio.

Christopher Hastings   Idie Hastings

American-Contemporary

Hot and Hot Heirloom Tomato Salad with
Fried Okra, Field Peas and Basil Vinaigrette.
Southern Bouillabaisse with Florida Hoppers, Low
Country Clams, Soft-Shell Crab and Black Grouper
with Spicy Tomato Rouille.

"A star team to watch. An old-fashioned idea with a
modern style: he's in the kitchen, she's in the dining
room..." "Very creative, delicious cuisine."

$$$

2

ALABAMA

Taj India

2226 Highland Avenue South
Birmingham, AL 35205
(205) 939-3805 • Fax (205) 939-0730
Lunch and Dinner 7 Days.
Decor: An Indian palace in the Southeast. 70 Seats.

 Manjeet Singh   Rosy

Indian

Tandoor Oven-Roasted Meats. Samosa Chat.
Curries.

"The gracious owners serve authentic and delicious
Indian food."

A gentleman came in to meet a woman he hadn't seen in 10 years. As he waited at the bar, a woman came in and threw her arms around him. We seated them, but not five minutes later the man came over to whisper, "I don't know this woman!" We gave him another seat on the other side of the restaurant, and soon his true friend turned up. Meanwhile, another man waiting for his date went to the podium to whisper that he'd seen the woman he planned to meet after ten years hugging, kissing and sitting with another guest...All ended well!

Tarbell's Restaurant

Tip: Remember...the eyes eat before the mouth. **Manjeet Singh** *Taj India*

The Marx Bros. Café

627 West 3rd Avenue, Anchorage, AK 99501
(907) 277-6279 • Fax (907) 258-6279
Website www.marxcafe.com
Dinner Only 7 Days.
Decor: An intimate restaurant located in a small,
historic Anchorage house with original Alaskan art
and stained glass. 45 Seats.

 Jack Amon   Van Hale

 Asian-Pacific Rim

 Halibut baked in a Macadamia Nut Crust
with Coconut Curry and Mango Chutney. Deviled
Crabcakes with Chipotle Mayonaise. Warm Wild
Berry Crisp with Alaskan Birch Syrup and Butter
Pecan Ice Cream.

"Definitely look this place up. They're getting a
very good reputation!" "The best in the area!"

ANECDOTES & COOKING TIPS

Tip: Soaked lemongrass sticks are great for skewering and grilling shrimp. *Janos Wilder, Janos Restaurant*

Following the tradition of the annual Festival of Colors, every patron is asked to wear white clothes and indulge freely in playing with colored chalk. It gets pretty wild sometimes!
Taj India

Tip: Use a heavy ceramic or marble pestle in a circular, stirring motion, to press raspberries or roasted tomatoes through a large sieve to remove seeds and skins. Much easier than a spoon!
Chrysa Kaufman, Rancho Pinot Grill

ARIZONA

Palo Verde-The Boulders

34631 North Tom Darlington Drive
Carefree, AZ 85377
(602) 488-9009 • Fax (602) 488-4118
Lunch and Dinner 7 Days.
Decor: A colorful, exciting restaurant featuring an exhibition kitchen, patio seating and a fabulous view of the golf course. 70 Seats.

 Jarett Forsberg  Anna Smith

 Regional Southwestern

Adobo-Braised Duck Tamale with Jicama-Radish Slaw. Red Chile-Roasted Chicken with Hominy-Squash Stew. Plantain-Crusted Gulf Snapper with Mole Amarillo.

"Innovative Southwestern cuisine! Bold flavors, dramatic presentations, everything expertly prepared." "Great food and service."

$$$ [AMERICAN EXPRESS] [VISA] [MasterCard] [◎] 👔

The Latilla at The Boulders

34631 North Tom Darlington Drive
Carefree, AZ 85377
(602) 488-9009 • Fax (602) 488-4118
Breakfast and Dinner Only 7 Days.
Decor: A rustic yet elegant Arizona adobe lodge with curved walls, soft lights and dramatic views of the famous boulders. 120 Seats.

 Mary Nearn Wayne Williams

 American

Apple, Endive and Walnut Salad with Port Vinaigrette. Peppered Scallops with Roasted Beets, Field Greens and Crisp Leeks. Pan-Seared Florida Gulf Snapper and Grilled Asparagus with Couscous and Tomatoes.

"New American cuisine, prepared with the finest ingredients, in a sophisticated and romantic atmosphere."

$$$ [AMERICAN EXPRESS] [VISA] [MasterCard] [◎] 👔

ARIZONA

Cave Creek

Crazy Ed's Satisfied Frog

6245 East Cave Creek Road
Cave Creek, AZ 85331
(602) 488-3317 • Fax (602) 488-2601
Website www.chilibeer.com
Lunch and Dinner 7 Days.
Decor: Down-home Western-style microbrewery
with views of the Sonoran Desert. Indoor and
outdoor dining. 250 Seats.

🍴 Maria Chilleen 🍽 Brian Straight

🔥 American 🍸 🍷

⭐ "Awesome" Mesquite Barbecue. Famous
Platters of Whole Fried Chicken. Prime Steaks.

"Fun, Fun, Fun!" "Delicious home cooking without
the cleanup. And the beer is outrageous!" "A place
for the whole family."

💲💲 AMERICAN EXPRESS VISA MasterCard DISCOVER 🛋

Phoenix

Fermier Brasserie

Biltmore Fashion Park, 2584 East Camelback Road
Phoenix, AZ 85016
(602) 522-2344 • Fax (602) 468-0188
Website www.fermier.com
Lunch and Dinner 7 Days.
Decor: A casual, fun restaurant with a South-of-
France ambiance, featuring 100 wines by the glass.
140 Seats.

🍴 Christopher Gross 🍽 Paola Embry Gross

🔥 French-Modern 🍸 🍷

⭐ House-Smoked Salmon. Terrine of Hudson
Valley Foie Gras ABC. Parnassienne of Chocolate
Mousse.

"Christopher and Paola are the reigning king and
queen of Phoenix cuisine!"

💲💲💲 AMERICAN EXPRESS VISA MasterCard DISCOVER 🛋

8

ARIZONA

Honey Bear's BBQ

5012 East Van Buren, Phoenix, AZ 85008
(602) 273-9148 • Fax (602) 273-0617
Lunch and Dinner 7 Days.
Decor: Country-style, down-home Southern feeling.

Mark Smith and Gary Clark

Sherry Leach

Barbecue

Pork Spare Ribs. Cowbro Beans. Pulled Pork.
"You don't need teeth to eat their meat!"

Los Dos Molinos

8646 South Central, Phoenix, AZ 85040
(602) 243-9113
Lunch and Dinner Tu.-Sa.
Decor: A funky, hip, colorful, New Mexican-style restaurant. 100 Seats.

Victoria Chavez

Regional Southwestern

Enchilada Dinner. Carne Adovada. Award-Winning Margaritas.

"Salsa like napalm, incredible Adovado Ribs, and great margaritas." "Excellent New Mexican that has been written up in The New York Times and every major magazine."

ARIZONA

Phoenix

Pizzeria Bianco

623 East Adams Street, Phoenix, AZ 85004
(602) 258-8300
Lunch Tu.-F. Dinner Tu.-Su.
Decor: The rustic restaurant features vaulted
ceilings, exposed brick and butcher block tables.
36 Seats.

Chris Bianco

Italian-Pizza

Wise Guy Pizza: House-Smoked Mozzarella,
Fennel Sausage, and Wood-Roasted Onions.
Antipasto of Wood-Roasted Seasonal Vegetables
with Soppressata and Italian Cheeses.

"Chris represents what I love about life and food;
keep it simple, have fun and do your best."
"Naturally-leavened crust, hand-selected, vine ripe
tomatoes, daily-made mozzarella and garden-fresh
herbs, all baked in his brick, wood-burning oven.
The ultimate pizza!"

Tarbell's Restaurant

3213 East Camelback Road
Phoenix, AZ 85018
(602) 955-8100 • Fax (602) 955-8181
Website www.tarbells.com
Dinner Only 7 Days.
Decor: A comfortable restaurant with warm
lighting, a wood-fired oven and a great bar crafted
of birdseye maple and cherrywood. 110 Seats.

Thomas Freimuth   Jim Gallen

American

Smoked Rock Shrimp with Plum Tomato
Relish and Focaccia Bread. Mr. Fish of the
Moment. Mark's Big Veg Plate with Mixed Grains,
Hummus and Parsley Gremolata.

"Creative cuisine in a fun and lively setting!"

10

ARIZONA

Mary Elaine's at The Phoenician

6000 East Camelback Road
Scottsdale, AZ 85251
(602) 941-8200 • Fax (602) 947-4311
Website www.thephoenician.com
Dinner Only Tu.-Sa.
Decor: Located on the upper level of the hotel,
Mary Elaine's is a sophisticated, elegant dining
room with breathtaking views of the sunsets and
city lights. 190 Seats.

George Mahaffey   Victorio Gonzales

American-Contemporary

Filet of Turbot with Almonds, Fresh Hearts of
Palm, Black Truffles and Whipped Potatoes.

"Passionate food, great view." "Simply some of the
best cuisine in America. An extraordinary
commitment to quality." "The place to go for top
ingredients prepared in surprisingly simple ways."
"Always exceptional."

Rancho Pinot Grill

6208 North Scottsdale Road
Scottsdale, AZ 85253
(602) 468-9463 • Fax (602) 443-7616
Dinner Only Tu.- Sa.
Decor: A comfortable, sophisticated room with a
vintage, cowboy-kitsch atmosphere featuring an
open kitchen. 60 Seats.

Chrysa Kaufman   Tom Kaufman

American-Contemporary

Nonni's Sunday Chicken. Mesquite-Grilled
Lamb Chops with Flageolet Beans and Preserved
Lemon. Lentil Cakes with Cucumber-Yogurt Sauce.

"This is a dynamic couple: Tom does the wine,
Chrysa does the food. They complement each other
well." "Beautifully prepared food, fabulous wine."

11

ARIZONA

Scottsdale

Restaurant Hapa

6204 North Scottsdale Road
Scottsdale, AZ 85253
(602) 998-8220 • Fax (602) 998-2355
Dinner Only M.-Sa.
Decor: A simple, elegant Asian decor of subtle
green tones, bamboo-framed mirrors, tropical plants
and Zen garden stone walls. 60 Seats.

James McDevitt   Stacey McDevitt

Asian

Chinese Mustard Beef Tenderloin and
Tempura Sweetwater Prawn. Fiery Squid Salad with
Papaya and Lychee in a Spicy Chile Lemongrass
Sauce. Caramelized Banana and Coconut Brûlée
Tart with Coconut Sorbet.

"Great Asian-American that isn't gimmicky, just
pure, wonderful flavor."

$$$ VISA   MasterCard

Roaring Fork

7243 East Camelback, Scottsdale, AZ 85251
(602) 947-0795 • Fax (602) 994-1102
Dinner Only M.-Sa.
Decor: A comfortably handsome American Western
lodge with a centerpiece bar and enclosed patio
featuring a stone hearth fireplace. 140 Seats.

Robert McGrath   Erin O'Brien

American-Regional

Sugar- and Chile-Cured Duckling with Green
Chile Macaroni. Barbecued Back Ribs and Pork
Tenderloin with Blue Cheese Bread Pudding.
"Campfire-Style" Salmon with Sweet Corn and
Tomato Fondue.

"Great chef, great restaurant." "You can smell the
mesquite when you open the car door! "The
experience starts as you drive up and park. Robert
is the consummate host and a fabulous chef!"

$$$ AMERICAN EXPRESS   VISA   MasterCard   DINERS CLUB   DISCOVER

Scottsdale

Sushi Ko

9301 East Shea Boulevard, #126
Scottsdale, AZ 88258
(602) 860-2960 • Fax (602) 860-8570
Lunch M.-F. Dinner 7 Days.
Decor: A cozy, traditional Japanese atmosphere.
70 Seats.

🐩 Dai Hayashi　　🍸 Michiko Hayashi

🚬 Japanese　🍸　🍷

⭐ Shabu-Shabu. Tempura. Sushi.

"Impeccably fresh fish selected and prepared by a
master. Attention to detail and integrity make this
neighborhood sushi bar the best in the state."

$$$　AMERICAN EXPRESS　VISA　MasterCard　① DISCOVER　🛋

Tucson

Café Terra Cotta

4310 North Campbell Avenue
Tucson, AZ 85718
(520) 577-8100 • Fax (520) 577-0615
Website www.cafeterracotta.com
Lunch and Dinner 7 Days.
Decor: An informal, contemporary Santa Fe dining
room overlooking the St. Philips Plaza. 244 Seats.

🐩 Matthew Lash

🚬 Regional Southwestern　🍸　🍷

⭐ Garlic Custard. Jennifer's Tortilla Soup.
Herbed Goat Cheese-Stuffed Prawns. Pork
Tenderloin Adovado with Apricot-Chile Conserve.

"For casual dining at its best, there is no other
choice in the Tucson area!"

$$$　AMERICAN EXPRESS　VISA　MasterCard　① DISCOVER　🛋

13

ARIZONA

Tucson

Janos Restaurant

3770 East Sunrise Drive, Tucson, AZ 85718
(520) 615-6100 • Fax (520) 615-3334
Website www.janos.com
Dinner Only M.-Sa.
Decor: A free-standing hacienda on the grounds of
the Westin La Paloma with spectacular panoramic
views of the entire Tucson Valley, private wine
room, banquet rooms and patio dining. 150 Seats.

 Janos Wilder Diane Gallardo

 French-Southwestern

 Lobster with Papaya in Champagne Sauce.
Wild Mushroom and Brie Relleno with Smoky
Tomato Coulis. Dark Chocolate Jalapeño Ice Cream
Sandwich.

"True to the art, Southwestern creativity."

ANECDOTES & COOKING TIPS

Tip: Use ground dried mushrooms
for an extra flavorful crust on
roasted meats. **Mary Nearn,
The Latilla**

We forgot one day to put the meat on
the bun, and the customer was saying,
"Where's my meat?!" **Honey Bear's BBQ**

Tip: Always cut cherry tomatoes in
half to avoid squirting juice when
eating. **Loretta Keller, Bizou**

One night, while Barry Goldwater was dining at Rancho Pinot, a customer at a nearby table was trying to be "polite" by using his knife and fork to cut corn off the cob. Suddenly, the corn cob slipped, went flying through the air, and landed on Goldwater's table. Unfazed, the Senator said, "No thank you...I've already finished my dinner." *Rancho Pinot Grill*

Tip: For guacamole that's the most nutty and creamy in flavor and texture, just mash the avocado lightly, to a chunky consistency, rather than a purée.
***Mary Sue Milliken
and Susan Feniger, Border Grill***

Berkeley

Café Fanny

1603 San Pablo Avenue
(Southeast Corner of Cedar Street)
Berkeley, CA 94704
(510) 524-5447 • Fax (510) 526-7486
Breakfast and Lunch 7 Days.
Decor: A bright, cheerful stand-up food bar with
high ceilings; original art from Italy and France.

Paula Blosky

French-Italian

Café Au Lait in a Bowl. Buckwheat Crêpes.
Soft-Boiled Farm Eggs, Levain Toast, House
Preserves. Prosciutto di Parma with Garlic Toast.

"I'm an ardent fan of Alice's vision. A simple egg or
a crêpe at Fanny's makes my day!"

Berkeley

Café Rouge

1782 4th Street, Berkeley, CA 94710
(510) 525-1440 • Fax (510) 525-2776
Lunch 7 Days. Dinner Tu.-Su.
Decor: A casual restaurant with a long zinc bar and
a retail meat market, featuring local meats, in the
back. 110 Seats.

Marsha McBride and Kelsie Kerr

John Mark

French Bistro

House Duck Prosciutto with Mâche, Endive
and Radishes in a Mustard Vinaigrette. New York
Steak with Frites, Red Wine and Shallot Butter.

"The charcuterie is celestial, the food a marriage of
Chez Panisse and Zuni Café, longtime homes of
the two chefs."

(ALIFORNIA

Berkeley

Chez Panisse Restaurant & Café

1517 Shattuck Avenue, Berkeley, CA 94709
(510) 548-5525 /5049 café • Fax (510) 548-0140
Website www.chezpanisse.com
Lunch and Dinner M.-Sa.
Decor: The restaurant has a homey feeling with
natural wood, copper fixtures and low lighting.
50 Seats Restaurant. 75 Seats Café.

Alice Waters   Peter Steiner

French-California

Baked Goat Cheese with Salad Greens.
Bouillabaisse Cooked in the Fireplace. Fresh Fruit.

"Simply the best." "Always a must when I visit San
Francisco. Even the most simple items are
mindblowing!" "The only restaurant in the world
that I dream about!"

$$$ AMERICAN EXPRESS   VISA   MasterCard   ①   DISCOVER

Calistoga

Catahoula Restaurant and Saloon

1457 Lincoln Avenue, Calistoga, CA 94515
(707) 942-2275 • Fax (707) 942-5338
Website www.catahoularest.com
Breakfast & Lunch Sa. & Su. Dinner 7 days.
Decor: This funky eatery features colorful, "found"
art work and a beautiful wood-burning oven.
100 Seats.

Jan Birnbaum   Leah Trefry and Scott Topa

Regional Southern

Pork Porterhouse Steak with Red-Eye Gravy,
Soft Sexy Grits and Pickled Cabbage. Tomatoes in
All Their Glory. Southern Fried Rabbit with Dirty
Rice and Collard Greens.

"This is food I could eat every night, great flavor!"
"Creative, REAL food from a Louisiana native."

$$$ VISA   MasterCard   DISCOVER

Eureka

Restaurant 301
at The Hotel Carter

301 L Street, Eureka, CA 95501
(707) 444-8062 • Fax (707) 444-8067
Website www.carterhouse.com
Dinner Only 7 Days.
Decor: An intimate dining room overlooking the tranquil waters of Humboldt Bay. 48 Seats.

Rodger Babel   Rene Pineda

Regional American

Humboldt Bay Oysters. Two Dégustation Menus Nightly, Meat or Seafood. Original preparations of grains and vegetables.

"The gardens are beautiful, there's a great wine list, and the food is some of the best in Northern California!"

$$$ AMERICAN EXPRESS   VISA   MasterCard   ○ DINERS   DISCOVER

Fresno

Echo

609 East Olive Avenue, Fresno, CA 93728
(209) 442-3246 • Fax (209) 229-4838
Lunch M.-F. Dinner 7 Days.
Decor: An open, bustling kitchen is framed by rich, textured colors and a unique blend of local artwork, original 1958 Frank Lloyd Wright chairs, a sleek patio and superb floral treatments. 80 Seats.

Tim Woods   R. Adams Hollard

California

An ever-changing, daily seasonal menu featuring the best meat and produce from a select group of organic, San Joaquin Valley farmers.

"Tim and Adams are offering disarmingly brilliant fare based on the most careful selection of local, organic products. Their effort is heroic and delicious, worth the trip to Fresno."

$$$ VISA   MasterCard   DISCOVER

CALIFORNIA

Mendocino

Café Beaujolais

961 Ukiah Street, Mendocino, CA 95460
(707) 937-5614 • Fax (707) 937-3656
Website www.cafebeaujolais.com
Dinner Only 7 Days.
Decor: California Rustic. 50 Seats.

 Chris Kump and Margaret Fox

French-California

Washington Sturgeon Filet, Pan-Roasted with Truffle Emulsion Sauce and served with House-Made Tagliatelle, Wild Mushrooms, Beets, Pearl Onions and Snap Peas.

"It could be the nearby ocean, it could be the romance, whatever it is, it's great!"

$$$

Monterey

The Sardine Factory Restaurant

701 Wave Street, Monterey, CA 93940
(831) 373-3775 • Fax (831) 373-4241
Website www.sardinefactory.com
Dinner Only 7 Days.
Decor: Four unique rooms: Cannery Row for clubby warmth; the Captain's Room for intimacy; the lush-gardened and glass-domed Conservatory; and the award-winning Wine Cellar. 260 Seats.

Bert Cutino and Karl Ilie Staub

Michael Zaouk

Seafood

Sesame-Crusted Tuna on Cucumber-Soba Noodle Salad with Maine Lobster Spring Roll and Wasabi-Soy Vinaigrette. Cornmeal-Crusted Prawns on Soft Polenta with Truffled Pan Sauce.

"Located on Cannery Row, this 20 year-old restaurant has won every fine dining award possible in the United States."

$$$

Brix Restaurant and Wine Shop

7377 St. Helena Highway, Napa, CA 94558
(707) 944-2749 • Fax (707) 944-8320
Website www.brix.com
Lunch and Dinner 7 Days.
Decor: An open, artisan-inspired dining room featuring an exhibition kitchen, fireplace, grand piano and spectacular views of our vineyards, herb gardens and olive groves. 100 Seats.

Tod Michael Kawachi

Curtis M. Jones and Matt Guyot

Fusion

Nori, "Black-n-Blue" Rare, Seared Ahi Tuna with Wasabi Aioli. Thai-Pesto-Grilled Rack of Lamb with Spicy Peanut Saté and Zinfandel Glace. Potato-Crusted Halibut with Asparagus, Braised Leek and Fennel Verjus and Truffle Oil.

"Cuisine prepared by skillful and passionate technicians."

Don Giovanni

4110 St. Helena Highway 29
Napa, CA 94558
(707) 224-3300 • Fax (707) 224-3395
Lunch and Dinner 7 Days. Seasonal.
Decor: A Mediterranean ambiance with terra cotta tile and a nice terrace overlooking the vineyards. 130 Seats.

Donna Scala   Howard Lane

Mediterranean

Grilled Filet of Salmon on a Bed of Mashed Potatoes. Whole Fish Prepared in a Wood-Burning Oven. Pastas.

"Family style. Great atmosphere on Sundays!"
"Deliciously rustic cooking, and a very good wine list!"

CALIFORNIA NORTHERN

Napa

Mustards Grill

7399 St. Helena Highway, Napa, CA 94558
(707) 944-2424 • Fax (707) 944-0828
Lunch and Dinner 7 Days.
Decor: A bright, cheery restaurant with a checkered floor and a covered patio. 85 Seats.

 Louise Branch and Cindy Pawlcyn

 California

Half-Slab of Baby Barbecue Ribs with Crispy Yams and Sweet & Sour Slaw. Grilled Mongolian Pork Chops with Mashed Potatoes.

"An amazing place, surrounded by small farms whose products are used in the kitchen."
"Deliciously hearty cuisine!"

$$$ AMERICAN EXPRESS VISA MasterCard ◎ DISCOVER

Oakland

Bay Wolf Restaurant

3853 Piedmont Avenue, Oakland, CA 94611
(510) 655-6004 • Fax (510) 652-0429
Website www.baywolf.com
Lunch M.-F. Dinner 7 Days.
Decor: A hip, elegant, festive restaurant. 70 Seats, Dining Room. 40 Seats, Terrace.

 Michael Wild

Mark McLeod and Jacinta Bouwkamp

California

Liberty Ranch Duck with Caramelized Onion Flan and Red Wine Sauce.

"No frills, just solid, really good food."

$$$ AMERICAN EXPRESS VISA MasterCard

Pacific Grove

The Fishwife at Asilomar Beach

1996 and-a-half Sunset Drive
Pacific Grove, CA 93950
(831) 375-7107 • Fax (831) 375-4650
Lunch and Dinner 7 Days.
Decor: A warm and friendly Caribbean feeling
done in sea-blue tones with great sunset views.
60 Seats.

Julio Ramirez

Darryl Brewer and Mark Churka

Seafood

Calamari Abalone-Style. Snapper Cancun.
Fresh Key Lime Pie.

"Simple, delightful, and always fresh!"

Palo Alto

L'Amie Donia

530 Bryant Street, Palo Alto, CA 94301
(650) 323-7614 • Fax (650) 323-6139
Dinner Only Tu.-Sa.
Decor: A charming French bistro with a fun and
lively atmosphere and original oil paintings by
Mitchell Johnson. 59 Seats.

Donia Bijan   Chloe Warren

French Bistro

New York Steak Bordelaise with Pommes
Frites. Pan-Braised Sea Bass Wrapped in Lettuce.
Rabbit in Mustard Sauce.

"I could eat this food every day!" "Food that warms
the soul. She cooks from the heart!"

Pebble Beach

Club XIX

17 Mile Drive, Pebble Beach, CA 93953
(408) 625-8519 • Fax (408) 622-8746
Lunch and Dinner 7 Days.
Decor: A bright, airy restaurant with a large patio
on the 18th hole, by the ocean. 64 Seats.

Lisa Magadini   Mario Beretti

French

Lobster Cassoulet. Rack of Lamb with
Roasted Shallots and Oven-Dried Tomatoes.

"The food is very much on a par with the view!"

$$$

Rohnert Park

Hana Japanese Restaurant

101 Golf Course Drive
Rohnert Park, CA 94928
(707) 586-0270
Lunch and Dinner Tu.-Su.
Decor: A modern Japanese restaurant with a patio
overlooking the golf course. 57 Seats.

Shobu Hasegawa & Ken Tominaga

Japanese

Extensive and Exotic Selection of Fresh Fish
from Japan. Grilled Ahi Tuna Steak, Served Rare
with a Creamy Wasabi Sauce.

"In my opinion, the best sushi in the Bay Area. The
five-course chef's menu is only $35. What a
bargain!" "A great Sake list!"

$$

San Anselmo

Insalata's Restaurant

120 Sir Francis Drake Boulevard
San Anselmo, CA 94960
(415) 457-7700 • Fax (415) 457-8375
Lunch M.-Sa. Dinner 7 Days. Sunday Brunch.
Decor: A warm, open, inviting interior with
windows providing lovely views. 130 Seats, Dining
Room. 16 Seats, Outdoor Patio.

Heidi Krahling   Jim Warren

Mediterranean

"Heidi's food is consistently bright, delicious and
generous in spirit. A gracious haven."

San Francisco

Aqua

252 California Street
San Francisco, CA 94111
(415) 956-9662 • Fax (415) 956-5229
Lunch M.-F. Dinner M.-Sa.
Decor: A dramatic triumph in contemporary
restaurant design and decoration. 125 Seats.

Michael Mina   Jean-Claude Persais

Seafood

Medallions of Ahi Tuna (Rare) with Foie Gras.
Tuna Tartare. Caviar Parfait.

"Excellent food and presentation." "One of the
finest young chefs in America. Dining at Aqua is
always a treat."

San Francisco

Betelnut Pejiu Wu

2030 Union Street
San Francisco, CA 94123
(415) 929-8855 • Fax (415) 929-8894
Website www.citysearch7.com/sfo/betelnut
Lunch and Dinner 7 Days.
Decor: An exciting, high-energy restaurant with a tropical, alluring ambiance. 136 Seats.

 Barney Brown   Robert Wellbeloved

Asian-Pacific Rim

Little Dragon Dumplings. Jumbo Black Pepper Prawns.

"By the people who brought us Fog City Diner, Tra Vigne, Bix, et al. It's authentic, it's bustling, it's a gas!" "Go here for truly exotic food."

$$

Bix

56 Gold Street, San Francisco, CA 94133
(415) 433-6300 • Fax (415) 433-4574
Website Microsoft Sidewalk
Lunch M.-F. Dinner 7 Days.
Decor: A 1930's-style supper club with live music nightly and an impressive bar. 100 seats.

Brian Lewis   Luigi Marateo

American

Chicken Hash. Steak Tartare.

"Great food, set in an historic San Francisco supper club. Catch the torch singer!" "It reminds me of the Roaring Twenties. Festive!"

$$$

Bizou Restaurant & Bar

598 Fourth Street
San Francisco, CA 94107
(415) 543-2222 • Fax (415) 543-2999
Website Microsoft Sidewalk
Lunch M.-F. Dinner M.-Sa.
Decor: A bright and lively bistro located in a sunny,
South- of-Market location with easy access from the
Convention Center. 80 Seats.

Loretta Keller   Sean Ellis

French-Italian

Bizou Crisp Italian Flatbread. Beef Cheeks.
Batter-Fried Green Beans.

"A charming room with rustic, delicious food."
"The best bistro in the Bay Area; warm,
approachable and energetic." "Great Beef Cheeks
and attentive, friendly service."

$$$

Boulevard

One Mission Street at Steuart
San Francisco, CA 94105
(415) 543-6084 • Fax (415) 495-2936
Website www.kuleto.com/boulevard
Lunch M.-F. Dinner 7 Days.
Decor: An industrial "Nouveau" interior with
spectacular views of the Bay Bridge and Ferry
Building. 145 Seats.

Nancy Oakes   Kathy King

American-Modern

Cider-Cured Pork Loin. Maine Crab Cakes.
Sautéed Sonoma Foie Gras.

"Fantastic combinations, superb service and
amazing decor." "Fabulous dining experience."
"The best contemporary comfort food in the US."

$$$$

(ALIFORNIA NORTHERN

San Francisco

Café For All Seasons

150 West Portal Avenue
San Francisco, CA 94127
(415) 665-0900 • Fax (415) 753-2480
Lunch M.-Sa. Dinner 7 Days. Sunday Brunch.
Decor: A warm, friendly American bistro with an
open kitchen and a homey appeal. 68 Seats.

Donna Katzl

American Bistro

Chicken Breast Scallopine with Wild
Mushroom Sauce. Café's Mexican Salad.

"As the name implies, you could eat their
unpretentious fare every day, and not tire of it!"

EOS Restaurant and Wine Bar

901 Cole Street, San Francisco, CA 94117
(415) 566-3063 • Fax (415) 566-2663
Dinner Only 7 Days.
Decor: Industrial style with steel accents and
granite tables. 70 Seats.

Arnold Eric Wong   Rajeeb Pradhan

Asian-New

Shiitake Mushroom Dumplings. Lemongrass-
Seared Ahi Tuna Tower. EOS Ginger Caesar Salad.
Blackened Asian Catfish.

"Fabulous exotic flavors!" "This is a young chef
to watch!"

Farallon

450 Post Street, San Francisco, CA 94102
(415) 956-6969 • Fax (415) 834-1234
Website www.kuleto.com/farallon
Lunch M.-Sa. Dinner 7 Days. Bistro Menu M.-Sa.
Decor: The interior is an underwater fantasy
complete with handmade jellyfish, sea urchin light
fixtures and a sweeping "caviar" staircase. 160 Seats.

Mark Franz   Lori Theis

Seafood

House-Made Duck Prosciutto with Red Beet
Gelée, Crisp Artichokes and Truffle. Farallon Hot
Pot with Lobster, Sweet Shrimp, Salmon, Scallops,
Oysters, Glass Noodles, Beech Mushrooms, Bok
Choy, Lotus Root and Ponzu Glaze.

"Wild, creative, technical mastery." "A beautiful
restaurant. Grand old style, cutting edge cuisine."

Fleur de Lys

777 Sutter Street
San Francisco, CA 94109
(415) 673-7779 • Fax (415) 673-4619
Dinner Only M.-Sa.
Decor: An incredibly romantic restaurant that feels
like an immense garden tent set in the French
countryside. 85 Seats.

Hubert Keller   Jeff Miller

French

Pan-Seared Foie Gras on Roasted Rhubarb
and Apples, with a Preserved Ginger and Sauternes
Reduction. Quail Stuffed with Sweetbreads,
Morels, and Spinach, with a Spicy Nutmeg Sauce.

"Gorgeous, delicious and creative food with
Alsatian influence, from a pioneer in modern
French-California cuisine." "The most romantic
spot I can think of."

San Francisco

Fringale

570 Fourth Street
San Francisco, CA 94107
(415) 543-0573 • Fax (415) 905-0317
Website www.citysearch.com/sfo/fringale
Lunch M.-F. Dinner M.-Sa.
Decor: A stylish, compact bistro in San Francisco's
SOMA district. 49 Seats.

 Gerald Hirigoyen   Jean-Baptiste Lorda

French Bistro

Pork Tenderloin Confit with Onion and
Apple Marmalade. Foie Gras Poached in Sauternes.
Crème Brûlée.

"Creative French bistro cooking." "This place is
always a taste treat!"

$$$

Hawthorne Lane

22 Hawthorne Street at Howard
San Francisco, CA 94105
(415) 777-9779 • Fax (415) 777-9417
Website www.hawthornelane.com
Lunch M.-F. Dinner 7 Days.
Decor: A private lane leads to a modern, elegant
restaurant offering a menu built around the
abundance of Northern California. 280 Seats.

Anne Gingrass

Jonathan Mayo and David Gingrass

California

Steamed Halibut with Shiitake Mushrooms,
Gingered Onions and Coriander. House-Smoked
Salmon with Sour Cream Waffles and Sweet Onion
Chutney with Mustard Seeds.

"Great food and service." "Wonderful
contemporary cooking."

$$$

Jardiniere Restaurant

300 Grove Street, San Francisco, CA 94102
(415) 861-5555 • Fax (415) 861-5580
Dinner Only 7 Days.
Decor: High ceilings, exposed brick, custom
metalwork and unique low lighting make this an
intimate and elegant dining experience. 145 Seats.

Tracy Des Jardins   Doug Washington

French-California

Strudel of Chanterelles and Lobster. Seared
Scallops with Truffle Mashed Potatoes. Terrine of
Foie Gras.

"Simple but exquisite, skillfully prepared food."
"Beautiful, updated versions of haute French
cuisine and an excellent wine list." "The best
French-California cuisine in the city. Always
refined, imaginative, fresh and satisfying."

La Folie

2316 Polk Street, San Francisco, CA 94109
(415) 776-5577 • Fax (415) 776-3431
Dinner Only M.-Sa.
Decor: Rich colors set off the dramatically
theatrical motif of La Folie: a cozy, romantic jewel
in the heart of San Francisco's Russian Hill.
60 Seats.

Roland Passot   Georges Passot

French

Roti of Quail and Squab stuffed with Wild
Mushrooms, wrapped in Crispy Potato Strings,
Natural Juice with Truffles. Maine Lobster Salad
with a Spicy Mango and Citrus Vinaigrette.

"Masterful cuisine. Roland is a legend amongst
fellow chefs."

San Francisco

Loongbar

Corner of Beach and Polk Streets
San Francisco, CA 94133
(415) 771-6800 • Fax (415) 771-5275
Dinner Only 7 Days.
Decor: Dramatic Asian restaurant on San Francisco
Bay with piano lounge and private dining room.
155 Seats.

 Mark Miller and John Beardsley

Asian

Kasu-Roasted Sea Bass. "Char Siu" Pork
Shanks.

"Great food, and an authentic, eye-catching,
cool decor."

$$$

Pastis

1015 Battery Street
San Francisco, CA 94111
(415) 391-2555 • Fax (415) 391-1159
Website www.citysearch7.com/sfo/pastis
Lunch M.-F. Dinner M.-Sa.
Decor: A chic, brasserie atmosphere with an
outdoor patio, in San Francisco's "media gulch"
area. 75 Seats.

Gerald Hirigoyen   Jean-Baptiste Lorda

French Bistro

Seared Oxtail Rouelle with Gribiche. Mussels
Steamed in Pastis with Fresh Herbs. Caramel and
Meringue Parfait.

"French-American fusion cuisine in a relaxing and
eclectic atmosphere." "Great place for a first date!"

$$$

Plumpjack Café

3127 Fillmore Street
San Francisco, CA 94123
(415) 563-4755 • Fax (415) 346-9879
Lunch M.-F. Dinner M.-Sa.
Decor: Whimsically theatrical, with subdued tones.
49 Seats.

Maria Helm   Pat Kelly

Mediterranean

Risotto of Baby Artichoke, Pancetta, and
Chèvre. Alsatian Onion Tart.

"Serious food with a sense of humor." "Great,
inexpensive fine dining." "A wine list full of great
finds at reasonable prices. A place you could eat in
every night!"

$$$

Postrio

545 Post Street, San Francisco, CA 94102
(415) 776-7825 • Fax (415) 776-6702
Website www.postrio.com
Breakfast & Lunch M.-F. Dinner 7 Days.
Sa. & Su. Brunch.
Decor: A tri-level design with a dramatic stairway
onto the main floor, featuring art by Rauschenberg,
Rosenquist and Dale Chihuly. 180 Seats.

Mitchell and Steven Rosenthal

Kim Beto

California

Sautéed Salmon with Plum Glaze, Wasabi
Mashed Potatoes and Miso Vinaigrette. Grilled
Squab with Herb Couscous, Date Purée and
Pomegranate Honey Glaze.

"One of the most exciting dining experiences, from
beginning to end." "There's a good reason why they
get those great reviews!"

$$$$

CALIFORNIA

San Francisco

Rose Pistola

532 Columbus Avenue
San Francisco, CA 94133
(415) 399-0499 • Fax (415) 399-8758
Lunch and Dinner 7 Days.
Decor: Rose Pistola has an aura of a long-established institution, with dark, rich woods, leather upholstery, a bustling open kitchen and wood-beamed ceiling. Floor-to-ceiling windows and sidewalk tables allow diners up front to take in the lively North Beach scene. 135 Seats.

Eric Cossolmon and Reed Hearon

John O'Neill

Italian

Cioppino. Grilled Calamari. Gnocchi.

"I love the beautiful display of food as you walk in, as well as the little plates of simple, best quality, tasty ingredients." "Polenta to die for!"

$$$

Straits Café

3300 Geary Blvd., San Francisco, CA 94118
(415) 668-1783 • Fax (415) 668-3901
Website www.citysearch.com/sfo/straitscafe
Lunch and Dinner 7 Days.
Decor: A whimsical look evoking a Singaporean street scene. 100 Seats.

Chris Yeo   Regina Papila

Asian-New

Wok-Roasted Black Pepper Mussels. Chilean Sea Bass En Papillote. Roti Prata.

"Stunning decor and very authentic cuisine from the cross-cultural tables of Singapore."

$$$

San Francisco

Swan Oyster Depot

1517 Polk Street, San Francisco, CA 94109
(415) 673-1101
Lunch Only M.-Sa.
Decor: The same marble counter and stools have been at Swan since 1912.

  Seafood

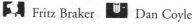 Cracked Dungeness Crab. Oysters and Clams on the Half Shell. Clam Chowder. Fresh and Smoked Fish.

"The absolute best oyster bar in the world."

Tadich Grill

240 California Street
San Francisco, CA 94111
(415) 391-1849 • Fax (415) 391-2373
Website www.citysearch.com/sfo/tadichgrill
Lunch and Dinner M.-Sa.
Decor: Early San Francisco traditional incorporating mahogany woodwork, stained glass and white tablecloths. 115 Seats.

 Fritz Braker Dan Coyle

 Seafood

Seafood Cioppino. Char-Broiled Lamb Chops. Crab and Prawns Casserole "A La Monza."

"The best seafood in the country; the pinnacle in the business."

San Francisco

The Dining Room

The Ritz-Carlton, 600 Stockton Street
San Francisco, CA 94108
(415) 773-6198 or 9518730 • Fax (415) 291-0147
Dinner Only M.-Sa.
Decor: Located in an 89-year-old Nob Hill
landmark, The Dining Room has a relaxed, yet
refined ambiance. 96 Seats.

Sylvain Portay   Kenneth Bryant

French-Modern

Menu changes seasonally.

"Innovative food, interesting menu concept, and
great service!" "Sylvain has cooked in some of the
best restaurants in the world, from Monaco's Alain
Ducasse to New York's Le Cirque!"

$$$$

Thep Phanom Thai Cuisine

400 Waller Street
San Francisco, CA 94117
(415) 431-2526 • Fax (415) 431-2526
Website www.thaitaste.com/thepphanom
Dinner Only 7 Days.
Decor: A cozy and homey candlelit Thai restaurant
reminiscent of an elegant Victorian parlor with
Thai artwork and fresh flowers. 49 Seats.

Miss Pathama Parikanont

Mr. Phonchai Wongsengam

Thai

Seafood and Eggplant Combination with
Southern Thai Spices. Stir-Fried Beef in Chef's
Famous Spicy Sauce with Crispy Basil. Prawns,
Scallops and Calamari in Chef's Special Coconut
Sauce.

"Great Thai food." "Exquisitely tantalizing flavors."

$$

Ton Kiang

5821 Geary Boulevard
San Francisco, CA 94121
(415) 386-8530 • Fax (415) 387-8012
Website www.citysearch.com/sfo/tonkiang
Lunch and Dinner 7 Days.
Decor: A modern-looking Chinese restaurant.
270 Seats.

 William Wong

 Chinese

 Salted Baked Chicken. Dim Sum. Seafood.

"The best dim sum in the world! I think it's better than in Hong Kong!"

Yank Sing

427 Battery Street
San Francisco, CA 94111
(415) 781-1111 • Fax (415) 391-3003
Website www.yanksing.com
Lunch Only 7 Days.
Decor: A modern setting with etched glass, wood floors and bamboo plants. 330 Seats.

CK Chan

Chinese

80 Different Kinds of Dim Sum. Steamed Shrimp Dumplings. Tempura-Style Prawns in a Cilantro Batter.

"My favorite dim sum, fresh, fresh, fresh!" "I always eat too much here!"

(ALIFORNIA NORTHERN

San Francisco

Zuni Café

1658 Market Street
San Francisco, CA 94102
(415) 552-2522 • Fax (415) 552-9149
Breakfast Tu.-Sa. Lunch and Dinner Tu.-Su.
Decor: A dramatic space in a wonderful 1913
building with huge windows and handsome old
brick and steel columns. The wood-burning oven is
a major feature, as is the sweeping bar. 110 Seats.

 Judy Rodgers Ben Caesar

French-Italian

Roast Chicken for Two with Bread Salad.
House-Cured Anchovies with Celery and Parmesan.
75% of the Menu Changes Daily.

"Still as delightful as when I left San Francisco
almost 20 years ago! A modern classic." "Like
home, but challenging." "For the best tarts in the
world, run to Zuni!" "Authentic, rustic, obscure
peasant dishes that are absolutely wonderful!"

$$$

St. Helena

Brava Terrace

3010 St. Helena Highway North
St. Helena, CA 94574
(707) 963-9300 • Fax (707) 963-9581
Lunch and Dinner Th.-Tu. Seasonal.
Decor: A romantic, airy restaurant with a terrace.
150 Seats.

Fred Halpert Lori Turk

French-California

Grilled Portobello Salad with Spinach.
Chocolate Chip Crème Brûlée.

"Imaginative food, and a great local wine list, in a
beautiful Wine Country setting."

$$$

Terra

1345 Railroad Avenue
St. Helena, CA 94574
(707) 963-8931 • Fax (707) 963-0818
Dinner Only W.-M.
Decor: A 114 year-old, native stone building that
feels like an Italian country house. 90 Seats.

🔲 Hiro Sone   🔲 Lissa Doumani

🔲 French-Italian   🔲

⭐ Petite Ragout of Sweetbreads with Wild
Mushrooms, Prosciutto and White Truffle Oil.
Broiled Sake-Marinated Sea Bass with Shrimp
Dumplings in Shiso Broth.

"This is a great husband-and-wife team, who have
fun and make their place fun." "Refined flavors and
elegant dining in a casual atmosphere. I have many
fond memories of this place!"

$$$ VISA   MasterCard   ◑   👔

Tra Vigne

1050 Charter Oak St., St. Helena, CA 94574
(707) 963-4444 • Fax (707) 963-1233
Lunch and Dinner 7 Days.
Decor: The dining room is grandiose, with 30-foot
ceilings, a hand-carved bar and Italian beaded light
fixtures. Like a Florentine Palazzo. 120 Seats,
Dining Room. 120 Seats, Courtyard.

🔲 Michael Chiarello and Carmen Quagliata

🔲 Kevin Cronin and Paul Leary

🔲 Regional Italian   🍸   🔲

⭐ Roasted Polenta with a Balsamic Game Sauce.
Rare-Seared Yellowfin Tuna Caponata. Gravenstein
Apple "Bom Baloni" in Rustic Pastry with Warm
Apple Sauce.

"I recently ate here three times in five days; the
food needs to be experienced to be believed!"

$$$ VISA   MasterCard   ◑   DISCOVER   🛋️

CALIFORNIA

Yountville

The French Laundry

6640 Washington Street
Yountville, CA 94599
(707) 944-2380 • Fax (707) 944-1974
Lunch F.-Su. Dinner 7 Days. Seasonal.
Decor: Country charm and elegance in a historic stone building that was once a French steam laundry. 62 Seats.

 Thomas Keller   Laura Cunningham

American-Progressive

Whole Roasted Foie Gras with Black Truffles and Pink Pearl Apples. Butter-Poached Maine Lobster with Wilted Green Leeks, Pommes Maxine and Red Beet Essence. Coffee and Doughnuts: Coffee Semifreddo with a Cinnamon-Sugar Glazed Doughnut.

"Thomas Keller has taken food to a new level; the Tongue and Cheek will blow your mind!" "A true innovator." "The French Laundry is THE restaurant in the Napa Valley." "This is one of the most romantic restaurants on Earth!" "Certainly one of my most memorable meals!" "A whirlwind of flavors, textures, ideas, and a never-ending stream of new china..."

$$$$ AMERICAN EXPRESS   VISA   MasterCard

Tip: Telling a boiled egg from a raw one: give it a spin. A hard boiled egg will spin easily; a raw egg won't spin at all. To coat something lightly with olive oil: fill a plastic squeeze bottle with olive oil. Holding the bottle 12 to 18 inches from the ingredients, give a couple of quick squeezes to provide a light, even coating of oil. **Hubert Keller, Fleur de Lys**

I'm not sure how funny, but we had a kitchen fire at 5:00 pm on Valentines Day, 1990! **The Marx Bros. Café**

Tip: When cooking meats or poultry, season before cooking and after cooking, and then let rest. The second seasoning helps to achieve a nice flavor and the resting period allows the juices that have collected in the center to redistribute throughout the meat or poultry. **Josiah Citrin, JiRaffe**

ANECDOTES & COOKING TIPS

Tip: When cooking with kaffir lime leaf, always split the leaf from the middle line. This brings more aroma to the food. **Miss Pathama Parikanont, Thep Phanom Thai**

One day, a line cook meticulously cut up what he thought was a truffle, for the truffled mashed potatoes. He discovered the truffle was actually a disk of squid ink when the mashed potatoes turned jet black! **Farallon**

Tip: When making mango puree, add part of the skin to intensify the flavor and brighten the color. **Roland Passot, La Folie**

Beverly Hills

Matsuhisa

129 North La Cienega Boulevard
Beverly Hills, CA 90211
(310) 659-9639 • Fax (310) 659-0492
Lunch M.-F. Dinner 7 Days.
Decor: A simple, elegantly comfortable Japanese
restaurant. 80 Seats.

Nobuyuki Matsuhisa   Eriko Sakai

Japanese

New-Style Sashimi. Sashimi Salad. Broiled
Black Cod Marinated in Miso Sauce.

"Asian 'tapas' at their finest!" "The best Japanese
food by the most creative and likeable chef in the
world." "The food of tommorrow."

Beverly Hills

Spago Beverly Hills

176 North Canon Drive
Beverly Hills, CA 90210
(310) 385-0880 • Fax (310) 385-9690
Lunch M.-Sa. Dinner 7 Days.
Decor: A large, bright, airy restaurant with pastels
and light wood tones. 200 Seats.

Wolfgang Puck and Lee Hefter

Chuck Craig

California

Roasted Beet Salad with Goat Cheese and
Citrus-Shallot Vinaigrette. Grilled Côte de Boeuf
with Braised Celery, Sweet Onions, Pommes Aligot
and Bordelaise Sauce. Kaiser Schmadden: Crème
Fraîche Pancake with Sautéed Chino Strawberries.

"I recently had one of the most inspiring meals of
my life here." "Wonderfully executed food." "Wolf
has found a fantastic chef in Lee Hefter!" "Design,
food and service, impeccable."

CALIFORNIA

Los Angeles

Campanile

624 South LaBrea Blvd.
Los Angeles, CA 90036
(323) 938-1447 • Fax (323) 938-5840
Lunch M.-F. Dinner M.-Sa. Sat.& Su. Brunch.
Decor: Located in Charlie Chaplin's office building, the restaurant features an original Malibu tile fountain, skylights and sophisticated upstairs balconies overlooking the dining room. 200 Seats.

Mark Peel and Nancy Silverton

Jay Perrin and Claudio Blotta

California

Grilled Prime Rib with Black Olive Tapenade, Flageolet Beans and Sautéed Bitter Greens. Risotto Corn Cake with Creamed Corn, Arugula and Roasted Cherry Tomatoes.

"The most honest, flavorful food I know, nothing contrived or fussy." "A sophisticated combination of California and the Mediterranean."

Citrus

6703 Melrose Avenue
Los Angeles, CA 90038
(213) 857-0034 • Fax (213) 939-2694
Website www.citrusinla.com
Lunch M.-F. Dinner M.-Sa.
Decor: A bright, sunny patio atmosphere with lots of plants. 220 Seats.

Michel Richard   Julio Iturbe

French-California

Shiitake Mushroom Torte. Pepper Tuna with Diablo Sauce.

"Simple and elegant preparations, beautifully shown off in an exciting room." "Michel has a great heart, and it shows in the food." "The desserts are just exquisite!"

Gardens Restaurant

The Four Seasons Hotel, 300 South Doheny Drive
Los Angeles, CA 90048
(310) 273-1314 • Fax (310) 385-4931
Website www.fourseasons.com
Breakfast, Lunch and Dinner 7 Days. Su. Brunch.
Decor: A recently renovated, elegantly comfortable
dining room overlooking private gardens. 70 Seats.

 Carrie Nahabedian

 Eric Vievard and Patrice Rozat

 California

 Hot Glazed and Smoked Salmon with Lentils,
Caramelized Onions, Cabbage and Trebbiano
Balsamic Syrup. Kansas City Sirloin, Soufflé of
Goat Cheese and Horseradish with Summer
Onions and Oxtail Red Wine Sauce.

"Creative cooking with a gentle hand." "Carrie is
an extremely talented chef."

$$$$

Hirozen Gourmet

8385 Beverly Boulevard
Los Angeles, CA 90048
(323) 653-0470 • Fax (323) 651-2367
Lunch M.-F. Dinner M.-Sa.
Decor: A tiny, friendly Japanese-style bistro in the
heart of glamorous Beverly Hills. 35 Seats.

 Hiroji Obayashi   Yasuyo Obayashi

 Japanese

 Assorted Seaweed Salad with Ginger Dressing.
Crispy Sautéed Orange Roughy in a Mixed
Mushroom Sauce. Steamed Soba-Stuffed Halibut
with Coconut Curry Sauce.

"Extremely creative sushi and Japanese cuisine as
well as incredible service and attention to detail."
"For a truly intimate Japanese experience..."

$$

Los Angeles

Mimosa

8009 Beverly Boulevard
Los Angeles, CA 90048
(323) 655-8895 • Fax (323) 655-9178
Lunch M.-F. Dinner M.-Sa.
Decor: A warm and earthy bistro with wooden tables, plank floors, antique mirrors and yellow walls filled with photos of family and friends. 48 Seats, Dining Room. 25 Seats, Patio.

Jean Pierre Bosc   Silvio DeMori

French

Bosc's Tomato Tarte Tatin. Veal Braised in a Clay Pot and Sealed with Dough Crust. Duck Confit Cassoulet.

"Hip spot, serving seriously heart-warming food."

$$$ AMERICAN EXPRESS   VISA   MasterCard   ○

Patina

5955 Melrose Avenue
Los Angeles, CA 90038
(213) 467-1108 • Fax (213) 467-0602
Website www.patina-pinot.com
Lunch Tu. Only. Dinner 7 Days.
Decor: Simple and airy, with an air of understated elegance. 100 Seats.

Joachim Splichal   Gary Gotcher

French-California

Perfect Potato Roll of Scallop with Brown Butter Vinaigrette. Grilled, Peppered Ahi Tuna with Baby Bok Choy, Shiitake and a Grilled Scallion Ponzu.

"This is a sophisticated restaurant with great talent in the kitchen. Joachim has a unique style that is much imitated." "Beautifully served New French-California, I love the Potato-Crusted Whitefish." "A unique chef who is rooted in tradition, yet modern." "One of the few places in the world for consistently exquisite dining!"

$$$$ AMERICAN EXPRESS   VISA   MasterCard   ○   DISCOVER

Shibucho

3114 West Beverly Boulevard
Los Angeles, CA 90057
(213) 387-8498 • Fax (213) 387-8498
Dinner Only M.-Sa.
Decor: Tiny, with a bright, classical design.
25 Seats.

 Shige Kudo

Japanese

No menu, only sushi, sashimi and rolls made to order. Traditional.

"The best sushi ever!"

$$$ AMERICAN EXPRESS   VISA   MasterCard

Taiko

11677 San Vicente Boulevard, #302
Los Angeles, CA 90049
(310) 207-7782 • Fax (310) 207-4172
Website www.taiko.net
Lunch and Dinner 7 Days.
Decor: An elegant restaurant featuring natural materials. 80 Seats.

Yasuhiro Fukada and Yoji Tajima

Noriko Fukada and Takeshi Saifo

Japanese

Homemade Soba and Udon Noodles. Sashimi. Grilled Seafood.

"Healthy, delicious, and wonderful!"

$$ AMERICAN EXPRESS   VISA   MasterCard   ◇

Los Angeles

Vida

1930 Hillhurst, Los Angeles, CA 90027
(213) 660-4446 • Fax (213) 660-4449
Dinner Only 7 Days.
Decor: A comfortable restaurant with booths and a slightly Japanese flair. 84 Seats.

Fred Eric   Sylvie Darr

American-Contemporary

Thai Cobb Salad: Crispy Duck on a Warm Spinach Salad with Traditional Cobb Salad Toppings. New Yorkshire: Roasted New York Steak, Yorkshire Pudding, Mashed Potatoes, Cream of Corn and Au Jus.

"Pushes the limits!"

$$

Vincenti Ristorante

11930 San Vincente Boulevard
Los Angeles, CA 90049
(310) 207-0127 • Fax (310) 207-0057
Lunch F. Only. Dinner Tu.-Su.
Decor: An urban, modern dining room with a view of the kitchen and rotisserie grill. 90 Seats.

Gino Angelini   Maureen Vincenti

Italian

Lobster Salad with Citrus Dressing. Green Lasagne with Meat Sauce. Mixed Fresh Rotisserie Fish.

"A perfect trattoria with a truly great chef."

$$$

Malibu

Granita

23725 West Malibu Road, Malibu Colony Plaza
Malibu, CA 90265
(310) 456-0488 • Fax (310) 456-8317
Dinner 7 Days. Sa. & Su. Brunch.
Decor: An abstract interpretation of the water, that
gives an illusion of a three-dimensional watercolor.
180 Seats.

Jennifer Naylor   Jannis Swerman

California

Crispy Potato Galette with Smoked Salmon,
Dill Cream and Salmon Caviar. Four-Cheese
Pansoti with Robiola, Bufala Ricotta, Tuscan
Pecorino and Parmesan Reggiano. Wood-Fire-
Roasted Atlantic Salmon with Red Chard and Five-
Bean Ragout.

"Unusual, creative interpretation of Mediterranean
and Italian dishes." "A superstar chef in the
making!"

$$$

Pasadena

Yujean Kang

67 North Raymond Avenue
Pasadena, CA 91103
(818) 585-0855 • Fax (818) 585-0856
Website www.ladining.com/yujeankangs
Lunch and Dinner 7 days.
Decor: A sophisticated, modern Chinese
atmosphere. 80 Seats.

Yujean Kang   Yvonne Kang

Chinese

Tea-Smoked Duck. Japanese Eggplant with
Garlic and Cilantro.

"Very inventive, yet authentic food!" "This place is
always a treat. The food is exquisitely tantalizing
and the wine list is a major surprise in its depth."

$$

(ALIFORNIA SOUTHERN

Rancho Santa Fe

Mille Fleurs

6009 Paseo Delicias
Rancho Santa Fe, CA 92067
(619) 756-3085 • Fax (619) 756-9945
Website www.millefleurs.com
Lunch M.-F. Dinner 7 Days.
Decor: A romantic, intimate restaurant with a
fireplace and a lovely courtyard, located in exclusive
Rancho Santa Fe. 80 Seats. Private Dining
Available.

Martin Woesle   Bertrand

French-Modern

Menu changes daily.

"Delicious, inventive, the best in the area!"

$$$$

Santa Barbara

Stonehouse Restaurant

San Ysidro Ranch, 900 San Ysidro Lane
Santa Barbara, CA 93108
(805) 969-5046 • Fax (805) 565-1995
Website www.sanysidroranch.com
Lunch and Dinner 7 Days.
Decor: Country elegance in the heart of the
Montecito Hills. 135 Seats.

David Adjey   Tom Fichera

California

Pan-Seared California Foie Gras with a Tarte
Tatin of our own Mission Figs. Lobster 3 Ways:
Broiled Tail, Claw Sausage and Delta Gumbo.
Banana Leaf-Wrapped Sea Bass with Tropical Root
Mash and Cracked Crab Escabèche.

"Creative California cuisine in a comfortable
setting."

$$$$

Santa Barbara

Wine Cask

813 Anacapa, in El Paseo
Santa Barbara, CA 93101
(805) 966-9463 • Fax (805) 568-0664
Website www.winecask.com
Lunch and Dinner 7 Days. Sa. & Su. Brunch.
Decor: High ceilings with gold-leafed exposed
beams, reminiscent of a Spanish hacienda. 80 Seats,
Dining Room. 40 Seats, Outdoors.

David Cecchini   Leslie Tucker

California

Ahi Tuna. Pheasant Ravioli. Foie Gras.

"Creative Californian cuisine!" "The wine list is
frankly one of the best in the world, and fairly
priced, to boot!"

$$$

Santa Monica

Border Grill

1445 4th Street, Santa Monica, CA 90401
(310) 451-1655 • Fax (310) 394-2049
Website www.bordergrill.com
Lunch Tu.-Su. Dinner 7 Days.
Decor: A stylishly funky, pleasantly raucous place,
with decor as wild as a fiesta to match the bold
foods and flavors of Mexico and Central America.
120 Seats.

Mary Sue Milliken & Susan Feniger

Kevin Finch

Mexican

Grilled Skirt Steak. Pescado Veracruzano.

"The place in L.A. for South-of-the-Border
cuisine." "If you think they're great on TV, you
should taste them in person!"

$$$

Santa Monica

Chinois on Main

2709 Main Street, Santa Monica, CA 90405
(310) 392-9025 • Fax (310) 396-5102
Lunch W.-F. Dinner 7 Days.
Decor: Bright, with an innovative and modern
look. 90 Seats.

Wolfgang Puck & Makoto Tanaka

Lisa Brady

Asian-French

Whole Sizzling Catfish with Ginger and
Ponzu Sauce. Cantonese Duck with Fresh Plum
Sauce.

"Great style, always tremendous service." "A world-
class adventure in eating!" "The original fusion, all
the rest should look to this master."

$$$

JiRaffe Restaurant

502 Santa Monica Boulevard
Santa Monica, CA 90401
(310) 917-6671 • Fax (310) 917-6677
Lunch Tu.-F. Dinner Tu.-Su.
Decor: Warm, elegant, French style with an airy
balcony and window seating; very welcoming and
friendly. 82 Seats.

Josiah Citrin and Raphael Lunetta

Allison Wetsel

French-American

Roasted Rabbit with Polenta Gnocchi, Oven-
Dried Tomatoes and Basil. Crispy Potato-Wrapped
Ahi Tuna and Foie Gras with Cepes and a Port
Wine Reduction. Crispy Maine Salmon with
Parsnip Purée, Braised Fennel and a Balsamic Nage.

"Great chefs that consistently put out great food."

$$$

Rockenwagner

2435 Main Street, Santa Monica, CA 90405
(310) 399-6504 • Fax (310) 399-7984
Dinner 7 Days. Sa. & Su. Brunch.
Decor: Reminiscent of the welcoming town squares
of Europe, Rockenwagner is a modern-day meeting
place where diners are expected to linger. 101 Seats.

 Hans Rockenwagner  Jacqueline Jo

 French-California

 Crab Soufflé. White Asparagus Dishes, in
season. Napoleon of Salmon with House-Cured
Tomatoes and Basil Sauce.

"A fun celebrity hangout that serves great food!"
"Very charismatic and talented chef-owner..."

$$$![AMEX] ![VISA] ![MasterCard] ![Diners] ![jacket]

Valentino

3115 Pico Boulevard
Santa Monica, CA 90405
(310) 829-4313 • Fax (310) 315-2791
EMail jenvalcat@aol.com
Lunch F. Only. Dinner M.-Sa.
Decor: Valentino is decorated in a subdued,
contemporary palette with lush fabrics from
Missoni. 215 Seats.

Angelo Auriana

Giuseppe Mollica and Arturo Nieto

Italian

Veal Chop with Cream, Prosciutto and
Marsala Wine. Pappardelle with Wild Greens, Fresh
Tomato and Aged Ricotta. Extravaganza Menu.

"Elegant food, great service." "The best Italian food
in the country." "Very gracious owner, impeccable
ingredients, awesome wine list." "The best
dégustation menu anywhere! I go there for great
service, a stupendous wine list and white truffles!"

$$$$![AMEX] ![VISA] ![MasterCard] ![Diners] ![jacket]

Sherman Oaks

Café Bizou

14016 Ventura Blvd
Sherman Oaks, CA 91423
(818) 788-3536 • Fax (818) 986-5550
Lunch and Dinner 7 Days. Su. Brunch.
Decor: Subtle colors. 150 seats.

Neil Rogers   Philippe Gris

French Bistro

Sesame-Coated Salmon on a bed of Potato
Pancakes with Mushrooms in a Red Wine Sauce.
Steak au Poivre with Mashed Potatoes.

"Well-executed, contemporary French cuisine
presented with finesse and priced lower than
anyone expects."

$$$

Posto

14928 Ventura Boulevard
Sherman Oaks, CA 91403
(818) 784-4400 • Fax (818) 986-0971
Lunch M.-F. Dinner M.-Sa.
Decor: A warm, contemporary style, decorated in
earth tones and washed with candlelight. 160 Seats.

Luciano Pellegrini   Santo Selvaggio

Italian

Smoked Bacon-Wrapped Snails on Garlicky
Spinach in a Red Wine Sauce. Spaghetti Alla
Chitarra with Butter and Sevruga Caviar. Grilled
Pork Loin with Fresh Figs and Roasted Garlic.

"Rustic country Italian by a chef who is full of
sensitivity and talent."

$$$

South Pasadena

Shiro

1505 Mission Street
South Pasadena, CA 91030
(626) 799-4774 • Fax (626) 799-9560
Dinner Only Tu.-Su.
Decor: Simple and elegant. 70 seats.

Hideo Yamashiro   Sherrill Bailey

Asian-French

Whole Sizzling Catfish. Ravioli with Shrimp Mousse and Shiitake Mushroom Sauce.

"Limited nightly menu with all items done to perfection. Expect a great meal!"

$$$

Venice

72 Market Street
Oyster Bar & Grill

72 Market Street, Venice, CA 90291
(310) 392-8720 • Fax (310) 392-8665
Website www.72marketst.com
Lunch M.-F. Dinner 7 Days.
Decor: An intimate, converted art gallery with armored steel, concrete and oxidized copper, designed by Morphosis. 94 Seats.

Roland Gibert   Michael Sorensen

Global

72 Market Street Meatloaf. Kickass Chili. Venice Banana Napoleon. Oysters. Mashed Potatoes.

"Home cooking like your mother used to make, but better!"

$$$

CALIFORNIA

West Hollywood

Raku

1106 North La Cienega Boulevard, #201 & 202
West Hollywood, CA 90069
(310) 657-4519 • Fax (310) 657-1587
Dinner Only W.-M.
Decor: A restaurant serving Korean and Japanese
family dishes with nice city views. 48 Seats.

Bangja Hong

Asian

Deep-Fried Zucchini Flower Stuffed with
Shrimp and Mushrooms. Korean Pancake. Halibut
Sashimi Salad.

"Simple, authentic, very fresh." "Homey and
relaxing. Great flavors!"

Spago Hollywood

1114 Horn Avenue at Sunset Boulevard
West Hollywood, CA 90069
(310) 652-3706 • Fax (310) 657-0927
Dinner Only Tu.-Su.
Decor: The main dining room overlooks Sunset
Boulevard and the LA basin. The garden room has
a tropical feeling with a waterfall. 150 Seats.

Wolfgang Puck   J. Michael Dargin

California

Smoked Salmon Pizza. Truffle Risotto
(seasonal). Chinese-Style Duck.

"Consistently great food."

Tip: Balance your sauces with acid, such as lemon juice, lime juice or vinegar. **Hans Rockenwagner, Rockenwagner Restaurant**

At the end of a very busy Saturday night, a prankster guest stole all of the car keys from our valet, and ran off with them...just imagine the panic!!! *Fleur de Lys*

Tip: Chicken cooked under a brick promotes even, crispy skin.
Eric Cossolman, Rose Pistola

ANECDOTES & COOKING TIPS

Tip: Do not cut squid into rings, but rather slice the tube lengthwise in half, then cut into 1½ inch-long strips, before a quick dunk in the hot oil. **Kent Rigsby, K2U Bar and Grill**

A recently divorced woman and her date were seated next to her recent ex-husband and his date... *Jardiniere*

Tip: Fish is done when it is firm but still juicy and has just turned from translucent to opaque. If you cook fish until it flakes, it will be tough and dried out. **Julio Ramirez, The Fishwife at Asilomar Beach**

COLORADO

Ajax Tavern

685 East Durant Avenue, Aspen, CO 81611
(970) 920-9333 • Fax (970) 920-2004
Lunch and Dinner 7 days. Seasonal.
Decor: A modern, tavern-style dining room at the base of Aspen Mountain. 76 Seats.

 Tobias Lawry

California

Pan-Roasted Sweet Potato Gnocchi in a Wild Mushroom Salad. Oven-Roasted Lamb Sirloin with Garlic-Oil Mashed Potatoes.

"Always good comfort food, attentive service, and an unbeatable location!"

$$$

Blue Maize

308 South Hunter, Aspen, CO 81611
(970) 925-6698
Dinner 7 Days.
Decor: An intimate restaurant with festive decor inspired by the owners' travels through Central America. 40 Seats.

Thomas Colosi   Richard Chelec

Regional Southwestern

Grilled Elk Tenderloin with Cranberry-Pasilla Sauce. Banana-Wrapped Sweet Potato Tamale. Wild Mushroom Burrito with Sundried Tomato Pesto and Smoked Yellow Pepper Sauce.

"This is a chef to watch! Amazing, creative flavors in a casual, fun environment."

$$$

COLORADO

Aspen

Cache Cache

205 S. Mill, Aspen, CO 81611
(888) 511-3835 • Fax (970) 544-8248
Website www.cachecache.com
Dinner Only 7 days. Seasonal.
Decor: An intimate room decorated in flesh-tone hues with soft lighting and leather banquettes. 100 Seats Restaurant 55 Seats Patio.

Michael Beary   Jodi Larner

French Bistro

Grilled Salmon with Spinach, Tomato Fondue, Basil, and Olive Purée with Grilled Eggplant. Spit-Roasted Pheasant, served with Grilled Shiitakes, Portobellos, Leeks, and Potato Croquettes.

"A lively place for intimate casual dining in Aspen." "Heart-warming country fare, and always a friendly greeting.""

$$$

Jimmy's
American Restaurant and Bar

205 S. Mill St., Aspen, CO 81611
(970) 925-6020 • Fax (970) 925-6048
Dinner Only 7 Days.
Decor: Rocky Mountain comfort with city sophistication. 105 Seats.

Jimmy Yeager and Kevin Ribich

Bernadette Williams

American Bistro

Chesapeake Jumbo Lump Blue Crab Cakes. Thirty-Five Day Dry-Aged Ribeye Steak. Veal Porterhouse Steak.

"For casually elegant dining with the whole family." "Some of the best crabcakes and chocolate chip cookies I've ever had!" "The best Mescal Bar in America. Watch out!"

$$$

Kenichi

533 East Hopkins, Aspen, CO 81611
(970) 920-2212 • Fax (970) 920-9831
Website www.kenichi.com
Dinner Only 7 Days. Seasonal.
Decor: A hip, high-energy restaurant with minimalist yet warm design features. Sculptures are by the chef-owner. 85 Seats.

Kenichi Kanada and Douglas Kesler

Scott Brasington

Asian

Blackened Tuna. Dynamite Shrimp. Bamboo Salmon. Cutting-Edge Sushi.

"Always the happening place to be!" "Excellent, creative entrées and super sushi!" "I never fail to be sated and surprised!"

$$$

Matsuhisa Aspen

303 East Main Street, Aspen, CO 81611
(970) 544-6628 • Fax (970) 544-6630
Dinner Only 7 Days.
Decor: A modern take on traditional Japanese design, featuring a bamboo ceiling, and a steel "water wall." 120 Seats.

Nobu Matsuhisa

Anthony Nocifera, Nobuko & Jeffrey Klein

Japanese

Yellowtail Jalapeño. Black Cod with Miso. Sashimi Salad.

"Amazing flavors, presentation and atmosphere." "The in-place to see and be seen while dining on masterfully prepared, healthy food."

$$$$

COLORADO

Aspen

Piñons

105 South Mill Street, Aspen, CO 81611
(970) 920-2021 • Fax (970) 920-9035
Website www.pinons.com
Dinner Only 7 Days. Seasonal.
Decor: An atmosphere evoking a warm mountain lodge tucked high in the Rockies. 110 Seats.

🔪 Rob Mobilian 🍴 Frank Chock

♨ American 🍸 🍷 Jeff Walker

⭐ Lobster Strudel. Pheasant and Foie Gras. Dover Sole.

"Heart-warming food in an elegant, typically Aspen environment." "The place to people-watch!"

$$$$ AMERICAN EXPRESS   VISA   MasterCard 👔

Renaissance and The R Bistro

304 East Hopkins Avenue, Aspen, CO 81612
(970) 925-2402 • Fax (970) 925-6634
Website www.renaissancerestaurant.com
Dinner Only 7 Days. Seasonal.
Decor: Warm earth tones, soft lighting and tented ceilings create casual mountain elegance and romance. The colorful and lively R Bistro features an outdoor patio and stupendous views. 50 Seats, Restaurant. 40 Seats, Bistro.

🔪 Charles Dale and Barclay Dodge

🍴 Pamela McLain

♨ French-Modern 🍸 🍷 Steve Humble

⭐ Sautéed Fresh Foie Gras with Honey-Roasted Pears and Maple-Candied Pecans; Expresso-Blackened Tenderloin of Beef with Tobacco and Shallot Sauce. Tasting Menu. Vegetarian Menu.

"Great-tasting, intelligent cuisine; Renaissance gets better all the time!" "A very good personal friend, a very passionate chef and a great musician, I'm most proud of my best alumni."

$$$$ AMERICAN EXPRESS   VISA   MasterCard 🌐 DISCOVER 👔

COLORADO

Aspen

Restaurant at The Little Nell

675 East Durant Street, Aspen, CO 81611
(970) 920-6330 • Fax (970) 920-6328
Lunch and Dinner 7 Days.
Decor: Elegant, spacious room, with a view of
Aspen Mountain. Summer patio with swimming
pool. 120 Seats.

Keith Luce   Keith Brown

American   Robert Stuckey

Mustard-Crusted Trout. Grilled Elk Loin with
Quinoa. Colorado Rack of Lamb.

"Another great chef comes to Aspen!"

$$$$

Syzygy

520 East Hyman, Aspen, CO 81611
(970) 925-3700 • Fax (970) 925-5593
Dinner Only 7 Days.
Decor: Syzygy is known for the warmth of its
contemporary art deco interior, intuitive
architectural detail, high class jazz acts and great
mountain views. 80 Seats.

Martin Oswald   Walt Harris

American-New   Jay Fletcher

Artichoke Salad with Roasted Bell Peppers,
Shaved Parmesan Reggiano, Limestone Lettuce and
Cavalli Balsamic. Seared, Ginger-Crusted Big Eye
Ahi with Coconut-Rice Cakes, Wasabi and Yellow
Pepper-Kaffir Lime Leaf Sauce. Elk Tenderloin with
Warm Sundried Fig Chutney, Ancho Chile Aioli
and Port Reduction.

"A very talented chef; lots of integrity in his style."

$$$

COLORADO

Aspen

The Century Room-Hotel Jerome

330 E. Main St., Aspen, CO 81611
(970) 920-1000 • Fax (970) 920-4190
Website www.hoteljerome.com
Dinner Only 7 Days.
Decor: Step back into history, with rich burgundy velvet banquettes, Italian tapestries, and overstuffed Victorian furniture. 75 Seats.

Todd Slossberg   Grant Maves

Regional American

Jerome Crabcakes with Spicy Fried Angel Hair Pasta and Orange-Chipotle Sauce. Maine Diver Scallops with White Truffle Gnocchi and Artichokes. Colorado Rack of Lamb with a Brown Barley Cassoulet and Pan Reduction.

"A wonderful, friendly place, serving deliciously creative cuisine in a stately environment." "When you want to be pampered, go here!"

$$$$

Avon

Masato's

92 Beaver Creek Place, Avon, CO 81620
(970) 949-0330 • Fax (970) 949-0337
Website www.sushi123.com
Lunch M.-F. Dinner 7 Days.
Decor: A simple, contemporary and traditional Japanese look. 90 Seats.

Masato Okamoto   Masato Okamoto

Japanese

Omakase: Chef's Choice. Albacore Tataki. Extra Crispy Tempura.

"Great sushi in the mountains!"

$$$

(OLORADO

Splendido at The Château

17 Chateau Lane, Beaver Creek, CO 81620
(970) 845-8808 • Fax (970) 845-8961
EMail splendid@vail.net
Dinner Only 7 Days.
Decor: A restaurant reminiscent of an Old World, European château with windows overlooking the ski slopes. 90 Seats.

 David Walford Joanie McVey

 American-New

Wood-Burning Oven-Roasted Lobster and Lamb. Chocolate Soufflé.

"Great American food, and an even better wine list!"

15 Degrees

1965 15th Street, Boulder, CO 80302
(303) 442-4222 • Fax (303) 444-1812
Dinner Only 7 Days.
Decor: A small, intimate dining room with live piano music nightly and an adjoining martini bar. 70 Seats.

 James Mazzio Stewart Allen

 Eclectic

Pacific Ahi Tuna Seared Medium Rare with a Panko-Crusted Potato Cake, Smoked Tomato-Shallot Compote and Wilted Organic Baby Spinach. Gnocchi with Smoked Wild Mushrooms and Essence of Black Truffle in Chicken Bordelaise.

"Creative cooking by a talented young chef."

COLORADO

Boulder

Q's Restaurant-Boulderado Hotel

2115 13th Street, Boulder, CO 80302
(303) 442-4880 • Fax (303) 442-4378
Breakfast, Lunch and Dinner 7 Days.
Decor: A casually elegant room featuring antiques
and historic architecture. 115 Seats.

John Platt   Peter Soutiere

American-Contemporary

Mango BBQ Shrimp Salad. Allspice-Cured
Rotisserie Pork Loin. Hoisin-Glazed Ahi with a
Wild Rice Cake and Carrot Butter.

"This food is as good as any in New York or San
Francisco."

$$$

Denver

Barolo Grill

3030 East Sixth Avenue, Denver, CO 80206
(303) 393-1040 • Fax (303) 333-9240
Dinner Only Tu.-Sa.
Decor: Rustic elegance with grape vines, sepia-
toned walls and hanging dried flowers, Barolo Grill
evokes the warmth and charm of a Tuscan
farmhouse. 120 Seats.

Antonio Walker   Blair Taylor

Italian

Barolo Duckling with Calamata Olives and
Garlic-Rosemary Hashbrown Potatoes.

"A wonderful wine program with true food from
the Tuscan region." "Outstanding wine list with
mind-blowing Barolos and Super Tuscans!"

$$$

Domo Japanese Country Foods

1365 Osage, Denver, CO 80204
(303) 595-8256 • Fax (303) 860-7452
Lunch and Dinner Th.-Sa.
Decor: A Japanese country inn complete with
flagstone tables, natural wood, Japanese gardens and
a folk art museum. 48 Seats.

Gaku Homma   Emily Busch

Japanese

Nabemono (Clay Pot Dishes). Tajimono
(Egg-Based Dishes). Teriyaki.

"An exquisitely different style of Japanese cuisine."

$$ VISA   MasterCard

Mel's Bar & Grill

235 Filmore Street, Denver, CO 80206
(303) 333-3979 • Fax (303) 355-7005
Website www.melsbarandgrill.com
Lunch M.-Sa. Dinner 7 Days.
Decor: A relaxed, happy and fun restaurant with a
lovely patio and live jazz nightly. 140 Seats.

Tyler Wiard and Frank Bonanno

Doug Fleischmann

American-Contemporary

Mussels La Cagouille. Smoked, Grilled Pork
Loin with Green-Chile Hash Browns, Sweet-Corn
Salsa and Shallot Jus. Lump Crab Cake with Asian
Slaw, Green Curry Vinaigrette and Pickled Ginger.

"Denver's most fun serious dining." "A great wine
list, full of hard-to-find gems."

$$$ AMERICAN EXPRESS   VISA   MasterCard   DINERS   DISCOVER

COLORADO

Denver

New Saigon Restaurant

630 South Federal Boulevard
Denver, CO 80219
(303) 936-4954 • Fax (303) 922-7780
Website www.newsaigonmsn.com
Lunch and Dinner Tu.-Su.
Decor: A Vietnamese-countryside feel. 150 Seats.

 Ha Pham

Vietnamese

Seafood in Curry Sauce and Coconut Milk.
Shrimp in Spicy Sauce.

"Fantastic spicy, flavorful food!"

Palace Arms-Brown Palace Hotel

321 17th Street, Denver, CO 80202
(303) 297-3111 • Fax (303) 297-2954
Website www.brownpalace.com
Lunch M.-F. Dinner 7 Days.
Decor: Richly decorated with Napoleonic artifacts
and antiques, the ambiance provides an Old-World
feeling. 76 Seats, plus 24 for Private Dining.

Mark Black and Karl Vogelbacher

Mehran Esmaili

Continental

Lobster Enchiladas. Roasted Colorado Rack of
Lamb. Pan-Seared Venison with Foie Gras.
Chocolate Soup.

"Haute elegance in downtown Denver!" "When
you want to celebrate, go here!"

COLORADO

Zino Ristorante

27 Main Street, Edwards, CO 81632
(970) 926-0444 • Fax (970) 926-0446
Dinner Only 7 Days.
Decor: A "mountain cosmopolitan" interior with
large arched windows that frame the Eagle River,
and a mahogany and zinc bar. 97 Seats, Dining
Room. 86 Seats, Patio. 75 Seats, Bar.

Brand Fibkins

Matt Morgan and Pollyanna Forster

Italian

Iron Skillet Roasted Mussels. Wood-Oven
Fired Pizzas. Veal Chop Milanese.

"Simple, down-to-earth good food."

$$

Sunflower Restaurant

19105 Highway 82, El Jebel, CO 81628
(970) 963-8373
Dinner Only 7 Days.
Decor: A small, casual restaurant with a
contemporary feel, featuring local artists and
modern jazz and blues in the background. 40 Seats,
Dining Room. 24 Seats, Seasonal Patio.

Jon Pell

Vegetarian

Sesame-Crusted Atlantic Salmon with a Miso-
Sake Glaze over Thai Rice Sticks in a Gingered
Vegetable Broth. Tempeh Scallopini with Organic
Brown Rice Pilaf and Steamed Organic Vegetables.
Corn- and Sage-Stuffed Free Range Chicken Breast
with a Shiitake Glaze and Colorado Red Potatoes.

"Our favorite place for dinner-and-a-movie dates."
"Healthy food prepared with love and finesse."

$$$

COLORADO

Morrison

The Fort Restaurant

19192 Route 8, off US 285
Morrison, CO 80465
(303) 697-4771 • Fax (303) 697-4786
Website www.thefort.com
Dinner Only 7 Days. Seasonal.
Decor: Located in the largest adobe building in
Colorado, the restaurant feels like a cozy, romantic
fort with a fireplace, candles and a beautiful view of
Denver. 350 Seats plus Lanai.

Mark Jakobsen   Chris Seres

Regional American

Game Platter: Grilled Medallions of Elk,
Buffalo Tenderloin and Quail. Rack of Lamb on a
Plank with Twice-Baked Orange-Mashed Potatoes.

"I would travel to Colorado just to eat at the Fort!"

$$$ VISA   MasterCard

Vail

Cucina Rustica

174 East Gore Creek Drive, Vail, CO 81657
(970) 476-5011 x177 • Fax (970) 476-7425
Website www.vail.net/thelodge
Seasonal. Dinner only 7 days.
Decor: Reflections of a charming, rustic Tuscan
inn, with large limestone fireplace, oversized
wooden tables and chairs and a spectacular view of
Vail Village. 120 Seats.

Dino DeBell   Shari Mason

Italian

Pork Porterhouse with Fontina Potato Torte
and Cipolinni Onions. Butternut Squash Gnocchi
with Balsamic-Molasses Glaze. Arugula Salad
with Oven-Dried Pears, Candied Walnuts and
Gorgonzola.

"One of the truly great restaurants in the Rocky
Mountains, serving food which has integrity."

$$$ AMERICAN EXPRESS   VISA   MasterCard   DINERS CLUB   DISCOVER

Sweet Basil

193 East Gore Creek Drive, Vail, CO 81657
(970) 476-0125 • Fax (970) 476-0137
Lunch and Dinner 7 Days. Seasonal.
Decor: A casual, comfortable, lively room
that opens onto the creek. 115 Seats, Winter.
140 Seats, Summer.

 Thomas Salamunovich   Mike Dennis

 American-Contemporary

 House-Cured Salmon with Meyer Lemon
Cream and Homemade Caviar. Seared Tuna and
Portobello Napoleon with Spinach and Merlot
Sauce. Nori and Wonton-Crusted Halibut with
Sticky Rice and Vegetable Stir Fry.

"Consistently fun!"

$$$$

The Wildflower Inn

174 East Gore Creek Drive, Vail, CO 81657
(970) 476-5011 x170 • Fax (970) 476-7425
Website www.vail.net/thelodge
Dinner Only 7 Days. Seasonal.
Decor: An elegant celebration of spring indoors
with giant flower arrangements and memorable
views of Vail Village. 80 Seats.

 Thomas Gay   Scott Engelman

 American-Contemporary

 Ahi Tuna Roll with Soy Vinaigrette, Radish
Sprouts and Pickled Ginger. Colorado Lamb T-
Bone with Butternut Squash, Cinnamon-Cap
Mushrooms and Potato Gnocchi.

"Always a vacation favorite!"

$$$

ANECDOTES & COOKING TIPS

Tip: Be focused.
Thomas Keller, French Laundry

One night we ran out of Lemon Sorbet, but a customer was insistent that because it was on the menu, he wanted it. We did our best by squeezing fresh lemon juice and running it through the ice cream machine, but the minute he tasted it his lips puckered so tightly he couldn't say a word. The expression was priceless! *Pastis*

Tip: The best way to store highly-perishable fish or shellfish is on ice. Place your fish in a perforated pan. This will allow the juices and water to drain away. The ice will keep the fish colder than the refrigerator, yet it won't freeze it. **Mark Franz, Farallon**

CONNECTICUT

Restaurant Jean-Louis

61 Lewis Street, Greenwich, CT 06830
(203) 622-8450 • Fax (203) 622-5845
Lunch F. Only. Dinner M.-Sa.
Decor: A bright, contemporary, very romantic
restaurant with lots of art. 45 Seats.

Jean-Louis Gerin   Linda Gerin

French-Modern

Imported Turbot Filet Steamed and Sautéed
with Saffron Mousseline. Breast of Duck and
Sautéed Foie Gras on a Bed of Spinach Salad with
an à l'Orange Sauce.

"Modern, classic cuisine with attentive service. Very
special!"

$$$$

The Lakeview Inn

107 North Shore Road
New Preston, CT 06777
(860) 868-1000 • Fax (860) 868-2595
Website lakeview@frenchculinary.com
Lunch and Dinner W.-M.
Decor: Metropolitan cuisine in a country setting
overlooking Lake Waramaus. 120 Seats, Dining
Room. 65 Seats, Outdoor Deck.

William Lopata

American

Live Lobsters. Sautéed Fresh Water Trout.
Devil's Food Cake.

"Fine dining in the country!"

$$$

Tip: With whole fish, make sure to check the eyes for clearness; the gills should be red, and the fish should have a salty smell which ensures its freshness. **Bert Cutino, The Sardine Factory**

A man was set to propose to his girlfriend, so we put the diamond ring on a crab claw and set the claw on a crab salad. When the waiter brought the first course the woman, seeing the crab salad, quickly declined saying she didn't like crab. The whole restaurant, which by this time was in on the secret, held its breath. Finally she looked down at the salad and saw the ring, let out a shriek and said "YES!" The entire room let out a collective sigh, along with a round of applause! The two are married now with twins. **The Fishwife at Asilomar Beach**

DISTRICT OF COL

1789 Restaurant

1226 36th Street Northwest
Washington, DC 20007
(202) 965-1789 • Fax (202) 337-1541
Website www.clydes.com
Dinner Only 7 Days.
Decor: A gracious, Federal townhouse with the
charm and elegance of a country inn, located in
residential Georgetown. 180 Seats.

Ris Lacoste   William Watts

Regional American

Roasted Rack of American Lamb with Creamy
Feta Potatoes. Alaskan Salmon with Mustard,
Cabbage and Sherried Beets. Macadamia-Crusted
Grilled Shrimp.

"Delicious food set in an elegant Virginia
mansion."

$$$ AMERICAN EXPRESS   VISA   MasterCard   DISCOVER

Aquarelle at The Watergate Hotel

2650 Virginia Avenue, Northwest
Washington, DC 20037
(202) 298-4455 • Fax (202) 337-7915
Breakfast, Lunch and Dinner 7 Days.
Decor: An elegant yet unpretentious setting with a
panoramic view of the Potomac River. 85 Seats.

Robert Wiedmaier   Carlos Mendes

French

Boneless Quail Stuffed with Foie Gras and
Confit of Duck. Napoleon of Icelandic Salmon
with Roasted Garlic Purée. Roasted Rack of Lamb
with White Bean Purée and Lardons of Bacon in a
Cumin-Madeira Sauce.

"Delicious food and wonderful service. What more
could you want?"

$$$ AMERICAN EXPRESS   VISA   MasterCard

DISTRICT OF COL

Washington

Asia Nora

2213 M Street Northwest
Washington, DC 20037
(202) 797-4860 • Fax (202) 797-1300
Website www.noras.com
Dinner Only M.-Sa.
Decor: A romantic, Asian oasis in the middle of the city with artifacts from every corner of the continent. 90 Seats.

Christian Thornton and Nora Pouillon

Scott Palmer

Fusion

Pan-Seared Duck Breast with Wild Mushroom Steamed Buns. Rare Ahi Tuna Tempura with Miso Vinaigrette and Field Greens. Spicy Thai Shellfish Stew in a Coconut-Lemongrass Broth.

"Delicious combinations of different Asian cuisines, prepared with Western techniques."

$$$ VISA   MasterCard   DISCOVER

Bistro Français

3128 M Street NW, Washington, DC 20007
(202) 338-3830 • Fax (202) 338-1421
Continuous from 11am to 3am 7 days.
Decor: Very Georgetown. 75 Seats Restaurant. 75 Seats Café.

Gerard Cabrol   Laurent Pieteres

French Bistro

"A beloved institution that never fails to deliver. Solid bistro cooking and a superb wine list."

$$ AMERICAN EXPRESS   VISA   MasterCard   ①

Café Atlantico

405 8th Street Northwest
Washington, DC 20004
(202) 393-0812 • Fax (202) 393-0555
Lunch M.-Sa. Dinner 7 Days.
Decor: A casual, lively, three-tiered restaurant
with an international, contemporary atmosphere.
120 Seats.

Jose Andres ▮ Andres Rivas

Nuevo Latino

"They're making their own rules when it comes to
food: fun, exciting flavors and presentations."

$$$

Cashion's Eat Place

1819 Columbia Road Northwest
Washington, DC 20009
(202) 797-1819 • Fax (202) 797-0048
Dinner Tu.-Su. Sunday Brunch.
Decor: A sophisticated yet warm and casual dining
room in the heart of D.C.'s lively Adams Morgan
neighborhood. 75 Seats.

Ann Cashion ▮ John Fulchino

American

Curried Mussels with Spinach. Lobster with
Truffle Emulsion. Spit-Roasted Leg of Lamb.

"The consummate neighborhood restaurant; always
expect a good meal!"

$$$

DISTRICT OF COL

Washington

Florida Avenue Grill

1100 Florida Avenue Northwest
Washington, DC 20009
(202) 265-1586 • Fax (202) 332-4655
Breakfast, Lunch and Dinner Tu.-Sa.
Decor: A Southern diner atmosphere. 42 Seats.

Mary Finch and Pauline Alston

Regional Southern

Barbecued Ribs. Baked Turkey. Chicken
Dumplings. Southern Pan-Fried Chicken.

"For 22 years, I've been enjoying their short ribs,
ham hocks, collard greens, and cornbread. I hope it
stays around forever!"

Kinkead's

2000 Pennsylvania Avenue Northwest
Washington, DC 20006
(202) 296-7700 • Fax (202) 296-7688
Lunch and Dinner 7 Days.
Decor: An urban, American brasserie with live
entertainment. 220 Seats.

Robert Kinkead   Mimi Schneider

Seafood

Pepita-Crusted Salmon with Chile, Corn and
Crab Ragout. Grilled Squid with Creamy Polenta
and Tomato Fondue. Tempura Soft-Shell Crab with
Green Papaya Salad.

"Kinkead is the master of the sea; the Fried Clams
will make you beg for more." "Bob puts out some
of the best seafood dishes I've ever had, and always
at a great value."

DISTRICT OF COL

Melrose

1201 24th Street Northwest
Washington, DC 20037
(202) 955-3899 • Fax (202) 785-5122
Breakfast, Lunch & Dinner 7 Days.
Decor: A modern, downtown restaurant
surrounded by windows and known for its fabulous
art work. 90 Seats.

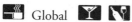 Brian McBride Ritu Duffy

Global

Thai Calamari with Lemongrass and Jalapeño.
Melrose Shrimp Ravioli with Sweet Corn and
Cracked Black Pepper. Colorado Lamb Rack with
Mustard Crust.

"Brian's cuisine is so exciting!"

$$$

Provence

2401 Pennsylvania Avenue Northwest
Washington, DC 20037
(202) 296-1166 • Fax (202) 296-6466
Lunch M.-F. Dinner 7 Days.
Decor: Typically French country. 200 Seats.

 Yannick Cam Carlos Mendes

French

Soup of Artichoke with Parmesan and Black
Truffle. Paupiette of Foie Gras in Cabbage Leaves.

"Good Mediterranean fare from the open wood
grill. The room is wonderful, and so is the service!"
"A great place for leisurely dining!"

$$$$

DISTRICT OF COL

Washington

Red Sage

605 14th Street Northwest
Washington, DC 20005
(202) 638-4444 • Fax (202) 628-8430
Website www.redsage.com
Lunch M.-F. Dinner 7 Days.
Decor: Incorporates the sense of adventure and
vitality of the American West, while preserving the
naturalness of its most mythic region. 385 Seats.

Morou Ouattara and Mark Miller

Bart Bonbrest

American-Contemporary

"Buffalo Bobs": Grilled Buffalo Sirloin,
Buffalo Mushroom Hash, and Chipotle Buffalo
Sope. Grilled Tuna with Shallot Confit Tamale and
Black Bean Sarsaparilla Salsa.

"You haven't eaten until you've had this food!"
"Tantalizing, spicy, awesome flavor combinations!"

$$$

Ruppert's Restaurant

1017 7th Street Northwest
Washington, DC 20001
(202) 783-0699 • Fax (202) 783-2921
Lunch Th. Only. Dinner Tu.-Sa.
Decor: A simple, elegant, romantic restaurant with
an American bistro feel. 65 Seats.

John Cochran   Kenan Forman

American Bistro

Venison Bresaola with Beets. Shad Roe with
Grits and Sorel. The Seasonal Menu Changes Daily.

"Because this place is so small, you get phenomenal
service, intimacy, and perfection!"

$$$

Vidalia

1990 M Street Northwest
Washington, DC 20036
(202) 659-1990 • Fax (202) 223-8572
Lunch M.-F. Dinner 7 Days.
Decor: A charming, American country home.
150 Seats.

 Peter Smith 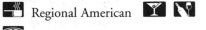 Michael Nevarez

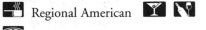 Regional American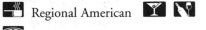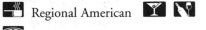

 Shrimp and Grits. Baked Vidalia Onion.
Sautéed Sweetbreads.

"Great New Wave American food." "I've got lots of favorites here."

Anecdotes & Cooking Tips

Tip: When making a tomato sauce from fresh, chopped summer tomatoes, bring the chopped and seasoned tomatoes to a boil to throw their liquid. Strain them, set the pulp aside and reduce the juice, then combine the juice and pulp and start your sauce. This helps the vine ripe tomatoes keep their fresh-tasting integrity by not overcooking the pulp. **Michael Chiarello, Tra Vigne**

One early evening, two men walked into the restaurant and ordered, "Chicken Coconut Soup" without looking at the menu. The soup was served and the men were enjoying it. Thirty minutes later five policemen walked in and handcuffed them. They had just robbed a grocery store. **Thep Phanom Thai**

FLORIDA

Chef Allen's Restaurant

19088 Northeast 29th Avenue
Aventura, FL 33180
(305) 935-2900 • Fax (305) 935-9062
Website www.chefallen.com
Dinner Only 7 Days.
Decor: Light and bright open spaces and an
elegant atmosphere. Glass-enclosed exhibition
kitchen. 120 Seats.

Allen Susser   Dale Lee LoSasso

Global

Caribbean Lobster and Crab Cakes with
Tropical Fruit Chutney. Chocolate Raspberry
Soufflé.

"One of the finest gentlemen in our industry;
outstanding food."

$$$$

Turnberry Isle Resort and Club

19999 West Country Club Drive
Aventura, FL 33180
(305) 932-6200 • Fax (305) 933-6904
Breakfast, Lunch and Dinner M.-Sa.
Decor: The Mediterranean-style, veranda restaurant
has French doors overlooking the courtyard and
pool area. 200 Seats.

Todd Weisz   Rebecca Akin

Regional American

Crispy-Skin Filet of Sea Bass and Cashew-
Dusted Soft-Shell Crab Legs with Citrus-Stewed
Hearts of Palm, Fava Bean, Corn Succotash and
Tamarind-Ginger Butter Sauce. Roast Squab and
Foie Gras with Manchego Cheese Polenta, Apple-
Smoked Bacon-Scented Cabbage, Rhubarb Jam and
Tart Cherry Sauce.

"Elegant dining."

FLORIDA

Boca Raton

Nick & Max

5050 Town Center Circle
Boca Raton, FL 33486
(561) 391-7177 • Fax (561) 392-9308
Website www.maxsrestaurants.com
Lunch M.-F. Dinner 7 Days.
Decor: A contemporary look with high-backed
banquettes and a wood-burning oven. 160 Seats.

Nick Morfogen   Ron Garcia

American

Twenty-Dollar Baked Potato, wrapped in
Bacon with Black Truffle and Gruyère Cheese.

"Bold flavors and extraordinary presentations."
"Elegant rustic cuisine."

$$$$

Coral Gables

Norman's

21 Almeria Avenue, Coral Gables, FL 33134
(305) 446-6767 • Fax (305) 446-7909
Website www.normans.com
Lunch M.-F. Dinner M.-Sa.
Decor: Mediterranean-style building with two huge
wood-burning ovens and interiors by local artists.
160 Seats, Dining Room. 80 Seats, Private Parties.

Norman Van Aken   Jeffrey Wolfe

Global

Yuca-Stuffed Crispy Shrimp with a Sour
Orange Mojo, Torn Greens and Habanero Tartar
Salsa. Down-Island French Toast with Curacao-
Scented and Seared Foie Gras, Brioche, Savory
Passion Fruit Caramel, Turmeric and Gingery
Candied Lime Zest.

"Indigenous is the word. It seems like Norman has
done a serious amount of research." "No one
combines New World ingredients like Norman!"

$$$$

FLORIDA

Brooks Restaurant

500 South Federal Highway
Deerfield Beach, FL 33441
(954) 427-9302 • Fax (954) 427-9811
Dinner Only 7 Days.
Decor: A quiet and sophisticated restaurant with traditional furnishings and wonderful art work. 287 Seats.

 Jon Howe Ali Kaptan and Bo Sanchez

 Continental

 Rack of Lamb with a Mustard-Rum Crust. Grand Marnier and Chocolate Soufflés.

"Large menu, great food and service."

$$$ AMERICAN EXPRESS VISA MasterCard

Delray Beach

32 East

32 East Atlantic Avenue
Delray Beach, FL 33444
(561) 276-7868 • Fax (561) 276-7894
Dinner Only 7 Days.
Decor: A casual but elegant restaurant on two floors with rich mahogany throughout. 190 Seats.

 Wayne Alcaide

 Butch Johnson and Michael Bilton

 American-Contemporary

 Seared Diver Scallops with Truffle Mashed Potatoes and Wild Mushrooms. Grilled Pork Porterhouse with Cuban Black Beans, Mojo and Boniato Chips. Summer Berry Pudding.

"Wonderful daily changing menus, and Butch, the owner, is a blast!"

$$$ AMERICAN EXPRESS VISA MasterCard DISCOVER

FLORIDA

Delray Beach

Damiano's
at The Tarrimore House

52 North Swinton Avenue
Delray Beach, FL 33444
(561) 272-4706 • Fax (561) 272-0858
Dinner Only W.-Su.
Decor: Restored Victorian dating back to 1924,
with a gas fireplace. 60 Seats.

Anthony Damiano   Phil Deberidinas

Florasian

Florasian Lacquered Duck. Phyllo-encased
Florida Grouper. Dessert soufflés.

"Chefs Anthony and Lisa: he's at the stove, and
she's in her 1924 bake shop. Together they make
grand New World Cuisine!"

$$$ AMERICAN EXPRESS   VISA   MasterCard

Fort Lauderdale

Mark's Las Olas Restaurant

1032 East Las Olas Boulevard
Fort Lauderdale, FL 33301
(954) 463-1000 • Fax (954) 463-1887
Lunch M.-F. Dinner 7 Days.
Decor: Floridian and Mediterranean design
elements combined to create a comfortable, boldly
contemporary feel. 126 Seats.

Mark Militello   Thomas Hillan

American-Contemporary

Potato and Goat Cheese Tart. Cracked Conch
with Black Bean-Mango Salsa and Vanilla-Rum
Butter Sauce. Spiny Lobster with Sweet Plantain
Mash and Conch Sauce.

"Mark has been at the forefront of modern
Caribbean cuisine. His food always surprises and
delights!"

$$$ AMERICAN EXPRESS   VISA   MasterCard

FLORIDA

Café Martorano

3343 East Oakland Park Boulevard
Ft. Lauderdale, FL 33308
(954) 561-2554 • Fax (954) 346-5308
Dinner Only M.-Sa.
Decor: Glossy black and white tiles envelop the
dining room and open kitchen from floor to ceiling.
38 Seats.

Steven Martorano   Steven Martorano

Italian

Rigatoni with Sunday Pork Gravy. Grilled
Calamari. Chicken Cutlet with Broccoli Rabe.

"Serious, South Philly-style Italian food, as good as
it gets!" "You feel like you're sitting right in the
chef's kitchen, and he's cooking just for you!"

$$$$

Grayton Beach

Criolla's

170 Scenic Highway 30 A
Grayton Beach, FL 32459
(850) 267-1267 • Fax (850) 231-4568
Website www.criollas.com
Winter, Dinner Only Tu.-Sa.
Summer, Dinner Only 7 Days.
Decor: A bright, casual Caribbean-style restaurant.
176 Seats.

Johnny Earles   Michel Thibault

Caribbean

Barbecued Shrimp. Cascabel Caesar Salad.
Ricotta-Rubbed, Banana-Leaf-Roasted Yellowedge
Grouper.

"Creatively delicious!"

$$$

FLORIDA

Lighthouse Point

Café Arugula

3150 North Federal Highway
Lighthouse Point, FL 33064
(954) 785-7732 • Fax (954) 346-9814
Dinner Only Tu.-Sa.
Decor: A comfortable, Southwestern-American
style restaurant. 120 Seats.

Dick Cingolani

Cuisine of the Sun

Jumbo Lump Crab Cake with Creole Mustard
Sauce. Pecan-Crusted Yellowtail Snapper.

"Great Southwestern and Italian blend!"

$$

Longboat Key

The Colony Dining Room

1620 Gulf of Mexico Drive
Longboat Key, FL 34228
(941) 383-6464 x2200 • Fax (941) 387-0250
Website www.colonybeachresort.com
Breakfast M.-Sa. Lunch & Dinner 7 Days.
Sunday Brunch.
Decor: Elegant surroundings and breathtaking Gulf
views. 200 Seats.

Daniel T. Jackson   Michael Moulton

American-Modern

Pan-Roasted American Snapper with Lump
Crab, Sundried Tomatoes and Basil Beurre Blanc.
Roasted Rack of Colorado Lamb and Merguez
Sausage with Fava Bean Cassoulet and Cracked
Peppercorn Demi Glace.

"The best dining, and a view on Longboat Key."

$$$

FLORIDA

Miami Beach

Astor Place

956 Washington Avenue
Miami Beach, FL 33134
(305) 672-7217 • Fax (305) 672-7607
Lunch and Dinner 7 Days.
Decor: Features a casually chic, open-air atrium with terrazzo floors. 144 Seats.

 Johnny Vinczencz and Dwayne Adams

Steve Monn and Amy Hammond

 Regional American

. Corn-Crusted Yellowtail Snapper with Smoked Pepper Relish and Roasted Corn Sauce. Wild Mushroom Pancake Short Stack, Grilled Portobello, Balsamic Syrup and Sundried Tomato Butter.

"Sophisticated tastes with a 'day-at-the-beach' attitude. I fell in love with the appetizer of velvety tomato soup with mini grilled cheese sandwiches!"
"Great Southwestern-meets-South Florida style."

$$$

China Grill Miami

404 Washington Avenue
Miami Beach, FL 33139
(305) 534-2211 • Fax (305) 534-2565
Lunch M.-F. Dinner 7 Days.
Decor: This 12,000-square-foot restaurant with an intimate champagne, sake and vodka bar is the hot spot for celebrity-watching. 390 Seats.

 Ephraim Kadish   Debra Sackin

Global

Shanghai Lobster. Szechuan Dry-Aged Beef. Pan-Seared Spicy Tuna.

"This place defines the South Beach scene! Fun and interesting food!"

$$$$

89

FLORIDA

Miami Beach

Joe's Stone Crab

227 Biscayne Street, Miami, FL 33139
(305) 673-0365 • Fax (305) 673-0295
Website www.joesstonecrab.com
Lunch Tu.-Sa. Dinner 7 Days. Seasonal.
Decor: A comfortable restaurant with mahogany, brass and terrazzo floors. 512 Seats.

Pedro Morales   Dennis Sutton

Seafood

Stone Crabs (the only place to have them). Fresh Fish.

"The best crabs anywhere!" "I love the rustic atmosphere!" "The quintessential Old South Beach style!" "An institution, need I say more?"

$$$

Nemo Restaurant

100 Collins Avenue, Miami Beach, FL 33139
(305) 532-4550 • Fax (305) 532-4187
Lunch M.-Sa. Dinner 7 Days. Sunday Brunch.
Decor: A funky, eclectic, indoor-outdoor setting with an open kitchen, great jazz and many different dining areas. 200 Seats.

Michael Schwartz and Frank Jennetti

Jeff Berke

American-New

Wok-Charred Salmon over a Four-Sprout Salad.

"Very cool decor, and Mike's the real deal." "A very relaxing Sunday brunch with great desserts."

$$$

FLORIDA

Pacific Time

915 Lincoln Road, Miami Beach, FL 33139
(305) 534-5979 • Fax (305) 534-1607
Lunch M.-F. Dinner 7 Days.
Decor: A loft-like space with distressed walls,
cobalt blue ceiling, theatrical lighting and an open
kitchen. 210 Seats.

 Jonathan Eismann   Gill Alexander

Asian-Pacific Rim

Wok-Sautéed Tuna with Sushi Bar Flavors.
One Duck, Two Flavors-One Hot, One Cold.
Warm Bittersweet Chocolate Bomb.

"Asian-American cuisine with a fabulous Whole
Yellowtail and a delicious Pasta with Miso and
Truffles." "Great seafood with Asian flavors, the
quintessential South Beach restaurant."

$$$ AMERICAN EXPRESS   VISA   MasterCard   DINERS

Tuscan Steak

433 Washington Avenue
Miami Beach, FL 33139
(305) 534-2233 • Fax (305) 534-4718
Dinner Only 7 Days.
Decor: An award-winning decor of wood floors,
mirrors and a field stone wall; a South Beach scene.
150 Seats.

Dewey LoSasso   Steven Haas

Steakhouse

28-ounce Florentine Tuscan T-Bone.
Homemade Gnocchi with Gorgonzola Cream
Sauce. Whole Grilled Garlic Snapper.

"Great Risotto, Gnocchi and a T-Bone not to be
missed!"

$$$ AMERICAN EXPRESS   VISA   MasterCard   DINERS

FLORIDA

Orlando

Chatham's Place

7575 Doctor Phillips Boulevard
Orlando, FL 32819
(407) 345-2992 • Fax (407) 345-0307
Lunch M.-F. Dinner 7 Days.
Decor: Fine dining in an Old New Orleans-style
atmosphere. 65 Seats.

Tony Lopez   Maurice Colindres

Continental

Rack of Lamb. Veal Piccata. Florida Black
Grouper. Mild Cajun Butter Jumbo Shrimp.

"Small, quiet room with creative cuisine."

$$$

Le Coq Au Vin

4800 South Orange Avenue
Orlando, FL 32806
(407) 851-6980 • Fax (407) 248-0658
Lunch Tu.-F. Dinner Tu.-Su.
Decor: A cozy little brown house with three dining
rooms. 95 Seats.

Louis Perrotte

French

Chicken Coq Au Vin. Eggplant Bayoutèche.

"All the chefs in town eat here."

$$$

FLORIDA

Darrel & Oliver's Café Maxx

2601 East Atlantic Blvd.
Pompano Beach, FL 33062
(954) 782-0606 • Fax (954) 782-0648
Website www.cafemaxx.com
Dinner Only 7 Days.
Decor: A comfortable, modern interior featuring an open kitchen and an award-winning wine bar. 110 Seats.

Oliver Saucy

Karen Ota and Darrel Broek

Regional American

Onion-Crusted Snapper with Madeira Sauce.
"Consistently creative, delicious food."

$$$

Michael's On East

1212 East Avenue South, Midtown Plaza
Sarasota, FL 34239
(941) 366-0007 • Fax (941) 955-1945
Website www.bestfood.com
Lunch M.-F. Dinner M.-Sa. Seasonal.
Decor: The newly renovated Michael's On East has a plush decor reminiscent of a 1940's private dining club. 125 Seats.

Keith Doherty   Linda White

Continental

Bowtie Pasta with Grilled Chicken, Pancetta, Shiitake Mushrooms, Sundried Tomatoes, Snow Peas and Light Cream. Seared Chilean Sea Bass with Quinoa Pilaf and Roasted Garlic Lemon Cream. Black Angus Filet of Beef with Wild Mushroom Ragout.

"Another hit from a long-standing local family of restaurateurs!"

$$$

FLORIDA

Tampa

Bern's Steakhouse

1208 South Howard Avenue, Tampa, FL 33606
(813) 251-2421 • Fax (813) 251-5001
Dinner Only 7 Days.
Decor: The restaurant is located on the dock and
features a great collection of antiques. 300 Seats.

 Kim Miller Paul Rainey

 Steakhouse

 Humongous Dry-aged Steak Cuts. Known for
its extensive wine list.

"Incredible steaks and an unbelievable wine list; but
everybody knows that. Just eat here!"

The first day of service at Tra Vigne in 1987, a manager (all 6'4 of him) fell through the ceiling from the attic, bounced off some shelving and landed on the hot line mats at the feet of Michael Chiarello. This set the stage for a never ending wild ride at *Tra Vigne*.

> *Tip: Poach whole garlic cloves for 10 minutes in unsalted water, then purée with a bit of olive oil to preserve and remove the unpleasant odor. Keeps in the fridge for two weeks. No more chopping garlic!*
> **Charles Dale, Renaissance**

ANECDOTES & COOKING TIPS

Sean, our neighborhood bum, was quoted in Los Angeles Magazine as saying: "Campanile is my favorite restaurant!"
Campanile

Tip: Add a little cracked black pepper to a strawberry coulis to bring the flavors out.
Tom Colosi, Blue Maize

GEORGIA

Anis

2974 Grandview Avenue, Atlanta, GA 30305
(404) 233-9889 • Fax (404) 233-4894
Lunch M.-Sa. Dinner 7 Days.
Decor: A candle-lit, romantic restaurant with fresh
flowers and a covered patio. 100 Seats.

 Dan Harrar Michel Arnaud

 Provençal

 Lamb Chops Grilled with Thyme and
Rosemary. Shrimp with Anise.

"A great Mediterranean bistro. We return many
times to have the best French food in town!"

$$ AMERICAN EXPRESS VISA MasterCard DISCOVER 🍽

Araxi

4651 Woodstock Road, Suite 305
Atlanta, GA 30075
(770) 587-2700 • Fax (770) 587-9951
Lunch M.-F. Dinner M.-Sa.
Decor: A contemporary look with lavish
surroundings. 172 Seats.

 Todd Annis George Papathanasiou

 Continental

 Open-faced Lobster Ravioli. Chilean Sea Bass
with Cornbread and Roasted Corn Relish. Cherry
and Chipotle Glazed Rack of Lamb.

"I love the wonderful Southwestern-style sea bass."

$$$ AMERICAN EXPRESS VISA MasterCard ◎ DISCOVER 👔

GEORGIA

Atlanta

Bacchanalia

3125 Piedmont Road, Atlanta, GA 30305
(404) 365-0410 • Fax (404) 365-8020
Dinner Only Tu.-Sa.
Decor: Sophisticated elegance in this French
country cottage in the heart of Buckhead. 50 seats.

Clifford Harrison and Anne Quatrano

Frances Quatrano

American-Contemporary

Blue Crab Fritter with Avocado, Blood Orange
and Thai Pepper Essence. Roasted Rack of
Colorado Lamb with Baby Artichoke Ragout.
Warm Valrhona Chocolate Cake with Vanilla Bean
Ice Cream.

"Finally, a great restaurant in Atlanta in which the
food outshines the social scene." "Creative use of
regional ingredients." "Well thought-out
combinations, always interesting."

$$$ **AMERICAN EXPRESS** **VISA** **MasterCard** **①**

Buckhead Diner

3073 Piedmont Road Northeast
Atlanta, GA 30305
(404) 262-3336 • Fax (404) 262-3593
Lunch M.-Sa. Dinner 7 Days. Sunday Brunch.
Decor: An upscale diner with a 1940's dining car
ambiance. 186 Seats.

Peter Kaiser

American-Modern

Veal and Wild Mushroom Meatloaf with
Celery Root-Mashed Potatoes and Thin Green
Beans in a Creamy Veal Jus. Grilled Smoked Pork
Chops, Triple Cut with Turnip Greens, Cheese
Grits and Black-Eyed Pea Salsa.

"Simple American food at its best!"

98

Bugatti Restaurant
at The Omni Hotel

100 CNN Center, Atlanta, GA 30335
(404) 818-4450 • Fax (404) 818-4340
Website www.menus.atlanta.com/bugatti
Lunch M.-F. Dinner 7 Days.
Decor: A beautiful restaurant with polished woods, gleaming brass, sparkling crystal and lovely views of the city. 120 Seats.

 Kevin Palm   Valerie Crawford

Mediterranean

Open-faced Seafood Ravioli. Veal Picatta with Creamy Risotto and Wilted Greens. Lunchtime Pasta Buffet with noodles cooked-to-order.

"Creative and elegant style."

$$$

Canoe

4199 Pace Ferry Road, Atlanta, GA 30339
(770) 432-2663 • Fax (770) 433-2542
Lunch M.-F. Dinner 7 Days. Sunday Brunch.
Decor: An elegant restaurant with polished cherry wood walls, washed riverstone slab floors and hand-made ironwork. 365 Seats.

Gary Mennie   Vincent Palermo

American-Contemporary

Herb-Crusted Florida Grouper with Roasted Sweet Corn and Lobster Succotash.

"Excellent, modern food with wonderful textures and flavors."

$$$

GEORGIA

Atlanta

Carbo's Café

3717 Roswell Road, Atlanta, GA 30342
(404) 231-4433 • Fax (404) 237-6826
Website www.menus.atlanta.com/carboscafe
Dinner Only M.-Sa.
Decor: An elegant, European chateau in the heart
of Buckhead. 88 Seats, Dining Room. 300 Seats,
Ballroom.

Scott Schwartz

Continental

Carbo's Carpetbagger: Grilled Filet Mignon
pocketed with Maine Lobster Tail finished with
Cardinal Sauce.

"Very innovative continental cuisine."

$$$

Cedars

2770 Lenox Road, Suite 201
Atlanta, GA 30324
(404) 261-0958 • Fax (404) 261-1826
Website www.cedars.com
Lunch Su.-F. Dinner 7 Days.
Decor: A romantic restaurant filled with fresh
seasonal flowers and a patio with fresh herbs and
tropical jasmine. 94 Seats.

Nasser Samad   Nasser Samad

Mediterranean

Kabobs and Kibbey. Tabouleh Salad.

"A wonderful taste of Lebanon, with class."

$$

GEORGIA

Chopstix

4279 Roswell Road, Atlanta, GA 30342
(404) 255-4868 • Fax (404) 256-2602
Lunch M.-F. Dinner 7 Days.
Decor: An elegant and romantic room with a piano
bar. 127 Seats.

Philip Chan   Alvin Yin

Chinese

Fresh Black Pepper Oyster. Steamed Sea Bass.
Golden, Sweet Pineapple Prawns.

"The best, elegant Chinese restaurant in the city;
fantastic food."

Fairlie Poplar Café and Grill

85 Poplar Street, Atlanta, GA 30303
(404) 827-0040 • Fax (404) 351-1272
Website www.imperialfez.com
Lunch M.-F. Dinner M.-Sa.
Decor: A very casual and cozy French, Latin-
Quarter style restaurant. 100 Seats.

Rita Benjelloun   Aziz Aztot

Mediterranean

Couscous. Grilled Sandwiches. Gourmet
Buffet.

"Fabulous international fare, very reasonably
priced."

GEORGIA

Atlanta

Horseradish Grill

4320 Powers Ferry Road, Atlanta, GA 30342
(404) 255-7277 • Fax (404) 847-0603
Website www.horseradishgrill.com
Lunch M.-F. Dinner 7 Days. Sunday Brunch.
Decor: Ralph Lauren-style makeover of an old horse barn. 150 Seats.

David Berry   David Abes

Regional Southern

Hickory-Grilled North Carolina Mountain Trout. Braised Rabbit Pot Pie. Wood-Grilled Pork Chop Stuffed with Goat Cheese and Pecans.

"Southern cuisine at its best!"

Hsu's Gourmet

192 Peachtree Center Avenue
Atlanta, GA 30303
(404) 659-2788 • Fax (404) 577-3456
Website www.hsus.com
Lunch M.-Sa. Dinner 7 Days.
Decor: Warm and cozy Chinese decor. 130 Seats.

Charlie Shan   Raymond Hsu

Chinese

Peking Duck In Two Courses. Steamed Sea Bass. Asparagus Shrimp in Black Bean Sauce.

"Upscale Chinese food prepared with love and grace."

Imperial Fez
Moroccan Restaurant

2285 Peachtree Road, Atlanta, GA 30309
(404) 351-0870 • Fax (404) 351-1272
Website www.imperialfez.com
Dinner Only 7 Days.
Decor: The palatial decor transports you to
Morocco, with red and blue velvet tented ceiling,
silks, gold leaf and low tables. 350 Seats.

Rafih and Rita Benjelloun

Driss Mohamed and Hamid Belghili

Moroccan

Couscous Fassi. Lamb M'shui. Tagines of
Lamb, Chicken and Fish. Vegetarian dishes.

"A lively atmosphere, with deliciously authentic
cuisine." "A great place for fun and fine dining!"

$$$

La Grotta Ristorante Italiano

2637 Peachtree Road, Atlanta, GA 30305
(404) 231-1368 • Fax (404) 231-1274
Dinner Only M.-Sa.
Decor: The intimate, elegant restaurant overlooks
the garden. 85 Seats.

Antonio Abizanda   Sergio Favalli

Italian-Northern

Black and White Linguine with Calamari.
Veal Chop with Shallots. Filet of Beef
Michelangelo.

"The best Northern Italian in town for over 20
years." "This restaurant will transport you to Italy
with its elegant, heavenly food."

$$$

GEORGIA

Atlanta

Nava

3060 Peachtree Road, Suite 160
Atlanta, GA 30305
(404) 240-1984 • Fax (404) 240-1831
Website www.buckheadrestaurants.com
Lunch M.-F. Dinner 7 Days.
Decor: Southwestern style, built on three levels, accentuated by dramatic color. 165 Seats.

Kevin Rathbun   Tim Stevens

Regional Southwestern

Cowboy-Cut Beef Tenderloin with Serrano-Polenta Fries and Ancho-Corn Butter Sauce. Suncorn-Crusted Snapper with Southwest Whipped Potato and Masa Tomato Broth. Green Chile Lobster Soft Taco with Cascabel Pepper Cream and Pico de Gallo.

"Surprising and satisfying combinations. Great desserts." "The best Southwest in the South!" "Very special and fantastic food from my favorite Southwestern chef."

$$$

Riviera

519 East Paces Ferry Road Northeast
Atlanta, GA 30305
(404) 262-7112 • Fax (404) 262-7335
Dinner Only M.-Sa.
Decor: A "homey" feeling. 110 Seats.

Jack Shoop

Contemporary European

Paella Riviera: Saffron Rice with Chicken, Salmon, Scallops, Shrimp, Calamari, Lamb Sausage, and Fresh Peas. Roast Duckling Laperouse and Smoked Breast with Rhubarb, Sweet Red Pepper, Wheat Berries, Snowpeas and Zinfandel Rouennaise Sauce.

"Top quality cuisine presented by an expert."

$$$$

GEORGIA

Ruth's Chris Steak House

5788 Roswell Road at I-285
Atlanta, GA 30328
(404) 255-0035 • Fax (404) 255-3111
Website www.ruthschris.com
Dinner Only 7 Days.
Decor: The casually elegant dining room has an air
of Old World charm with dramatic two-story-high,
draped windows and original artwork by Charles
Reinike. Five Private Rooms. 295 Seats.

Tina Faucher   John Harof

Steakhouse

Ruth's Chris features the finest custom-aged,
USDA prime, Midwestern corn-fed beef. New
York Strip and T-Bone are stand-outs. Live
Maine Lobster.

"Meat that melts in your mouth, and excellent
service."

$$$

Seeger's

111 West Paces Ferry Road
Atlanta, GA 30305
(404) 846-9779 • Fax (404) 846-9217
Dinner Only M.-Sa.
Decor: An elegant, contemporary European
restaurant housed in a craftsman-style bungalow.
86 Seats.

Guenter Seeger   Claude Guillaume

French-American

The menu changes daily, but two standouts
are the Foie Gras and the Scallops Layered with
Truffles and Cocobean Croustillant.

"Superb food." "Ever-changing precision cuisine
that is pure, simple and elegant."

$$$$

GEORGIA

Atlanta

South City Kitchen

1144 Crescent Avenue, Atlanta, GA 30309
(404) 873-7358 • Fax (404) 873-0317
Lunch and Dinner 7 Days.
Decor: A glass and steel bungalow in the heart of midtown, featuring original art. 128 Seats.

🍴 Jay Swift　🔲 Chris Martha

♨ Regional Southern　🍸 🍴

⭐ Jerk-Spiced Pork Tenderloin with Sweet Potato Boniato Mash and Raspberry Sauce. Skillet Crab Cake with Chow-Chow and Mustard Sauce. Shrimp and Scallops with Creamy Stone-Ground Grits and Garlic Gravy.

"For gourmet adventure-seekers." "Food prepared with love and deep attention to detail."

$$$　AMERICAN EXPRESS　VISA　MasterCard　◑　👔

The Abbey Restaurant

163 Ponce de Leon Avenue
Atlanta, GA 30308
(404) 876-8532 • Fax (404) 876-8832
Dinner Only 7 Days.
Decor: Landmark church with 60-foot vaulted ceilings, stained glass windows and waiters dressed as monks, as well as an award-winning wine list. 250 Seats.

🍴 Philippe G. Haddad

🔲 Karriem Simmons

♨ American-Contemporary　🍸 🍴

⭐ Game Duo: Venison Loin and Roasted Squab with Calvados and Lingonberry Sauce. Grilled Maine Lobster with Leek and Morel Fondue. Free Range Chicken Breast with Port-Truffle Sauce.

"An institution in Atlanta for fun and fine dining!"

$$$$　AMERICAN EXPRESS　VISA　MasterCard　◑　DISCOVER　👔

GEORGIA

Toulouse

2293B Peachtree Road, Atlanta, GA 30309
(404) 351-9533 • Fax (404) 351-2299
Dinner 7 Days. Sunday Brunch.
Decor: A cozy, sensual dining room with an open kitchen, floor-to-ceiling windows, exposed brick, and hardwood floors. 135 Seats.

 Brian Travot Michael Anderson

French-American

Oven-Roasted Chicken with Arugula Bread Salad. Grilled Salmon with Jasmine Rice. Braised Cabbage and a Balsamic Beurre Blanc. Braised Lamb Shank with a Calamata Olive, Sweet Pepper Sauce served over Oven-Roasted Vegetables.

"My favorite restaurant! I love the creative flavors of Southern France and the Mediterranean." "The enticing aromas waft from the wood-burning grill and oven and dance throughout the restaurant."

$$$ 🍸 🍷

Marietta

Los Reyes

1869 Cobb Parkway, Suite 150
Marietta, GA 30062
(770) 953-4150
Lunch M.-F. Dinner 7 Days.
Decor: Tiny, bright, festive. An authentic Mexican joint. 15 Seats.

Gumaro Reyes

Mexican

Fajitas Rancheros. Quesadillas Rellenos.

"Cheap and authentic, great Mexican! I like the Tongue Tacos, but the Tacos al Pastor and any of the Tortas are exceptional!"

$

GEORGIA

Philadelphia

Ciboulette

The Bellevue, 200 South Broad Street
Philadelphia, GA 19102
(215) 790-1210 • Fax (215) 790-1209
Website www.ciboulette.com
Dinner Only 7 Days.
Decor: French Renaissance architecture with circa-1904 original features including mosaic tile floor, gold-leaf moldings, marble columns and ceiling frescos. 140 Seats.

 Bruce Lim    Ian Mark

 French-Modern

 Sautéed N.Y. State Foie Gras of Duck with Asparagus. Rack of Lamb with Sweet Garlic-Rosemary Sauce.

"One of Philadelphia's more talented chefs, a great place for business meetings." "What I think contemporary French should be."

$$$$ AMERICAN EXPRESS   VISA   MasterCard   ◑   /Λ\

Roswell

dick and harry's

1570 Holcomb Bridge Road
Roswell, GA 30076
(770) 641-8757 • Fax (770) 641-8884
Website www.dickandharrys.com
Lunch M.-F. Dinner M.-Sa.
Decor: A casually chic place. 122 Seats, Dining Room. 40 Seats, Outdoor Patio.

Harold Marmulstein

Richard Marmulstein

American French Brasserie

Hand-Rolled Roasted Vegetable Ravioli. Jambon de Paris and Fennel Slaw. Pan-Roasted Squab.

"Simple and super 'real food' and great service."

$$$ AMERICAN EXPRESS   VISA   MasterCard   ◑

Elizabeth on 37th

105 East 37th Street, Savannah, GA 31401
(912) 236-5547 • Fax (912) 232-1095
Website www.savga.com/businesses/e37
Dinner Only M.-Sa.
Decor: A 1900's Victorian mansion with hardwood floors and a fireplace in each of the four dining rooms. 95 Seats.

 Elizabeth Terry

 Regional Southern

 Stir-Fried Grits with Shrimp and Red-Eye Gravy. Grouper Celeste with a Sesame-Almond Crust and Peanut Sauce. Grilled Venison with Red Cabbage and Sweet Potato Cake.

"I love to eat here!" "Just plain great Southern cooking!"

ANECDOTES & COOKING TIPS

Tip: To check the temperature of a roast, insert a metal skewer into the roast, leave in ten seconds, remove and place the center on your upper lip. If it feels warm, it is medium rare. **Thomas Salamunovich, Sweet Basil**

As it became time to lock up for the evening, a couple was found in the restroom, 'in flagrante delicto'. When informed that we were closing, they responded, "We're coming!" **Mimosa**

Tip: For better tomato flavor in salads, cut the tomatoes and salt them 30 minutes before using, then use the resulting juices in your vinaigrette. **Martin Oswald, Syzygy**

Haliimaile, Maui

Haliimaile General Store

900 Haliimaile Road
Haliimaile, Maui, HI 96768
(808) 572-2666 • Fax (808) 572-7128
Lunch M.-F. Dinner 7 Days. Sunday Brunch.
Decor: A former general store, built in 1929. Old-fashioned feeling front room, and a cozy, art-filled ambiance in the back room. 130 Seats.

Beverly Gannon and Tom Lelli

Stacy Wood

Regional Hawaiian

Rack of Lamb Hunan-Style. Szechuan Barbecued Salmon. Pariolo Ribs.

"Consistently some of the best food in the state."

$$$

Honolulu

Alan Wong's Restaurant

1857 South King Street
Honolulu, HI 96826
(808) 949-2526 • Fax (808) 951-9520
Website www.alanwongsrestaurant.com
Dinner Only 7 Days.
Decor: Warm Koa wood enhances the casual island ambiance. The exhibition kitchen allows diners to watch the chefs at work. 90 Seats.

Alan Wong

Mark Shishido and Charly Yoshida

Regional Hawaiian

Ginger-Crusted Onaga with a Miso-Sesame Vinaigrette. Nori-Wrapped Tempura Bigeye Ahi with Tomato Ginger Relish and Soy Sauce Mustard.

"One restaurant, one focus, awesome!" "Alan IS Hawaiian Regional cuisine." "Masterful." "The best, most creative Hawaiian Regional-Fusion chef."

$$$

HAWAII

Honolulu

David Paul's Diamond Head Grill

2885 Kalakana Avenue, Honolulu, HI 96815
(808) 922-3734 • Fax (808) 791-5154
Lunch M.-F. Dinner 7 Days.
Decor: A modern and eclectic room using a variety
of marble, wood, brushed metals and colored-glass
lighting in an exciting atmosphere. 200 Seats,
Dining Room. 125 Seats, Banquet.

 David Paul Johnson   William Lee

American-New

Kona Coffee-Roasted Rack of Lamb.
Napoleon of Hamachi, Lobster and Unagi. Pepper-
Seared Ahi with Goose Liver and Balsamic Demi
Glace.

"David Paul cooks consistently delicious New
Hawaiian Cuisine. A must try!"

$$$

Sushi Sasabune

1417 South King Street
Honolulu, HI 96814
(808) 947-3800 • Fax (808) 941-1122
Website www.members.aol.com/nobib/index.html
Dinner Only M.-Sa.
Decor: "Decoration is secondary. Our sushi are
cozy and heavenly on your tongue." 36 Seats.

Seiji Kumagawa

Tomoko and Seiji Kumagawa

Japanese

This restaurant serves only Sushi.

"For the purist only."

$$$

Wasabi Bistro

1006 Kapahulu Avenue, Honolulu, HI 96816
(808) 735-2800 • Fax (808) 739-5651
Lunch M.-Sa. Dinner 7 Days.
Decor: An art-filled dining room with French doors that open onto a patio in a lovely garden setting. 90 Seats.

 Jimmy Ueda   Kumi Iseki

Japanese

East-West Combination. Wasabi #1 Special. Papaya Motoyaki.

"Inventive use of traditional ingredients."

$$$

Yanagi Sushi

762 Kapiolani Boulevard
Honolulu, HI 96813
(808) 597-1525 • Fax (808) 591-8223
Lunch and Dinner 7 Days.
Decor: This mainly sushi restaurant features two sushi bars and six private rooms. 131 Seats.

Haruo Naka Yama

Japanese

Sushi and Sashimi. Tempura and Classic Japanese Entrées.

"For consistently great fresh sushi until 2am."

$$

HAWAII

Kailua, Kona

Sam Choy's Restaurant

73-5576 Kauhola Street
Kailua, Kona, HI 96740
(808) 334-1213 • Fax (808) 334-1213
Website www.places.com/samchoy
Breakfast & Lunch 7 Days. Dinner Tu.-Sa.
Decor: Festive family-style dining in a warehouse-like room with an open kitchen. 70 Seats.

Sam Choy

Regional Hawaiian

Sam's Award-Winning Seafood Lau Lau.
Chinese-Style Honey Duck served with Kau
Orange Sauce and Sam's Homemade Marmalade.

"Local food for local people."

Kapalua

Sansei Seafood Restaurant & Sushi Bar

115 Bay Drive, Ste. 115
Kapalua, HI 96761
(808) 669-6286 • Fax (808) 669-0667
Dinner Only 7 Days.
Decor: A bright, casual, fun restaurant with Otsuka
paintings and contemporary Jazz music. 90 Seats.

D.K. Kodama   Kennan Randolph

Asian-Pacific Rim

Asian Rock Shrimp Cake with Ginger-Lime
Chili Butter and Cilantro Pesto. Panko-Crusted Ahi
Sashimi with Soy Wasabi Butter. Japanese Nori
Ravioli of Shrimp and Salmon with a Shiitake
Mushroom Sauce.

"DK is one of the most creative chefs, especially
with sushi."

Erik's Seafood Grotto

4242 L. Honoapiilani Road
Lahaina, HI 96761
(808) 669-4806 • Fax (808) 669-3997
Lunch and Dinner 7 Days.
Decor: A romantic, nautical feeling on the Pacific Ocean with a 180-degree view of neighboring islands. 195 Seats.

■ Erik Jakobsen   ■ Renate Soares

■ Contemporary European ■ ■

★ Steamed Clams and Oysters.

"Great, super fresh seafood."

$$$ AMERICAN EXPRESS VISA MasterCard ① DISCOVER ■

Avalon

844 Front Street, Lahaina, Maui, HI 96761
(808) 667-5559 • Fax (808) 661-4492
Website www.maui.net/~eatmaui
Lunch and Dinner 7 Days.
Decor: An eclectic, cutting-edge eatery. 130 Seats.

■ Mark Ellman   ■ Judy Ellman

■ Regional Hawaiian ■ ■

★ Seared Sashimi. Avalon Summer Rolls. Whole Opakapaka in Garlic Black Bean Sauce. Luau Roasted Garlic Clams. Caramel Miranda.

"Wonderfully innovative Pacific Rim cuisine!"
"This place is always hopping!"

$$$ AMERICAN EXPRESS VISA MasterCard ① DISCOVER ■

HAWAII

David Paul's Lahaina Grill

127 Lahainaluna Road
Lahaina, Maui, HI 96761
(808) 667-5117 • Fax (808) 661-5478
Website www.maui.net/~paradise/restaurants/
davidpauls.html
Dinner Only 7 Days.
Decor: A bright, bistro-style restaurant. 50 Seats.

David Paul Johnson   Michel Ray and

Alex Lavery

American-New

Tequila Shrimp with Firecracker Rice. Kona
Lobster Crab Cakes. Kahlua Duck.

"A chef who uses the best products no matter what
the cost and gives his full attention to perfection."

Maui Tacos

Lahaina Square, Lahaina, Maui, HI 96761
(808) 661-8883 • Fax (808) 661-4492
Website www.maui.net/~eatmaui
Lunch and Dinner 7 Days.
Decor: Cool fast-food environment.

Sergio Perez

Mexican

"Healthy Maui Mex." Fresh Salsa Bar.

"Maui-Mex food in an inexpensive, fun
environment."

HAWAII

Roy's Kahana Bar & Grill

4405 Honoapiilani Highway
Lahaina, Maui, HI 96761
(808) 669-6999 • Fax (808) 669-6909
Website www.roysrestaurants.com
Dinner Only 7 Days.
Decor: A casually elegant Island Style with an open kitchen. 135 Seats.

David Abella and Roy Yamaguchi

Adam Flier and Jasmine Peterson Quele

Asian-Pacific Rim

Hibachi Salmon with Japanese Sprouts and Ponzu Sauce. Blackened Island Ahi with Spicy Mustard-Soy Butter Sauce.

"Consistently excellent and tantalizing!" "Great Pacific Rim-Fusion." "My favorite restaurant in my favorite state of the Union, and what a great union it is with David and Roy."

$$$

Eggs & Things

1911 B Kalakau Avenue, Waikiki, HI 96815
(808) 949-0820 • Fax (808) 247-5689
Breakfast Only 7 Days.
Decor: A bright and cheerful breakfast place. 65 Seats.

Tom Warwicke   Jerry Fukunaga

Breakfast **BYOB**

Crêpes. Daily Omelette Specials.
"The best breakfast anywhere!"

$

HAWAII

Wailea

Joe's Bar and Grill

131 Wailea Ike Place, Wailea, HI 96753
(808) 875-7767 • Fax (808) 875-1827
Dinner Only 7 Days.
Decor: A contemporary bar and grill feel, like
dining in a treehouse with an ocean view and
spectacular sunsets. 110 Seats.

Beverly Gannon and Bryan Bresnahan

Richard Clark

American

Two-Inch Thick Grilled Pork Chop with
Dried Fruit Compote. Meatloaf and Mashed
Potatoes. Fresh Catch of the Day.

"Simple, honest down-home cookin'!"

$$$

Seasons

3900 Wailea Point, Wailea, HI 96753
(808) 874-8000 • Fax (808) 874-6449
Dinner Only Tu.-Sa.
Decor: Open-air dining with spectacular ocean
views. 80 Seats.

George Mavrothalassitis

Ashraf Hassan

Regional Hawaiian

Ahi Tartare and Caviar on a Taro Wafer.
Charbroiled Keahole Lobster and Molokai Sweet
Potato Purée with Mango Coulis. Onaga Baked in a
Salt Crust.

"Worth every dime." "George is probably one of
the best chefs in the country!"

$$$$

Tip: Simmer an unopened can
of sweetened condensed milk for
one and a half to two hours for a
perfect caramel sauce. Allow to cool
and cover. **Jimmy Yeager,
Jimmy's American Restaurant**

A group of tourism officials from Spain got
everybody in the restaurant, including the
busboys and dishwashers to dance to a salsa
CD. **Blue Maize**

Tip: Salt early and well.
**Ann Cashion,
Cashion's Eat Place**

We forgot to unlock the front door at opening time and we waited for one hour wondering why no customers had arrived.
Domo Japanese Country Foods

> *Tip:* Dust your fish with Wondra flour. This makes your sautéed fish crispy and moist. The flour may be seasoned with ground herbs or spices, mushroom powder, etc.
> **Peter Smith, Vidalia**

ILLINOIS

Le Titi de Paris

1015 West Dundee Road
Arlington Heights, IL 60004
(847) 506-0222 • Fax (847) 506-0474
Lunch Tu.-F. Dinner Tu.-Sa.
Decor: A comfortable, elegant room decorated with original art and fresh flowers. 150 Seats.

 Pierre Pollin & Michael Maddox

Marcel Flori

French-Modern

Sautéed Norwegian Salmon with Cider Sauce and Apples. Loin of Venison with Sauce Grand Veneur and Chestnuts.

"A really cool French bistro. Authentic in every way."

$$$

Arun's Restaurant

4156 North Kedzie Avenue
Chicago, IL 60618
(773) 539-1909 • Fax (773) 539-2125
Dinner Only Tu.-Su.
Decor: A bright, elegant room filled with Thai paintings and antiques. 95 Seats.

Arun Sampanthavivat

Lauren Merrill and Joe O'Brien

Thai

Golden Baskets. Steamed Rice Dumplings. Three-Flavored Red Snapper.

"Thai food taken to a new level, elegant and sophisticated." "Arun's dishes are seductive, intriguing and delicious; magical exotic flavors." "The best Thai food I've ever had."

$$$$

ILLINOIS

Chicago

Big Bowl

6 East Cedar Street, Chicago, IL 60610
(312) 640-8888 • Fax (312) 640-1555
Website www.bigbowl.com
Lunch and Dinner 7 Days.
Decor: A casual Asian restaurant with a make-it-yourself stir fry bar and open-air seating. 158 Seats.

 Matt McMillin   Geoffrey Alexander

Asian

Chicken Potstickers. Vietnamese Shrimp Summer Rolls. Sesame Peanut Noodle Salad.

"This place makes Asian fun! Great noodle dishes, stir fry bar and a house-made spicy Ginger Beer."

Bistro Zinc

3443 North Southport, Chicago, IL 60657
(773) 281-3443 • Fax (773) 281-3446
Dinner Only 7 Days. Closed M. Seasonally.
Decor: A very authentic, classic café and bistro: burgundy and cream banquettes, mirrors, and a zinc bar made in Paris. 225 Seats.

John Moore

French Bistro

Sautéed Skate Served with Tomato, Artichoke, French Green Beans and Red Onion Salad. Bouillabaisse every Friday.

"This is a neighborhood restaurant, and they do really good food in a wonderful atmosphere!"

Café Absinthe

1954 West North Avenue, Chicago, IL 60647
(773) 278-4488 • Fax (773) 278-5291
Dinner Only 7 Days.
Decor: A fun, casual restaurant, great for people-watching. 66 Seats.

 Joshua Young   Michael Nahabedian

French-American

Napoleon of Artichokes with Feta Mousse. Seared Red Snapper with Grapes, Almonds and Tarragon, Grape Juice Reduction.

"A unique restaurant with great style and excellent food."

$$$

Charlie Trotter's

816 West Armitage Avenue
Chicago, IL 60614
(773) 248-6228 • Fax (773) 248-6088
Website www.charlietrotters.com
Dinner Only Tu.-Sa.
Decor: The split-level, beautifully appointed, 19th Century townhome has been completely renovated in Viennese detail. 90 Seats.

Charlie Trotter   Mitchell Schmieding

American-Contemporary

The Grand Dégustation and Multi-Course Vegetable Dégustation.

"Food, food, wine, wine!" "Total perfection." "Consistently the best dining experience in America." "The attention to detail and the quality of food is the finest around." "A genius, a purist, a creator full of personality."

$$$$

ILLINOIS

Chicago

Don Juan Restaurant

6730 Northwest Highway, Chicago, IL 60631
(773) 775-6438 • Fax (773) 775-1052
Lunch and Dinner 7 Days.
Decor: A bright, cherry-colored, informal place
decorated with Mexican art. 95 Seats.

 Patrick Concannon

Mexican

Six-Chili Amish Chicken. Pork Tenderloin in
a Pasilla Sauce.

"For authentically spicy food, eat here!"

Everest

440 South LaSalle Street, 40th Floor
Chicago, IL 60605
(312) 663-8920 • Fax (312) 663-8802
Website www.brasseriejo.com
Dinner Only Tu.-Sa.
Decor: A luxuriously elegant restaurant featuring
the personalized cuisine of Jean Joho. 75 Seats.

Jean Joho   Jean-Pierre Sire

French

Chef's Multi-Course Dégustation Dinner.

"Exceptional food, setting and service" "Alsatian
heart and palette brought to the USA."

Frontera Grill

445 North Clark Street, Chicago, IL 60610
(312) 661-1434 • Fax (312) 661-1830
Lunch and Dinner Tu.-Sa. Sunday Brunch.
Decor: A high-energy, colorful restaurant with a
Mexican folk art collection. 65 Seats.

Rick Bayless

Mexican

Chile Rellenos. Carne Asada.

"Better Mexican food than you find in Mexico!"
"Flavors that come from the soul; great definition
of Mexican food in America." "Rick is an artist, his
food is always exciting and original."

Gordon

500 North Clark Street, Chicago, IL 60610
(312) 467-9780 • Fax (312) 467-1671
Website www.gordon.com
Lunch Tu.-F. Dinner 7 Days.
Decor: Eclectic, theatrical design, with an open and
cheery atmosphere. 150 Seats.

Don Yamauchi

Tad Edwards & R.C. Castro

American-Contemporary

Fresh Water Prawn with a Brandade Cake,
Yellow Tomato Coulis and Osetra Caviar. Grilled
Australian Lamb Loin with a Vegetable Tian, Goat
Cheese and a Grainy Mustard Sauce.

"Fantastic dining experience." "Killer
combinations!" "An elegant hand in the kitchen,
coupled with super service."

ILLINOIS

Chicago

Heaven on Seven

111 North Wabash, Chicago, IL 60602
(312) 263-6443 • Fax (312) 782-6016
Breakfast and Lunch M.-Sa.
Decor: A fun, casual diner setting with an open kitchen and a "Wall of Fire": over 1000 bottles of hot sauce! 120 Seats.

Jimmy Bannos

Regional American

Jamaican Jerk Pork Tenderloin and Portobello Mushroom Stack with a Jerk Cream Reduction Sauce. Yukon Gold Potato-Crusted Mahi Mahi with Parmesan Reggiano Cheese Grits and Creole Meunière Butter Sauce.

"Great Cajun food, up North!" "The best, most creative creole cookin' I've had!" "For creative, spicy food in a bustling atmosphere, this is it!"

Kiki's Bistro

900 North Franklin, Chicago, IL 60610
(312) 335-5454 • Fax (312) 335-0614
Lunch M.-F. Dinner M.-Sa.
Decor: Reminiscent of a French country inn. 120 Seats.

Mike Gregson   Gerard Kelley

French

Sautéed Breast of Duck with Leg Confit, Wild Rice and Green Peppercorn Sauce.

"Great service and the Duck Liver Mousse Pâté is awesome!" "Heart-warming cuisine at a reasonable price..."

Le Bouchon

1958 North Damen, Chicago, IL 60647
(773) 862-6600 • Fax (708) 524-1208
Dinner Only M.-Sa.
Decor: A Parisian bistro housed in a tiny storefront
with closely spaced tables, wall sconces, a pressed
tin ceiling and walls filled with French paintings
and murals. 45 Seats.

Jean-Claude Poilevey

French Bistro

Onion Tart. Sautéed Chicken with Garlic.
Saddle of Rabbit with Potato Galette.

"Authentic bistro cuisine that makes me feel like
I'm in Paris." "The best bistro food in Chicago."

Printer's Row Restaurant

550 S. Dearborn, Chicago, IL 60605
(312) 461-0780 • Fax (312) 461-0624
Lunch and Dinner M.-Sa.
Decor: The warm room is done in dark woods and
mauve tones. Located on a sunny corner. A great
spot for early theatre and lunch or dinner.
140 Seats.

Michael Foley   Philip Gaven

American-Contemporary

Lime-Scented Salmon with Miso. Chicken
Roasted with Mediterranean Lemon. Venison with
Tart Cherries.

"Michael continues to be one of the most
innovative and creative culinarians in America. His
accolades are too numerous to mention."

ILLINOIS

Chicago

Spiaggia

980 North Michigan Avenue, 2nd Floor
Chicago, IL 60611
(312) 280-2750 • Fax (312) 943-8560
Lunch Tu.-Sa. Dinner 7 Days.
Decor: Expansive, comfortable, with elegant design elements. 120 Seats.

Paul Bartolotta

Ron Reiff, Arthur Greenan

Italian

Steamed Mussels and White Beans. Lamb Wrapped in Basil with Squash Purée.

"In my opinion, the best Italian restaurant in the USA."

$$$$

The Dining Room at The Ritz Carlton

100 East Pearson, Chicago, IL 60610
(312) 573-5223 • Fax (312) 266-9623
Dinner 7 Days. Sunday Brunch.
Decor: An elegant European decor consisting of rich rosewood panelling and crystal chandeliers. 228 Seats.

Sarah Stegner   Steven Lande

French-Modern

Applewood Home-Smoked Salmon with Traditional Garnish. Roasted Rack of Colorado Lamb with Peppers, Olives, Raisins, Balsamic Glazed Onions and Coach Farm Goat Cheese Gratin. Maine Lobster with Avocado and Grilled Corn Salad with Shellfish-Corn Sauce.

"Beautifully orchestrated cuisine which is all-American, with the perfect amount of French sensibility. This is dining on a completely different level, only the very finest of everything."

$$$$

Topolobampo

445 North Clark Street, Chicago, IL 60610
(312) 661-1434 • Fax (312) 661-1830
Lunch and Dinner Tu.-Sa.
Decor: A brightly painted dining room with art from Mexico. 70 Seats.

🔲 Rick Bayless 🔲 Larry Butcher

🔲 Mexican 🔲

🔲 Sopa Astera. Nightly Specials.

"Rustic, soulful food with deeply complex flavors. This is a place where chiles are expertly used and traditions respected." "Rick's cuisine in this atmosphere is unbeatable." "Transcends America's idea of Mexican cooking."

🔲 $$$ 🔲 AMERICAN EXPRESS 🔲 VISA 🔲 MasterCard 🔲 🔲 DISCOVER 🔲

Vivere

71 West Monroe Street, Chicago, IL 60603
(312) 332-4040 • Fax (312) 332-2656
Lunch M.-F. Dinner M.-Sa.
Decor: A very modern restaurant with copper, wood and marble accents and a relaxing atmosphere. 100 Seats.

🔲 Marcelo Gallegos 🔲 Fred Ashtari

🔲 Regional Italian 🔲 🔲

🔲 Lobster-Filled Tomato Pasta with a Light Lobster Cream Sauce and Leeks. Duck Breast with Zucchini Purée, Crispy Leeks, and Celery Root Chips, Finished with Red Wine Balsamic Vinegar Sauce.

"Undoubtedly one of the best wine lists in the world!" "Best Italian outside of Italy!"

🔲 $$$ 🔲 AMERICAN EXPRESS 🔲 VISA 🔲 MasterCard 🔲 🔲 DISCOVER 🔲

ILLINOIS

Evanston

Trio Restaurant

1625 Hinman Avenue, Evanston, IL 60201
(847) 733-8746 • Fax (847) 733-8748
Website www.trio-restaurant.com
Lunch F. Only. Dinner Tu.-Su.
Decor: A cozy, French country-style dining room
with contemporary accents. 72 Seats.

Shawn McClain   David Ligon

Asian-French

Palette of Caviars with Lobster Ceviche and
Warm Brioche. Potato and Nori-Wrapped Salmon
with Japanese Crab Salad. Grilled Kobe Beef with
Oxtail, Shiitakes and Sweet Soy. Three Levels of
Dégustation, $48, $75, $100.

"Haute luxe and finesse in the suburbs!"

$$$$

Glen Ellyn

The Glen Ellyn Brewing Company

433 North Main Street
Glen Ellyn, IL 60137
(630) 942-1140 • Fax (630) 942-1143
Lunch and Dinner 7 Days.
Decor: Located in downtown Glen Ellyn, the
dining room has views of brewing equipment and
local artwork. 125 Seats.

Robert Matzig   Nolan Schiff

American Bistro

Drunken Steak Salad. Ancho Stout Pork
Tenderloin. Spentgrain Spice Cake.

"A great restaurant that also brews beer, not a
brewery with food."

$$

Gabriel's Restaurant

310 Green Bay Road, Highwood, IL 60046
(847) 433-0031 • Fax (847) 433-7499
Dinner Only Tu.-Sa.
Decor: A European, country-manor-style
restaurant. 75 Seats.

■ Gabriel Viti

■ French-Italian ■ ■

■ Roasted Rack of Lamb with Ratatouille and
Thyme Sauce. Papillotte of Bass with Lemon and
Herb Vinaigrette.

"It was flawless!"

$$$ ■ ■ ■ ■ ■

Wheeling

Le Francais

269 South Milwaukee Avenue
Wheeling, IL 60090
(847) 541-7470 • Fax (847) 541-7489
Lunch Tu.-F. Dinner M.-Sa.
Decor: A very comfortable, expansive room that
feels like a French country inn. 85 Seats.

■ Roland Liccioni ■ Mary Beth Liccioni

■ French-Modern ■ ■

■ Terrine of Roasted Salmon, House-Smoked
Salmon, Tuna and Crab. Sautéed Foie Gras with
Ginger Sauce and Oven-Dried Pineapple. Smoked
Maine Lobster with Vietnamese Broth.

"Delicious marriage of French and Asian flavors!"
"I always feel so welcome here!"

$$$$ ■ ■ ■ ■ ■ ■

Tip: When cooking dried beans, add a little oil to the water to soften the skins. **Wayne Alcaide, 32 East**

Several years ago, a server unknowingly spilled teriaki sauce on Clint Eastwood's head. Clint leaned over and softly said, in his inimitable way: "You are spilling s... on my head..." Guess that made the waiter's day... **Kenichi**

Tip: Only use the highest quality ingredients and believe in yourself. **Steven Martorano, Café Martorano**

Lexington

Lexington Barbecue

1029 70 South, Lexington, KY 27295
(910) 249-9814
Lunch and Dinner M.-Sa.
Decor: Comfortable, basic Americana. 25 Seats.

 Ricky Monk

 Barbecue

 Chop Sandwich with Slaw and Dip. Chop
Plate with Slaw, Fries and Dip.

"Best chopped pork barbecue, with vinegary slaw
and sweet iced tea!"

Louisville

Asiatique Restaurant

106 Sears Avenue, Louisville, KY 40207
(502) 899-3578 • Fax (502) 899-5859
Dinner Only 7 Days.
Decor: An art deco interior with an elegant but
relaxed ambiance. 102 Seats.

Peng S. Looi

Pablito Sembillo and Ron Bacigallipi

Asian-Pacific Rim

Wok-Seared Salmon. Roasted Quail with
Noodle Pancake and Spicy Shiitake Sauce.

"I love their everything, but especially the
appetizers!"

KENTUCKY

Louisville

Brasserie Dietrich

2862 Frankfort Avenue
Louisville, KY 40206
(502) 897-6076
Dinner Only Tu.-Su.
Decor: A very French brasserie in a 1920's theatre, with an open kitchen, wood-burning grill and oversized vintage posters. 145 Seats.

Jack Tapp   Diana Baker

French

Sea Bass with Potato Crust and Cabernet Reduction. Rib Chop of Beef with Marrow and Beaujolais Glaze.

"I love their new, exciting menu."

\$\$\$

Equus Restaurant

122 Sears Avenue, Louisville, KY 40207
(502) 897-9721 • Fax (502) 897-0535
Dinner Only M.-Sa.
Decor: An elegant room decorated with fresh flowers and crystal stemware. 120 Seats.

S. Dean Corbett and David Cuntz

James Cover

Regional American

Crabcakes. Shrimp Jenkins. Pan-Seared Fresh Sea Bass.

"Wonderful dining in elegant surroundings."

\$\$\$

Lilly's

1147 Bardstown Road, Louisville, KY 40204
(502) 451-0447 • Fax (502) 458-7546
Lunch and Dinner Tu.-Sa.
Decor: Elegant and cozy dining rooms with hand-painted murals and large fresh flower arrangements.
120 Seats.

Kathy Cary   Kevin Casserro

Regional American

Hudson Valley Foie Gras and Grit Cake with a White Peach, Cuban Oregano Glaze, Laced with Pomegranate. Warm Cheese Soufflé with Toasted Pecans, Country Ham and a Champagne Vinaigrette. Smoked Pork Tenderloin with a Mango-Hoisin Barbecue Sauce, Wasabi Slaw and Grilled Corn Pone.

"They use the best locally available ingredients, and always cook with the seasons." "A must when I'm in Louisville."

$$$

Shariat's Restaurant

2901 Brownsboro Road
Louisville, KY 40206
(502) 899-7878 • Fax (502) 899-3677
Dinner Only M.-Sa.
Decor: Modern look with copper accents and contemporary artwork. 110 Seats.

Anoosh Shariat   Mehrzad Sharbaiani

Global

Portobello-Lentil Tower with Seared Spinach, Red and Yellow Roasted Peppers and Smoked Tomato Sauce. Cardamon Cake with Saffron Ice Cream Rolled in Pistachios and Drizzled with Rose Water.

"The chef is extremely creative, and combines cultures very well!" "Some of my finest meals ever!"

$$$

KENTUCKY

Louisville

The English Grill

The Camberley-Brown Hotel, 335 West Broadway
Louisville, KY 40202
(502) 583-1234 • Fax (502) 561-8443
Website www.camberleyhotels.com
Dinner Only 7 Days.
Decor: A stately dining room with elegant white
jacquard linen-draped tables, dark oak paneling,
soft candlelight and oil portraits of thoroughbreds.
120 Seats.

 Joe Castro  Jeff Jarfi

 Regional American

 Tempura Soft-Shell Crabs with Mustard
Greens and Hominy. Hickory-Smoked Pork
Tenderloin with Honeysuckle Honey Glaze. Chef's
Nightly Five-Course Prix-Fixe Dinner.

"I love the atmosphere."

$$$ VISA MasterCard

Shelbyville

Science Hill Inn

525 Washington Street
Shelbyville, KY 40065
(502) 633-2825
Lunch Tu.-Su. Dinner F. & Sa. Only. Su. Brunch
Decor: The original dining room in a historic old
girls' school, quaint and lovely with a fireplace and
rose garden. 100 Seats.

 Donna & Ellen Gill  Terrence Gill

 Regional American

 Carolina Shrimp and Grits: Shrimp Sautéed
with Butter, Onion, Herbes de Provence and Cajun
Spices, served over Cheese Grits topped with
Crumbled Bacon. Crispy Pan-Fried Chicken. Hot
Cornbread and Buttermilk Biscuits.

"Ths is true Kentucky cookin'!"

$$ VISA MasterCard

Tip: Never boil miso broth.
Johnathan Eismann, Pacific Time

Our hoods failed on the hottest night of summer. Who was in the dining room but Julia Child, Jacques Pepin, Patricia Wells and a dozen other culinary luminaries, all at one table! We cooked our hearts out despite the heat and everything went smoothly with one exception. Julia's chocolate sorbet was more like chocolate soup when she received it! Polite and sympathetic as ever, she complimented it anyway... *Renaissance*

Tip: Beefsteak tomatoes taste best when served at room temperature.
Todd Weisz, Turnberry Isle Resort

Anecdotes & Cooking Tips

Wolfgang, our local mushroom picker, sometimes runs through the dining room with his basket of mushrooms while yodeling. *Splendido at The Château*

Tip: A little lemon juice on fruit is like salt on meat, it brings out the flavor. **Anne Quatrano and Clifford Harrison, Bacchanalia**

LOUISIANA

Lafitte's Landing Restaurant

Sunshine Bridge Access Road West Bank
Donaldsonville, LA 70346
(504) 473-1232 • Fax (504) 473-1161
Website www.jfolse.com
Lunch Tu.-Su. Dinner Tu.-Sa.
Decor: Situated in an ancient Acadian cottage with
views of Sunshine Bridge. 90 Seats.

John Folse   Scott Cart

Cajun/Creole

Louisiana Seafood Gumbo. Boiled Crawfish,
Corn and Potato Soup. Colossal Veal Shank.
Charbroiled Rack of Venison with Jumbo Crab.
Blackeyed Pea-Battered Shrimp.

"Excellent innovations on classical Louisiana
cuisine, coupled with exemplary service."

$$$

Metairie

Andrea's Restaurant

3100 19th Street, Metairie, LA 70002
(504) 834-8583 • Fax (504) 834-6698
Lunch M.-F. Dinner 7 Days.
Decor: A very homey restaurant with five dining
rooms. 300 Seats.

Andrea Apuzzo   Erhard Thumfart

Italian-Northern

Filet Andrea. Stuffed Veal Valdostana.
Tiramisu.

"It's Northern Italian cuisine, serving homemade
pastas and pastries, all very authentic. They also do
fresh seafood, game, and lobster."

$$$

139

LOUISIANA

Metairie

R&O's Pizza Restaurant

216 O. Hammond Highway
Metairie, LA 70005
(504) 831-1248
Lunch and Dinner W.-M.
Decor: Casual family atmosphere. 140 Seats.

🔥 Roland Jr. and U.J. Mollere

♨️ Italian-American 🍸

⭐ Fried Seafood. Roast Beef. Pizza.

"Having grown up in New Orleans, it was tough to come to this conclusion, but there is no better Po-Boy in the city."

New Orleans

Bayona

430 Rue Dauphine Street
New Orleans, LA 70112
(504) 525-4455 • Fax (504) 522-0589
Website www.bayona.com
Lunch M.-F. Dinner M.-Sa.
Decor: A romantic, Creole cottage located in the historic French Quarter complete with a lush courtyard, fountain, and scenic countryside murals. 130 Seats.

🔥 Susan Spicer   🍴 David Payne

♨️ Mediterranean 🍸 🍷

⭐ Cream of Garlic Soup. Grilled Duck Breast with Pepper Jelly Glaze. Grilled Shrimp with Black Bean Cake and Coriander Sauce.

"Bayona offers a unique Asian influence that is masterfully done." "Tasty starters; I love lunch in the courtyard."

Bella Luna Restaurant

914 North Peters, New Orleans, LA 70116
(504) 529-1583 • Fax (504) 522-4858
Dinner Only 7 Days.
Decor: An elegant atmosphere with far-reaching
Mississippi river views through floor-to-ceiling
windows. 220 Seats.

Horst Pfeifer   Gino Capriotti

Eclectic

Sautéed Redfish in a Sweet Basil Pesto Crust
served with Fresh Fennel. House-Cured Pork Chop
in a New Orleans-Style Pecan Crust with a Beer
Sauce.

"An exquisite dining experience, featuring
outstanding preparations of quality ingredients."

$$$

Brigtsen's

723 Dante Street, New Orleans, LA 70118
(504) 861-7610 • Fax (504) 866-7397
Dinner Only Tu.-Sa.
Decor: A renovated Victorian cottage in the
Riverbend neighborhood with an interior painted
by local artist Ivy Sherman. 60 Seats.

Frank Brigtsen

Marna Brigtsen and Rhonda Madach

Cajun/Creole

Roasted Duck with Cornbread Dressing and
Honey-Pecan Gravy. Blackened Tuna with Smoked
Corn Sauce, Red Bean Salsa and Avocado Sour
Cream. Filé Gumbo with Rabbit and Andouille
Sausage.

"The courageous and absolute commitment to his
small-scale, non-commercial operation, makes this
guy's interpretation of Cajun-Creole a real standout.
A special, special experience." "Fabulous duck and
rabbit dishes!"

$$$

LOUISIANA

New Orleans

Clancy's

6100 Annunciation, New Orleans, LA 70118
(504) 895-1111 • Fax (504) 899-4203
Lunch Tu.-F. Dinner M.-Sa.
Decor: Bistro-style, neighborhood restaurant.
120 Seats.

Brian Larson   John Vodanovich

Cajun/Creole

Fried Oysters with Brie. Smoked Soft-Shell
Crab. Veal Liver Lyonnaise.

"Wonderful, local feel. Great, simple food."

$$$

Commander's Palace

1403 Washington Avenue
New Orleans, LA 70130
(504) 899-8221 • Fax (504) 891-3242
Website www.commanderspalace.com
Lunch M.-F. Dinner 7 Days. Sa. & Su. Brunch.
Decor: The restaurant is located in an old Victorian
mansion. 98 Seats.

Jamie Shannon   George Rico

Cajun/Creole

Gulf Fish Pecan with Haricots Verts and
Carrots. Bread Pudding Soufflé with Whisky Sauce.

"Always a great meal." "State-of-the-art Haute
Creole cuisine in a high volume setting; a
professional, well-run New Orleans institution."
"Perfect food, service and atmosphere."

$$$

Dominique's

1001 Rue Toulouse, New Orleans, LA 70112
(504) 522-8800 • Fax (504) 525-5334
Website www.maisondupuy.com
Lunch and Dinner 7 Days.
Decor: An intimate and comfortable room, with upholstered armchairs and linen tables adorned with orchids. 72 Seats.

🍴 Dominique Macquet

🚬 Asian-French 🍸 🍷

⭐ Sugarcane Brochette of Sweetbreads. Flash-Broiled Whole Maine Lobster with Mauritian-Spiced Couscous.

"Great young chef from Mauritius, who is not afraid to experiment; wonderful flavors and an excellent technician."

$$$ AMERICAN EXPRESS VISA MasterCard ◑ DISCOVER ⫍⫎

Emeril's Restaurant

800 Tchoupitoulas, New Orleans, LA 70130
(504) 528-9393 • Fax (504) 558-3925
Website www.emerils.com
Lunch M.-F. Dinner M.-Sa.
Decor: Located in a historic pharmacy warehouse with exposed brick, a glass wall and a food bar on the open kitchen where guests can watch Chef Emeril and his crew in action. 180 Seats, Dining Room. 50 Seats, Private Parties.

🍴 Emeril Lagasse   👔 Tony Lott

🚬 Cajun/Creole 🍸 🍷

⭐ Emeril's Homemade BBQ Shrimp with Petite Rosemary Biscuits. American Roasted Rack of Lamb with a Creole Mustard Crust and Rosemary Au Jus. "Mr. Louisiana Real and Rustic" Banana Cream Pie with Caramel Drizzles and Chocolate Shavings.

"Emeril's is one of the friendliest restaurants I've been to and the pork chop is to die for!"

$$$$ AMERICAN EXPRESS VISA MasterCard ◑ DISCOVER ⫍⫎

LOUISIANA

New Orleans

Galatoire's

209 Bourbon Street, New Orleans, LA 70130
(504) 525-2021 • Fax (504) 525-5900
EMail galatoir@iamerica.net
Lunch and Dinner Tu.-Sa.
Decor: Classic French bistro style. 138 Seats.

Milton Prudence

Arnold Chabaud and Kenneth Solis

Cajun/Creole

Shrimp Rémoulade. Oysters Rockefeller.
Pompano with Sautéed Crabmeat.

"The best place for brunch in New Orleans."
"An institution, not to be missed! And they're so
friendly here." "For classic N.O. cooking, this is it!"

$$$

Palace Café

605 Canal Street, New Orleans, LA 70130
(504) 523-1661 • Fax (504) 523-1633
Lunch and Dinner 7 Days.
Decor: A Parisian grand café ambiance. 300 Seats.

Gus Martin

Cajun/Creole

Crabmeat Cheesecake. Seafood Boil. White
Chocolate Bread Pudding.

$$$

LOUISIANA

Peristyle

1041 Dumaine, New Orleans, LA 70116
(504) 593-9535 • Fax (504) 529-6942
Dinner Tu.-Sa. Lunch F. Only.
Decor: An old French Quarter structure with
Bentwood chairs, slow-moving fans, murals, and a
copper bar. 56 Seats.

Anne Kearney   Lee Ingold

American French Brasserie

Hand-Rolled Roasted Vegetable Ravioli.
Jambon de Paris and Fennel Slaw. Pan-Roasted
Squab.

"Elegant flavors, relaxed atmosphere, great bar."
"A charming French Quarter bistro with creative,
well executed food, and one of the nicest chefs you
will ever meet." "Anne is one of the 10 hottest new
chefs in America...need I say more?"

Uglesich's Restaurant

1238 Baronne Street
New Orleans, LA 70113
(504) 523-8571 • Fax (504) 899-8256
Lunch Only M.-F.
Decor: A small, old-time New Orleans restaurant.
40 seats.

Gail Uglesich   Anthony Uglesich

Cajun/Creole

Paul's Fantasy. Shrimp Uggie. Fried Green
Tomatoes Topped with Boiled Shrimp and
Rémoulade.

"A down-home joint with the best seafood in
town." "A Creole neighborhood hangout in the
Crescent City with the best oyster bar and local
cuisine available in New Orleans."

145

LOUISIANA

New Orleans

Vaqueros Restaurant

4938 Prytania Street
New Orleans, LA 70115
(504) 891-6441 • Fax (504) 899-8005
Website www.vacqueros-restaurant.com
Lunch M.-F. Dinner 7 Days. Sunday Brunch.
Decor: Located just above the Garden District in uptown New Orleans, locals gather for margaritas, Latin jazz and tortillas hand-rolled to order in the main dining room. 140 Seats.

James Didier II   Craig Cassioppi

Regional Southwestern

Habanero Fish Soup with Corn and Potatoes. Ancho-Tamarind-Glazed Shrimp with Wilted Spinach and a Cornbread, Black Bean and Goat Cheese Tower. Navajo Filet of Beef with Chipotle Demi Glace, Garlic Mashed Potatoes, Navajo Flat Bread and Grilled Vegetables.

"Authentic, creative Mexican, a real treat!"

Windsor Court Hotel Grill Room

300 Gravier Street, New Orleans, LA 70130
(504) 522-1992 • Fax (504) 596-4649
Website www.windsorcourthotel.com
Breakfast, Lunch and Dinner 7 Days.
Decor: A traditionally elegant restaurant with stunning glass tables and an extensive art collection. 150 Seats.

Rene Bajeux   Ali Sharifi

American-Contemporary

Black Bass with Peruvian Potatoes and Basil Vinaigrette. Roasted Maine Lobster with Morel Risotto. Roasted Rack of Antelope with Black Onyx Beans.

"Simple elegance, great sauces."

146

Tip: When shucking oysters and
clams, tap them first. If they sound
hollow, discard them, they are dead.
Harold Marmulstein,
dick and harry's

A customer said that it was very difficult to
get the meat out of the shell of a soft-shell
crab. **The Wildflower**

Tip: The success of a crabcake
depends more on the crab meat
than on the recipe. Use only
jumbo-lump blue crab meat.
Jay Swift, South City Kitchen

The garde manger cook gets scared
of lobsters when they jump!
The Lakeview Inn

Tip: *Use only the freshest
ingredients, the boldest
imagination, and a dash of
attitude. Temper this with the
humility of experience and serve
immediately.* **Brian Travot,
Toulouse**

MAINE

The White Barn Inn

35 Beach Street, Kennebunkport, ME 04046
(207) 967-2321 • Fax (207) 967-1100
Website www.whitebarninn.com
Dinner Only 7 Days.
Decor: A romantic, elegant dining room filled with 15th-century antiques, wildlife woodcarvings and collectibles in a restored barn from 1820. 120 Seats, Dining Room. 14 Seats, Private Wine Room.

Jonathan M. Cartwright

Laurence Bongiorno

Regional American

Lobster Spring Roll with Carrot, Daikon Radish, Snowpeas, Cilantro and Thai-Inspired Spicy Sweet Sauce. Steamed Maine Lobster Nestled on a Bed of Homemade Fettucine. Pan-Seared Maine Halibut Filet on a Red Onion Marmalade.

"Great, formal service in a beautiful room."

The Lobster Pound

U.S. 1, P.O. Box 118
Lincolnville, ME 04849
(207) 789-5550
Lunch and Dinner 7 Days. Seasonal.
Decor: Weathered wood and nautical artifacts. Featuring an outdoor patio. 300 Seats.

Peter McLaughlin   Richard McLaughlin

American

Baked and Stuffed Lobster. Berry Desserts of the Season.

"For an authentic New England experience. The freshest seafood served by true professionals."

149

MAINE

Ogunquit

98 P-R-O-V-E-N-C-E

104 Shore Road, Ogunquit, ME 03907-0628
(207) 646-9898 • Fax (207) 641-8786
Website www.98provence.com
Dinner Only W.-M.
Decor: Cozy, French country style, reminiscent of
Provence. 55 Seats.

 Pierre Gignac  Johanne Haseltin

 Provençal

 Mussels, Shrimp, Scallops and Fish in a Fresh
Fennel Broth. Pan-Seared Loin of Venison with
Wild Berry Sauce. Fish of the Day.

"Innovative, French country dining with
wonderfully light and flavorful food."

$$$ AMERICAN EXPRESS VISA MasterCard

Arrows Restaurant

Berwich Road, 1.8 miles West of Route 1
Ogunquit, ME 03907
(207) 361-1100
Dinner Only Tu.-Su.
Decor: Arrows is situated in a Colonial farmhouse
dating back to 1765. It is surrounded by acres of
flowers, herbs and vegetable gardens, which provide
most of the produce for the restaurant. 65 Seats.

Clark Frasier and Mark Gaier

Clark Frasier

Regional American

Menu changes daily.

$$$$ AMERICAN EXPRESS MasterCard

Fore Street

288 Fore Street, Portland, ME 04101
(207) 775-2717 • Fax (207) 772-6778
Dinner Only 7 Days.
Decor: Rustic, wood-fired cooking in a restaurant with great views of Portland Harbor. 130 Seats.

Sam Hayward

Regional American

Turnspit-Roasted Pork Loin. Wood Oven-Roasted Maine Lobster. Applewood-Grilled Bluefin Tuna Loin.

"Delicious regional cooking!"

$$$

Walter's Café

15 Exchange Street, Portland, ME 04101
(207) 871-9258
Website www.walterscafe.com
Lunch M.-Sa. Dinner 7 Days.
Decor: An eclectic café in a period brick building with large windows and hardwood floors, located in the historic Old Port section of town. 68 Seats.

Jack Neal   Blaik Watson

American-New

Angel Hair Pasta with Lobster. Crazy Chicken. Mediterranean Linguine.

"A fun place for lunch."

$$

ANECDOTES & COOKING TIPS

Tip: Remember that even fine restaurant chefs make mistakes, so don't let yours deter you from going right back into the kitchen, or from turning one of your mistakes into a signature dish. To avoid food sticking to the pan, remember, "Hot pan, cold oil." **David Paul Johnson, David Paul's**

President Clinton came to eat at Kinkead's the same evening we were having a going-away party for my sous-chef of 13 years. A local food critic had brought Rus a new chef's knife as a going-away present. Secret Service took it away from him with the comment, "Great gift...bad night!" *Kinkead's*

Tip: The higher the temperature when cooking fish, the more tender and juicy the result. **Erik Jensen, Erik's Seafood Grotto**

MASSACHUSETTS

Ambrosia on Huntington

116 Huntington Avenue, Boston, MA 02116
(617) 247-2400 • Fax (617) 247-4009
Lunch M.-F. Dinner 7 Days.
Decor: An open, spacious restaurant with high
ceilings, rich Tuscan colors and lots of glass and
metal work. 85 Seats.

Tony Ambrose Gary Sullivan

French

Lobster Sashimi Served in a Martini Glass
with Stoli-Anise Noodles. Game in season. Fresh
Shellfish.

"Tony Ambrose is always out on the edge, but
always in control!"

$$$

Aujourd'hui at The Four Seasons

200 Boylston Street, Boston, MA 02116
(617) 351-2071 • Fax (617) 351-2293
Website www.fourseasons.com
Breakfast and Dinner 7 Days. Lunch M.-F.
Sunday Brunch.
Decor: Very sophisticated and elegant, with
windows overlooking the public gardens.
124 Seats.

Ed Gannon Steven Davis

Continental

Sea Scallops with Sweet Potato and Lobster
Glaze. Vegetarian and Traditional Tasting Menus.

"Simply perfect."

$$$$

153

MASSACHUSETTS

Boston

Biba

272 Boylston Street, Boston, MA 02116
(617) 426-7878 • Fax (617) 426-9253
Website www.boston.sidewalk.com/detail/10241
Lunch M.-Sa. Dinner 7 days.
Decor: Designed by Adam Tihany, the romantic,
warmly-colored restaurant is on two floors and
overlooks the swan boats in the Public Garden. 150
Seats.

 Lydia Shire and Susan Regis

 Frank King, Peter Nelson, Sara Finnerty

 American-Eclectic

Biba's Own Lobster Pizza. Calves' Brains with
Crisp Fried Capers and Sherry Vinegar. Cedar-
Planked Club Sirloin with a Sauce of White
Burgundy.

"Fun, inventive and out there, yet always perfect."

$$$$　　AMERICAN EXPRESS　VISA　MasterCard　◎

Café Louis

234 Berkeley Street, Boston, MA 02116
(617) 266-4680 • Fax (617) 375-9427
Lunch and Dinner M.-Sa.
Decor: A small, intimate restaurant with a modern
European design. 50 Seats, Dining Room. 18 Seats,
Outdoors.

 David Reynoso Craig Bledsoe

 Italian

Al Forno Grilled Pizza, Made to Order. Made-
to-Order Garden Minestrone Soup.

"Incredibly bold flavors, and a wonderful
atmosphere."

$$$　　AMERICAN EXPRESS　VISA　MasterCard

MASSACHUSETTS

East Ocean City

25 Beach Street, Boston, MA 02111
(617) 542-2504 • Fax (617) 348-2878
Lunch M.-F. Dinner 7 Days.
Decor: A bright, elegant, contemporary Oriental restaurant. 154 Seats.

Sung-Chi Tam

Chinese

Chinese-style Seafood.

"The best roasted duck on the planet! I also love the sweet shrimp sashimi."

Ginza Japanese Restaurant

16 Hudson Street, Boston, MA 02111
(617) 338-2261 • Fax (617) 426-3563
Lunch M.-Sa. Dinner 7 Days.
Decor: Upscale, featuring authentic Japanese woodwork. 110 Seats.

Toru Oga   George Chan

Japanese

Ginza Surprise. Spider Maki. Caterpillar Maki.

"Deliciously innovative!"

MASSACHUSETTS

Boston

Hamersley's Bistro

553 Tremont Street, Boston, MA 02116
(617) 423-2700 • Fax (617) 423-7710
Dinner Only 7 Days.
Decor: A light, airy dining room with large
windows and an open kitchen, housed in an old
piano factory in Boston's historic South End.
120 Seats.

Gordon Hamersley

Sophia Schueler and Fiona Hamersley

French Bistro

Duck Confit with Prunes and Walnuts.
Roasted Lobster with Vegetable Confetti. Lemon
Custard Soufflé.

"The best bistro in Boston! I love the chicken with
garlic, lemon and rosemary."

$$$$

L'Espalier

30 Gloucester Street, Boston, MA 02115
(617) 262-3023 • Fax (617) 375-9297
Website www.lespalier.com
Dinner Only M.-Sa.
Decor: Situated in a Back Bay townhouse from
1876, featuring a mahogany spiral staircase, three
dining rooms with carved moldings, bay windows,
original fireplaces and crystal candelabras. 75 Seats.

Frank McClelland   Louis Risoli

French-Modern

Steamed Vidalia Onion, Cashew and Foie
Gras Pudding with Grilled Foie Gras in a Pinot
Noir Cherry Sauce. Poached Young Atlantic
Halibut in Summer Black Truffles and Vin Jaune.
Blue Potato and Maine Crabmeat Gratin.

"One of my greatest dining experiences in America!
The wine list will blow you away!" "This renowned
chef just keeps getting better!"

$$$$

156

MASSACHUSETTS

Boston

Legal Sea Foods

Park Plaza, 35 Columbus Avenue
Boston, MA 02116
(617) 426-4444 • Fax (617) 426-3321
Website www.legalseafoods.com
Lunch and Dinner 7 Days.
Decor: A casual restaurant with a nautical feel.
300 Seats.

 Jasper White

Seafood

Blue Fish Pâté. Halibut with Crab
Imperial Sauce.

"Jasper White is a chef who's not afraid to go all
out!" "This place is committed to quality."

Pignoli

79 Park Plaza, Boston, MA 02116
(617) 338-7500 • Fax (617) 338-7691
Website www.boston.sidewalk.com/detail/5382
Lunch M.-Sa. Dinner 7 Days.
Decor: An ultramodern, baroque design with a
casual elegance and private dining available.
110 Seats.

Daniele Baliani and Lydia Shire

Jerry Rosa

Italian

"Elephant Ear...Walking" (A Curly Pizza).
Gorgonzola Ravioli with Roasted Peaches and
Pistachio Pesto. Roast Duck "Marco Polo" with
Minted Couscous and a Macedonia of Fruits.

"An awesome, ever-changing antipasto table, and
unique hand-crafted pastas and bread." "Daniele's
gnocchi are to die for! His food is smart and
creative."

157

MASSACHUSETTS

Boston

Sonsie

327 Newbury Street, Boston, MA 02115
(617) 351-2500 • Fax (617) 351-2565
Website www.avenue.com/sonsie
Lunch M.-F. Breakfast & Dinner 7 Days.
Saturday Brunch.
Decor: A lively restaurant with a street-side café,
reading salon, mahogany bar, brick oven and
colorful dining rooms. 120 Seats.

⬛ Bill Poirier **⬛** Brian O'Neill

⬛ Global **⬛** **⬛**

⬛ Vietnamese Spring Rolls. Mee Krob: Spicy,
Thai Crispy Noodles. Angry Pizza: Sausage, Hot
Pickled Pepper and Cheese.

"Foods from grandma to the rest of the map...cool
folks."

$$$ **AMERICAN EXPRESS**   **VISA**   **MasterCard**   **⬤**   **⬛**

Brighton

Pho Pasteur

137 Brighton Avenue, Brighton, MA 02134
(617) 783-2340 • Fax (617) 783-2060
Lunch and Dinner 7 Days.
Decor: An old-fashioned Country Vietnamese-style
restaurant with three dining rooms. 180 Seats.

⬛ Quyen Long

⬛ Vietnamese **BYOB**

⬛ Vietnamese-Style Hot and Sour Soup. Fresh
Spring Roll with Peanut Sauce. Chicken with
Lemongrass.

"Wonderfully light Vietnamese cuisine, with very
direct flavors."

$$ **AMERICAN EXPRESS**   **VISA**   **MasterCard**   **⬛**

MASSACHUSETTS

Cambridge

Chez Henri

One Shepard Street, Cambridge, MA 02138
(617) 354-8980 • Fax (617) 441-8784
Dinner 7 Days. Sunday Brunch.
Decor: A funky, creatively designed room with
great lighting, done in burgundy reds and mustard
yellows. 80 Seats.

Paul O'Connell   Erik Bevans

French Eclectic

Spinach Salad with Duck Tamales and
Mustard Vinaigrette. Roast Chicken with Achiote,
Lime and Yuca Con Mojo.

"Excellent French-Cuban food, just outside
Harvard Square." "I think this is the best bistro in
the Boston/Cambridge vicinity! Highly original."

East Coast Grill and Raw Bar

1271 Cambridge Street
Cambridge, MA 02139
(617) 491-6568 • Fax (617) 868-4278
Website www.eastcoastgrill.com
Dinner 7 Days. Sunday Brunch.
Decor: A funky, world-inspired, hip restaurant with
an open kitchen and a great raw bar. 90 Seats.

Chris Schlesinger   Maureen Rubino

Eclectic

White Pepper-Crusted Tuna. Grilled Latin-
Style Mahi Mahi. Eastern North Carolina Pulled
Pork.

"The most fun restaurant experience in the Boston-
Cambridge area, Chris' food is great!" "Fun, hot
barbecue."

MASSACHUSETTS

Cambridge

Rialto

1 Bennett Street, Cambridge, MA 02138
(617) 661-5050 • Fax (617) 497-5552
Dinner Only 7 Days.
Decor: A chic, sophisticated restaurant in Harvard
Square with a rich and welcoming feel. 130 Seats.

Jody Adams

Kate Tsoi, Michael Dinsmore &
Sharon Cohen

Mediterranean

Provençal Fisherman's Soup with Rouille,
Gruyère and Basil Oil. Tuscan-Style Sirloin Steak
with Sliced Portobello Mushrooms and Arugula
Salad, Shaved Parmesan Reggiano and Truffle Oil.
Hot Chocolate Cream with Vodka-Spiked
Peppermint Chip Ice Cream.

"The food is tops and the atmosphere, incredibly
welcoming and comfortable." "Award-winning
cuisine!"

$$$ AMERICAN EXPRESS   VISA   MasterCard

Salamander Restaurant

Carter Ink Building, One Athenaeum Street
Cambridge, MA 02142
(617) 225-2121 • Fax (617) 494-8871
Website www.salamander-restaurant.com
Take-out Lunch Only. Dinner M.-Sa.
Decor: Spacious and comfortable with beautiful
silver, china and crystal. 120 Seats.

Stan Frankenthaler   Jim Smith

Global

Lightly-Fried Lobster with Chilis, Lemongrass
and Thai Basil. Tea-Scented Chicken over Stir-Fried
Chow Foon Noodles with Shrimp, Spicy Greens
and Chinese Sausage.

"Very interesting, eclectic world cuisine."

$$$ AMERICAN EXPRESS   VISA   MasterCard   ◯   DISCOVER

160

MASSACHUSETTS

Olives

10 City Square, Charlestown, MA 02129
(617) 242-1999 • Fax (617) 242-1333
Dinner Only M.-Sa.
Decor: A charming restaurant with hardwood
floors, antiques, Italian ceramic dishes and
embroidered seats. 100 Seats.

Todd English   Darren Wright

Mediterranean

Tortelli of Butternut Squash with Brown
Butter, Sage and Parmesan. Black Truffle-Foie Gras
Flan with a Ragu of Exotic Mushrooms and Seared
Foie Gras. Wood-Grilled Sirloin served over a
Tuscan Bruschetta with a Vidalia Onion and
Roquefort Cream, Georgian Peas and a Sweet and
Sour Shiitake Glaze.

"Robust flavors, generous portions and divine
pastas." "Full-flavored, high-energy cooking, a must
for any food lover."

$$$$

Roadhouse Café

488 South Street, Hyannis, MA 02601
(508) 775-2386 • Fax (508) 778-1025
Website www.roadhousecafe.com
Dinner Only 7 Days.
Decor: A clubby feeling with dark mahogany wood
and oriental carpets. 180 Seats.

Tim Souza   Dave Colombo

Italian

Veal Chop. Cioppino. Calamari Marinara.

"A yearly ritual to eat here in the summer; great
Cioppino!"

$$$

MASSACHUSETTS

Salem

Red Ravens Havana

90 Washington Street, Salem, MA 01970
(978) 740-3888
Dinner Only 7 Days.
Decor: The look is a cross between a 1920's French bistro and 1500's gothic. 145 Seats.

 Dave Chicane  Michael Frechet

 American-New

 Grilled, Marinated Duck Breast with Braised Lentils, Balsamic-Roasted Red Onion and Seasonal Fired Vegetables. Herb and Fresh Horseradish-Crusted Sirloin Steak with Classic Veal Sauce, Roasted Red Bliss Potatoes and Vegetable Saute.

"Best dining experience north of Boston!"

$$$

Siasconset

The Chanticleer

9 New Street, Siasconset, MA 02504
(508) 257-6231 • Fax (508) 257-4154
Website www.thechanticleer.com
Lunch and Dinner Tu.-Su.
Decor: A romantic, classically French restaurant overlooking a rose garden. 120 Seats.

 Jean-Charles Berruet  David McCoy

 French

 Roasted Lobster with Champagne Butter. Fresh Local Fish and Shellfish.

"Excellent French cuisine and service, beautiful surroundings and one of the best wine lists in the country."

$$$$

MASSACHUSETTS

Dali Restaurant

415 Washington Street
Sommerville, MA 02143
(617) 661-3254 • Fax (617) 661-2813
Website www.dalirestaurant.com
Dinner Only 7 Days.
Decor: Typically Spanish, romantic and inspiring.
90 Seats.

Jorge Ramirez

Spanish

Pescado a la Sal: Fresh Sea Bass Baked Under a
Bed of Sea Salt, De-salted and De-boned Tableside.
Over 40 Different Tapas (Small Plates of Food).

"For the best Tapas; and it's casual and FUN!"

$$

Il Capriccio

888 Main Street, Waltham, MA 02154
(617) 894-2234
Dinner Only M.-Sa.
Decor: A small, elegant Venetian-style restaurant.
45 Seats.

Richard Barron

Italian-Northern

Porcini Mushroom Soufflé. Foie Gras and
Portobello Mushroom Ravioli.

"A small, funky restaurant, yet solidly professional
and classical in its approach."

$$$

Tip: *Always add fresh herbs at the end of cooking any dish. Also, slightly freeze meats in order to thinly slice them more easily.*
Beverly Gannon, Haliimaile General Store

Dom DeLuise paraded through the kitchen announcing his dietary restrictions to all.
Pacific Time

Tip: *Try using a teaspoon when peeling ginger. Hold the ginger in one hand and with the teaspoon facing away, use the edge and scoop lightly. It works better than anything else, with less waste.*
DK Kodama, Sansei Sushi

MICHIGAN

The Rattlesnake Club

300 River Place, Detroit, MI 48207
(313) 567-4400 • Fax (313) 567-2063
Website www.rattlesnakeclub.com
Lunch M.-F. Dinner M.-Sa.
Decor: A contemporary room with panoramic views of the river and Canada. 200 Seats.

■ Jimmy Schmidt   ■ Robert Sereno

■ American-New   🍸 📋

⭐ Rack of Young Lamb Grilled with a Mint Crust, Artichoke and Asparagus Ragout and a Red Pepper Polenta Pyramid. White Chocolate Ravioli with Hazelnut Anglaise.

"The original, quintessential American dining spot!" "Always fresh and interesting ideas..."

$$$ AMERICAN EXPRESS VISA MasterCard ◑ DISCOVER 👔

Tapawingo

9502 Lake Street, Ellsworth, MI 49729
(616) 588-7971 • Fax (616) 588-7881
Website www.members.aol.com/tapdining
Dinner Only. Seasonal.
Decor: A warm spot featuring softly-colored fabrics and oak with many windows overlooking the lake and the gardens. 116 Seats.

■ Harlan Peterson and Richard Travis

■ Pram Acharya and Joel Hauswirth

■ American-Modern   🍸 📋

⭐ Morel Mushroom and Fiddlehead Cassoulet. Barbecued Duck Salad with Grilled Pineapple and Mango. Seared Sea Scallops in Lemongrass Broth.

"Great food and ambiance." "Reminds me of the great country restaurants of France."

$$$$ AMERICAN EXPRESS VISA MasterCard 👔

MICHIGAN

Farmington Hills

Tribute Restaurant

31425 West 12 Mile Road
Farmington Hills, MI 48334
(248) 848-9393 • Fax (248) 848-1919
Website www.tribute-restaurant.com
Dinner Only Tu.-Sa.
Decor: A breathtaking fusion of contemporary and classical design. 100 Seats.

Takashi Yagihashi   Mickey Bakst

Asian-French

Japanese Kaiseki. Braised Wild Sea Bass with Eggplant Confit, Glazed Baby Corn, Cream of Leeks and Haricots Verts. Herbal Sea Water with Razor Clams. Char-Grilled Wild Mushroom-Crusted Beef Tenderloin with Tortellini of Beef Marrow, Purple Sticky Rice and Zinfandel Sauce.

"I think Takashi is one of the most talented chefs in America today!"

Milford

Five Lakes Grill

424 North Main Street, Milford, MI 48381
(248) 684-7455 • Fax (248) 684-5935
Dinner Only M.-Sa.
Decor: An urban environment in a small town setting with wood floors and open rooms overlooking Main Street. 124 Seats.

Brian Polcyn   Ron Edwards

American-Contemporary

Potato-Crusted Whitefish with Lobster Mousseline and Armaganac Sauce. Pan-Seared, Unsoaked Sea Scallops on Sweet Corn Sauce with Chanterelles. Roast Crisp Duckling with Red Currant Sauce, Lentils and Sweet Potato Haystack.

"Great food!"

MICHIGAN

Mon Jin Lau

1515 East Maple Road, Troy, MI 48083
(248) 689-2332 • Fax (248) 689-6709
Lunch M.-F. Dinner 7 Days.
Decor: A friendly, lively, eclectic, Euro-Asian restaurant with an unusual collection of Hollywood memorabilia. 160 Seats.

Marshall Chin   Sharon Taylor

Asian-New

Ginger-Garlic Eggplant. Chili Pepper Squid. Mongolian Rack of Lamb.

"Wonderful contemporary Asian cuisine."

$$$

The Lark

6430 Farmington Road
West Bloomfield, MI 48322
(248) 661-4466 • Fax (248) 661-8891
Dinner Only Tu.-Sa.
Decor: A Southern European-style country inn. 60 Seats.

Marcus Haight   Jim Lark

French

Rack of Lamb Genghis Khan (41,000 sold). Curried Duck Salad.

"A tradition because they attend to every detail. The owner is always there, and it shows!"

$$$$

Tip: Never serve asparagus al dente; it should be fully cooked.
George Mavrothalassitis, Seasons

One of our dishwashers went to polish our brand new stainless steel walk-in refrigerator door, only to find out too late that what he thought was cleaner was actually white spray paint! **Brooks Restaurant**

Tip: Everything tastes better on a tortilla! **Rick Bayless, Frontera Grill and Topolobampo**

MINNESOTA

Tejas

3910 West 50th Street, Edina, MN 55424
(612) 926-0800 • Fax (612) 926-8444
Website www.tejasrestaurant.com
Lunch and Dinner M.-Sa.
Decor: A warm, cozy, Santa Fe-style restaurant with an adobe fireplace and an outdoor patio with tiled fountain. 140 Seats.

 Mark Haugen  Francoise Paradiese

 Regional Southwestern

 Tortilla Soup. Smoked Chicken Nachos. Barbecued Shrimp Enchiladas.

"Really interesting Southwestern cuisine with worldwide influences."

Giorgio's

2451 Hennepin Avenue, South
Minneapolis, MN 55405
(612) 374-5131
Website www.sidewalk.minnesota.com
Dinner Only 7 Days.
Decor: A tiny back street, Florentine-style trattoria. 55 Seats.

 Mike Hart  Dan Tomassetti

 Italian

 Lamb Pasta Sardinian-Style with Feta, Rosemary, Black Olives, Roasted Tomato Sauce, Mushrooms and Homemade Pappardelle Pasta. Focaccia with Goat Cheese, Roasted Garlic and Spicy Puttanesca Sauce.

"Very simple but incredibly well thought-out dishes and great service." "Real Tuscan food, many of the recipes have been in the Cherubini family for generations."

MINNESOTA

Minneapolis

Goodfellow's

40 South Seventh Street
Minneapolis, MN 55402
(612) 332-4800 • Fax (612) 332-1274
Lunch M.-F. Dinner M.-Sa.
Decor: Comfortably elegant, vintage art deco interior with mirrors, chandeliers and creative metal work. 120 Seats.

Kevin Cullen   John Day

Regional American

Pecan-Crusted Star Prairie Brook Trout. Wisconsin Veal Chop with Minnesota Sweet Corn Custard. Sliced Iowa Lamb Loin with Rosemary Butter and Huckleberries.

"The best example of Midwest regional cooking, very careful attention to detail, incredible wine list." "An institution!"

South Minneapolis

Rainbow Chinese Restaurant

2739 Nicollet Avenue
South Minneapolis, MN 55408
(612) 870-7084 • Fax (612) 870-6204
Lunch and Dinner 7 Days.
Decor: Open and soothing ambiance with a slate floor, Chinese garden mural and bamboo bar. 70 Seats.

Tammy Ying Wong

Fong Wong and Trinh Wong

Chinese

Chinese Noodles. Szechuan Wontons with Black Bean Sauce. Shrimp Cakes.

"The best Chinese food in Minneapolis; very fresh, well-spiced and authentic; excellent noodle dishes."

170

ANECDOTES & COOKING TIPS

Tip: When adding butter to a sauce, always make sure your reduction is boiling so the sauce doesn't separate. **Pierre Polin, Le Titi de Paris**

While filming "Dining Around" for TV Food Network, the fire sprinkler system went off, dousing everyone. *Astor Place*

Tip: Always loosely cover meats like duck and chicken breast with a piece of foil so the steam and heat will continue to cook the breast, moistening it and giving it a better texture. Never cut hot meat, let it rest. **Michael Foley, Printers Row**

One of our guests was dissatisfied with the whipped cream on top of her after-dinner coffee. She asked to speak to the manager to tell him how disappointed she was that a four-star restaurant would serve something out of a can instead of real whipped cream. The manager told her it was real, fresh whipped cream and offered to have the chef demonstrate how he made it for her. She said that would be the only way she would believe it was not out of a can, so the manager escorted her into the kitchen, where the chef proceeded to make the whipped heavy cream. Despite the demonstration by the chef, she refused to believe it was not out of a can and proclaimed as she left, "I haven't been convinced." *Vidalia*

MISSISSIPPI

KC's

Highway 61 North at 1st Street
Cleveland, MS 38732
(601) 843-5301 • Fax (601) 843-7006
EMail winetrmntr@aol.com
Lunch Su.-F. Dinner M.-Sa.
Decor: A California Mission-style building with a
funky New York interior. 165 Seats.

 Wally Joe   Don Joe

 American-Modern

 Seared Diver Sea Scallops with Foie Gras,
Summer Vegetable Salad, Lemon Oil and 25-year-
old Balsamic Vinegar. Grilled Muscovy Duck Breast
with Chinese Spices, Confit Leg and Wild Rice.
Shiitake Risotto and Purple Plum Hoisin Sauce.

"Great food and atmosphere in the middle of
nowhere!" "Elegant setting, excellent food and an
extensive wine selection."

Big Apple Inn

509 North Farish Street
Jackson, MS 39202
(601) 354-9371
EMail apple nms@aol.com
Breakfast, Lunch and Dinner M.-Sa.
Decor: A rustic, Southern-style restaurant.
25 Seats.

 Gene Lee

 Soul Food

 Smoked Sausage Sandwich. Hot Tamales.

"Where else can you get a Fried Pig's Ear
Sandwich and House-rolled Tamales from behind
bullet-proof glass?"

MISSISSIPPI

Jackson

Times Change

4800 I-55 North, Suite 6B
Jackson, MS 39211
(601) 366-8147 • Fax (601) 366-8112
Dinner Only M.-Sa.
Decor: A modern black and white restaurant with constantly changing artwork. 45 Seats.

Thomas Lambing Jr.

Kimberly Lambing

American

Fresh Game and Seafood.

"The best wood-fired grill chef to walk the planet. The wild game selections are second to none!"

$$$

Nesbit

Bonne Terre

4715 Church Road West, Nesbit, MS 38651
(601) 781-5199 • Fax (601) 781-5466
Website www.bonneterre.com
Dinner 7 Days. Sunday Brunch.
Decor: Simple, Country French. 70 Seats.

Andy Bouchard   Max Bonnin

French-Country

Shrimp and Calamari Pasta. Crêpe de Légumes en Julienne.

"Very relaxing country cooking."

$$$

City Grocery

152 Courthouse Square, Oxford, MS 38655
(601) 232-8080 • Fax (601) 281-8876
Lunch and Dinner M.-Sa.

Decor: A charming dining room with exposed brick walls and cypress hardwood floors. Also a casual, eccentric bar upstairs with the best jukebox on the planet! 100 Seats.

 John M.Currence

Jim Weems and Catherine Ladner

 Eclectic

Sautéed Shrimp and Tabasco Cheese Grits. Napoleon of Seared Foie Gras with Blueberry Glaze. Ginger Crème Brûlée.

"A fun atmosphere, and great cuisine. Perfect in a college town!" "Terrifically progressive Southern/ Creole cuisine!" "Accessibly eclectic American food, great atmosphere, great wine list, and the chef-owner is a swell guy!"

Tip: *When utilizing beer in a food preparation, it is essential to also add some form of sugar.* **Robert Matzig, Glen Ellyn Brewing Co.**

During a wedding rehearsal dinner, a fight broke out between the two families! *Araxi*

Tip: *To perk up parsley, wash it in soapy water and rinse very well.* **Cathy Cary, Lily's**

MISSOURI

Chesterfield

Annie Gunn's

16806 Chesterfield Airport Road
Chesterfield, MO 63005
(314) 532-7684 • Fax (314) 532-0561
Lunch and Dinner Tu.-Su.
Decor: A comfortable bistro with two wood-burning fireplaces and a patio overlooking the award-winning perennial garden. 100 Seats.

Lou Rook III   Dan O'Connor

Regional American

Jumbo-Lump Crabcakes with Chipotle Aioli. Grilled Muscovy Duck Breast with Smoke House Bacon and Juniper Glaze with Whipped Yukon Gold Potatoes.

"This place is one-of-a-kind: great food and friendly service."

$$$

Clayton

Cardwell's Restaurant & Bar

8100 Maryland, Clayton, MO 63105
(314) 726-5055 • Fax (314) 726-1909
Lunch and Dinner M.-Sa.
Decor: An upscale, elegant dining room accented with dark wood. Private dining available and a separate café with French doors that flows onto a patio. 220 Seats.

Gary Suarez   Marc D. Ray

American

Pecan-Wood-Smoked Shrimp, Wild Rice Salad and Cheddar Cheese Pecan Wafer. Roasted Rack of Lamb Crusted with Mustard and Herb Crumbs, Merlot Jus and Potato-Gruyère Gratin.

"Terrifically elegant down-home cookin'!"

$$$

177

MISSOURI

Kansas City

Saigon 39

1806 West 39th Street
Kansas City, MO 64111
(816) 531-4447
Lunch and Dinner M.-Sa.
Decor: Tiny and simple, traditional Vietnamese.
60 Seats.

Mimi Perkins

Vietnamese

Spring Rolls.

"A small Vietnamese café, serving very solid food to a young, hip crowd."

$$ [O]

The American Restaurant

2450 Grand Avenue at 25th
Kansas City, MO 64108
(816) 426-1133 • Fax (816) 426-1190
Lunch M.-F. Dinner M.-Sa.
Decor: A beautiful room with vaulted ceilings, banquettes and a great view of Kansas City.
160 Seats.

Michael Smith and Debbie Gold

Rose Rudi, Solomon Melesse and
Victor Berndt

American-Contemporary

Gulf Blue Crab Cakes with Grain Mustard Sauce and Wild Mushrooms. Grilled Veal Tenderloin with Foie Gras, Celery Root Puree, Sweetbreads, Hazelnuts and Madeira Sauce.

"This is a restaurant to watch. But in the meantime, go eat there!"

$$$$

MISSOURI

Fiorella's Smokestack Barbecue

13441 Holmes, Martin City, MO 64145
(816) 942-9141 • Fax (816) 942-5166
Website www.smokestack.com
Lunch and Dinner 7 Days.
Decor: Country French ambiance. 50 Seats.

Chris Dorman

Barbecue

Crown Prime Short Ribs of Beef. Fresh Grilled Salmon.

"This place serves great food, and it's not all barbecue! The service is friendly and knowlegeable, and the product is always consistent."

$$

St. Louis

Tony's

410 Market Street, St. Louis, MO 63102
(314) 231-7007 • Fax (314) 231-4740
Dinner Only M.-Sa.
Decor: A contemporary Italian restaurant.
110 Seats.

Vincent P. Bonmarito

James D. Bonmarito

Italian

Veal Loin Chop with Black Truffles. Filet Mignon of Swordfish with Olives, Capers and Tomato. Spinach-and-Veal-Stuffed Agnolotto.

"Classy, Classy, Classy." "One of the oldest and best-known Italian restaurants in America. Vincent Bonmarito is a household name among restaurateurs internationally."

$$$$

MISSOURI

St. Louis

Trattoria Marcella

3600 Watson Road, St. Louis, MO 63109
(314) 352-7706
Dinner Only Tu.-Sa.
Decor: A warm, casual restaurant. 70 Seats.

 Steve Komorek   Patricia Komorek

Italian

Frito Misto: Fried Calamari and Spinach, Dusted with Garlic, Parmesan and Lemon. Homemade Veal Ravioli with Roasted Garlic, Mushroom Broth and Escarole with Wild Mushrooms.

"Besides a great neighborhood atmosphere, this restaurant has personality!"

Tip: When making brown roux, start on top of the stove and finish in a 350-degree oven. It will take about three to four hours, but you only have to stir every 30 minutes or so. **Frank Brigsten, Brigsten's**

The garland on the mantle caught fire on New Year's Eve at about 11:30pm. That certainly welcomed in 1994! **Bacchanalia**

Tip: Cajun and Creole cuisine should not be considered hot and spicy, but rather a perfect blend of seasonings. When creating a new dish, always remember to be true to your region... and "more ain't better." **John Folse, Lafitte's Landing**

There is a display grand piano in the restaurant that a guest went to play. After a few chords, the back leg fell out and the piano collapsed, the desserts slid off the top and the guest ran out the door. *Bugatti*

Tip: Start mashed potatoes with cold water and no salt. Only salt water halfway through the cooking time.
Rene Bajeux, Windsor Court

Las Vegas

Emeril's New Orleans Fish House

3799 Las Vegas Boulevard South
Las Vegas, NV 89109
(702) 891-7374 • Fax (702) 891-7338
Lunch and Dinner 7 Days.
Decor: An upscale, casual restaurant located in the MGM Grand Hotel. 170 Seats.

Emeril Lagasse

Scott Farber

Cajun/Creole

New Orleans BBQ Shrimp and Campfire Steak. Banana Cream Pie.

"The food and service are great."

$$$

Las Vegas

Napa

Rio Suite Hotel and Casino,
3700 West Flamingo Road
Las Vegas, NV 89103
(702) 247-7961 • Fax (702) 247-7923
Dinner Only W.-Su.
Decor: A classy, elegant restaurant with a bright, ethereal feeling and an amazing art collection. 120 Seats.

Jean-Louis Palladin   George Arfuso

French-Country

Fresh Hudson Valley Foie Gras with Mango. Chorizo-Crusted Halibut with a White Bean Broth. Stuffed Artichoke with Farm-Raised Squab.

"There is no better restaurant in the Southwest!" "Truly a great chef." "Excellent menu." "Innovative, always surprising, and a fantastic wine list!"

$$$$

NEVADA

Las Vegas

Spago Las Vegas

3500 Las Vegas Boulevard,
In The Forum Shops at Caesar's
Las Vegas, NV 89109
(702) 369-6300 • Fax (702) 369-0361
Lunch & Dinner 7 Days.
Decor: A colorful, eclectic space with unique
artwork and patio dining. 200 Seats, Dining Room.
120 Seats, Café. 14 Seats, Bar.

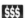 David Robins and Wolfgang Puck

Andre Binard

American

House-Smoked Salmon Pizza with Dill
Cream, Chives and Black Caviar. Foie Gras Two
Ways with Crisp Galette. Seared Red Snapper with
Baby Spinach Risotto, Lemon Crème Fraîche and
Lobster Nage.

"Great food every time." "Best food in town."
"Inspired, delicious combinations!"

One person, seated at table seven, received seven sandwiches of the same one he ordered, because the kitchen thought the table number was the number of people at the table. *Fairly Poplar Café*

Tip: When making risotto, most people tell you that the stock must be hot when you add it to the rice. I disagree. The hot stock causes the rice to spatter, which has the potential to break the grains. The trick is to create a slow, low simmer that enables the grains to slowly absorb the room-temperature liquid. When you spoon it out, risotto should sink on the plate, run a bit, and then stop.
Todd English, Olives

ANECDOTES & COOKING TIPS

Tip: *To prepare risotto ahead, cook until rice is slightly underdone and spread out in a sheet pan. Pour cold stock over it to cover. Chill until ready to serve.*
Jack Amon
The Marx Bros. Café

A man and his son dressed in tutus for his daughter's 18th birthday... *Imperial Fez*

Tip: *Cooking is like flying a plane... take off and landing are tricky, the rest is just simmering.*
Daniele Baliani, Pignoli

NEW HAMPSHIRE

The Creamery

288 Shaker Road, Canterbury, NH 03224
(603) 783-9511 • Fax (603) 783-9152
Website www.shakers.org
Lunch and Dinner 7 Days. Seasonal.
Decor: A quaint, New England country restaurant set in a 1905 creamery, with lots of windows and picturesque views of the historic 1792 Canterbury Shaker Village. Guests eat at community tables of 16. 48 Seats.

Jeffrey Paige   Rene Paquette-Paige

Regional American

Applewood-Smoked Loin of Pork with Cider Gravy and Sage Cakes. Maine Crab Bisque with Pan-Roasted Corn and Scallion Purée. Hot Apple Charlotte with Homemade Vanilla Bean Ice Cream and Gentleman Jack Caramel.

"Contemporary preparation of traditional Shaker recipes."

$$$

Café Buon Gustaio

72 South Main Street, Hanover, NH 03755
(603) 643-5711
Dinner Only Tu.-Su.
Decor: A relaxed, cozy atmosphere with a lovely terrace. 70 Seats, Dining Room. 24 Seats, Terrace.

Jim Oronte   Theo Simpson

Italian

Cioppino. Veal with Porcini and Marsala Cream. Lobster Lasagna.

"Great Italian bistro with a wonderful staff and well-chosen wines."

$$$

NEW HAMPSHIRE

Salem

The Colosseum Restaurant

264 North Broadway, Suite 101
Salem, NH 03079
(603) 898-1190 • Fax (603) 898-4490
Website www.dining-out.com/restaurant/colosseum
Lunch Tu.-F. Dinner Tu.-Su.
Decor: Elegant, modern, and contemporary with a
touch of glass...lots of windows. 225 Seats.

Annibale   Coty Todesca

Italian

Stuffed Portobello Mushrooms. Veal
Scalloppini Sautéed with Wild Mushrooms and
Ziti. Chicken Stuffed with Shrimp, Mozzarella and
Sautéed in Pizzaiolo Sauce. Seafood Spaghetti
Frutti di Mare al Cartoccio.

"The only place you get food like this is in Rome:
pure, unadulterated Italian cooking."

Wolfeboro

East of Suez

775 South Main Street
Wolfeboro, NH 03894
(603) 569-1648
Dinner Only Tu.-Su. Seasonal.
Decor: Located in America's oldest summer resort,
this former lodge is decorated with Asian artifacts
and has two tatami rooms. 60 Seats.

Charles and Elizabeth Powell

Katsuhito Gorac

Asian

Kim Chee, Made In House. Sushi and
Sashimi. Szechuan Filet Mignon and Scallops.

"Open only July-August for 28 years, this is a
summer ritual, a unique blending of Philippino and
Thai cooking."

ANECDOTES & COOKING TIPS

Tip: Soak garlic in warm water before peeling. **Mark Gaier and Clark Frasier, Arrows**

On his last day at Toulouse, a sous-chef leaving to man the helm of his own kitchen arrived to find his knives frozen in a block of ice. *Toulouse*

Tip: Grilled fish almost always has more flavor if the skin is left intact, but remember to scale the fish before cooking. **Sam Hayward, Fore Street**

ANECDOTES & COOKING TIPS

One night, after cooking 300-plus dinners and banquets, I fell asleep on a prep table. I awoke in the morning to find the prep cook covering me in vegetables!
David Paul's Diamond Head Grill

Tip: Roll lemons on the counter before juicing, they will release more juice... **Bryan Polcyn, Five Lakes Grill**

NEW JERSEY

Le Petit Château

121 Claremont Road
Bernardsville, NJ 07924
(908) 766-4544 • Fax (908) 766-9244
Website www.powerpg.com/nj1/lepetit
Lunch Tu.-F. Dinner Tu.-Su.
Decor: An elegant, country-style restaurant.
95 Seats.

Scott Martin Cutaneo

Kimberly Anne Ross

French

Rabbit Loin with Squab Breast, Foie Gras,
Black Truffle Ravioli and Savoy Cabbage with
Spinach. Frog's Legs Stuffed with Lemon Compote,
Garlic Aioli and Asparagus. Strawberries of the
Woods Baked on a Tart with a Honey Glaze.

"This guy's a howl, and he's talented!" "Very
complex flavors, and a well-executed, personal
cuisine."

$$$

Highland

Doris & Ed's

348 Shore Drive, Highland, NJ 07732
(732) 872-1565 • Fax (732) 872-2299
Website www.doris-and-eds.com
Dinner Only W.-Su.
Decor: A bright, cheerful restaurant overlooking
Sandy Hook Bay. 90 Seats.

Russell Dare   Jim Filip

Seafood

Lobster Bisque. Grilled Tuna Steak with
Wasabi and Soy Ginger Sauce.

"They serve the freshest seafood this side of the
Atlantic, and have a fine American wine list!"

$$$

191

NEW JERSEY

Rumson

Fromagerie

26 Ridge Road, Rumson, NJ 07760
(732) 842-8088 • Fax (732) 842-6625
Lunch M.-F. Dinner 7 Days.
Decor: French Provençal. 140 Seats.

🐾 Hubert Peter 🍸 Michael Doman

🚬 Provençal 🍸 🍷

⭐ Sautéed Duck Breast with Plum Wine Demi Glace. House-Smoked Salmon with Apple Mousse and Horseradish Crème.

"Top-notch, well-seasoned food and a really good wine list, served by an accommodating staff, in charming surroundings."

$$$ AMERICAN EXPRESS VISA MasterCard ◎ 🏧

Short Hills

The Dining Room
at The Hilton at Short Hills

41 JFK Parkway, Short Hills, NJ 07078
(973) 379-0100 • Fax (973) 379-1153
Website www.hiltonatshorthills.com
Dinner Only M.-Sa.
Decor: A large but intimate dining room done in rich cherrywood, plush couches and elegant touches such as silver, china, fine linens and floral arrangements. 68 Seats.

🐾 Paul Sale 🍸 George Staikos

🚬 American-New 🍸 🍷

⭐ Warm, Marinated Goat Cheese and Grilled Vegetables with Tomato-Tarragon Drizzle. Herb-Crusted Lamb Loin with Goat Cheese Risotto, Oven-Roasted Fennel and Smoked Tomato Natural Jus.

"A talented chef!" "Paul has brought the prestige back to the Hilton at Short Hills."

$$$$ AMERICAN EXPRESS VISA MasterCard ◎ DISCOVER 🏧

NEW JERSEY

The Ryland Inn

Route 22 West, Whitehouse, NJ 08888
(908) 534-4011 • Fax (908) 534-6592
Website www.rylandinn.com
Lunch Tu.-F. Dinner Tu.-Su.
Decor: An elegant, country atmosphere in a 200-year-old building set on a 50-acre estate. 120 Seats.

 Craig Shelton Steve Gallagher

 French-American

 Warm Tart of Maine Lobster, Potatoes and Chanterelle Mushrooms. Crispy Black Sea Bass with Sunchokes, Maine Crab and Beurre Meunier. Seared Veal Medallions Dusted in Root Vegetable Flours.

"I've had some of the best dishes ever from Craig."
"Craig has created a place that provides top quality food, wine and service."

Tip: Keep fragile sauces (such as Beurre Blanc) hot in Thermos bottles to avoid reduction or breaking. **Harlan Peterson, Tapawingo**

The dining room aquarium broke during the dinner hour, and the saltwater fish flopped onto a customer's plate, now that's service! **Erik's Seafood Grotto**

Tip: When grating citrus peel, use a piece of wax paper over the grater so that the zest is easy to remove, and does not stick to the grater. **Mark Haugen, Tejas**

Santa Fe

Bistro 315

315 Old Santa Fe Trail
Santa Fe, NM 87501
(505) 986-9190
Lunch M.-Sa. Dinner 7 Days.
Decor: A downtown, French country bistro with a
beautiful patio and incredible sunset views.
100 Seats.

 Matt Yohalem 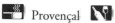 Louis Moskow

Provençal

Stuffed Portobello Mushroom with
Potato Galette and Truffle Creme. Steak Frites.
Potato-Crusted Salmon with Horseradish and
Cucumber Salad.

"Fine Modern French cuisine, intimate atmosphere,
friendly but proper service and a very good wine
cellar."

$$$ AMERICAN EXPRESS   VISA   MasterCard

Santa Fe

Bobcat Bite Restaurant

Route 3, Bobcat Ranch, Santa Fe, NM 87507
(505) 983-5319
Lunch and Dinner W.-Sa.
Decor: Simple diner with bobcat pictures
everywhere. 25 Seats.

 Bob Amos

Regional Southwestern

Green Chili Cheeseburger. Ribeye Steak.

"Flat, grilled burgers, no fries (hash browns
instead). Informal counter service, and oddly, they
close at 7:10 pm!???"

NEW MEXICO

Santa Fe

Cowboy of Santa Fe

331 Sandoval Street, Santa Fe, NM 87501
(505) 982-8999
Dinner Only 7 Days.
Decor: A contemporary Southwestern feel with a comfortable, expansive dining room. 120 Seats.

 Zach Calkins   Chris Hervey

Regional Southwestern

Dungeness Crab Poblano Relleno with Saffron Cream. Dry-Aged Rib Chop with Ranch Mashed Potatoes. Mini Chocolate Torte with Rum Bananas and Honey Ice Cream.

"The best eclectic Cowboy-Southwestern food in the state!" "A real taste treat!"

$$$ AMERICAN EXPRESS   VISA   MasterCard

Coyote Café

132 Water St., Santa Fe, NM 87501
(505) 983-1615 • Fax (505) 989-9026
Lunch and Dinner 7 Days.
Decor: High ceilings, bright colors, open kitchen. Evokes the fun and fantasy of the Southwest. 100 seats restaurant. 60 seats café.

Mark Miller, Mark Kiffin and Jeff Drew

Brett Kemmerer

Regional Southwestern

Buttermilk Corn Cakes with Chipotle Shrimp. Cowboy Rib Chop. Roasted Banana Flan.

"Fantastic wine list, and I loved the salmon."
"Always tantalizing to the tastebuds! They're still going strong after so many years!"

$$$ AMERICAN EXPRESS   VISA   MasterCard   DINERS CLUB

NEW MEXICO

Santa Fe

Geronimo

724 Canyon Road, Santa Fe, NM 87501
(505) 982-1500 • Fax (505) 820-2083
Lunch Tu.-Sa. Dinner 7 Days.
Decor: A casually elegant 1756 adobe hacienda on
the historic Canyon Road. 95 Seats.

 Eric DiStefano Ken Brown

 American-New

Mesquite-Grilled Lobster on Herb-Spun Pasta
with Sirachi Vinaigrette. Elk Tenderloin with
Scallion Risotto and Apple-Cranberry Jus. French
Chocolate Walnut Strudel with Banana-Orange Ice
Cream.

"Deliciously innovative Southwestern cuisine!"
"The tiny bar is very cool; you feel as though you
were in someone's private home!"

Harry's Roadhouse

Old Las Vegas Highway, Santa Fe, NM 87501
(505) 989-4629 • Fax (505) 989-5623
Breakfast, Lunch and Dinner 7 Days.
Decor: A real roadhouse with an extraordinary
patio and garden in the back. 80 Seats, Summer.
40 Seats, Winter.

Harry Shapiro, Peyton Young, and
David Holupchinski

Regional American

Blue Corn Waffle with Honey Butter and
Strawberries. Shrimp, Black Bean, Feta and Spinach
Quesadilla. Cornmeal-Dusted Trout Stuffed with
Mushrooms, Pumpkin Seeds and Sage with a Wild
Rice Corn Cake.

"Fresh, hearty, home-style American diner food,
and delicious homemade desserts."

NEW MEXICO

Santa Fe

India Palace

227 Don Gaspar Street, Santa Fe, NM 87501
(505) 986-5859 • Fax (505) 983-3851
Lunch and Dinner 7 Days.
Decor: Very elegant, intimate Indian interior.
43 Seats.

Ashok Virui

Indian

Chicken Tikka Kabob. Saag Paneer:
Homemade Cheese with Spinach.

"Great classical East Indian cooking!"

$$ AMERICAN EXPRESS   VISA   MasterCard   ◑   DISCOVER

Julian's Restaurant

221 Shelby Street, Santa Fe, NM 87501
(505) 988-2355 • Fax (505) 988-5071
Dinner Only 7 Days.
Decor: Warm and romantic, reminiscent of a
Tuscan home. 120 Seats.

Wayne Gustafson   Elizabeth McLeod

Regional Italian

Roasted Chicken in Agrodolce with Onions.
Duck Two Ways with Pomegranate Sauce and
Polenta. Taglialini with Lobster and Tomato.

"Marvelous Italian food!"

$$ AMERICAN EXPRESS   VISA   MasterCard   ◑   DISCOVER

Mu Du Noodles

1494 Cerillos Road, Santa Fe, NM 87501
(505) 983-1411
Lunch M.-F. Dinner M.-Sa.
Decor: Traditional Thai design.
54 Seats, Dining Room. 24 Seats, Patio.

🔪 Mu Jing Lau 🍴 Mu Jing Lau

🚬 Asian-Southeast 🍷

🎯 Pad Thai. Rangoon. Orange Blossom Custard.

"A great taste of Thai and Vietnamese in the middle of the desert!"

💲💲 AMERICAN EXPRESS VISA MasterCard ⊘ DISCOVER 🛋

Old House Restaurant

309 West San Francisco Street
Santa Fe, NM 87501
(505) 995-4530 • Fax (505) 995-4555
Website www.eldoradohotel.com
Dinner Only 7 Days.
Decor: A cozy restaurant with a Southwestern flair.
95 Seats.

🔪 Martin Rios 🍴 Kevin Guidon

🚬 American-Contemporary 🍸 🍷

🎯 Sautéed Escargots in Potato Crust with Spinach, Potatoes and Herb Butter Sauce. Mustard and Pepper-Crusted Lamb Rack with Roasted Red Chile-Infused Lamb Sauce. Warm Liquid Center Chocolate Cake with Crème Anglaise and Caramel Sauce.

"When you want a romantic getaway, this is the place!"

💲💲 AMERICAN EXPRESS VISA MasterCard ⊘ DISCOVER 👔

NEW MEXICO

Santa Fe

Pasqual's

121 Don Gaspar, Santa Fe, NM 87501
(505) 983-9340 • Fax (505) 988-4645
Breakfast & Lunch M.-Sa. Dinner 7 Days.
Sunday Brunch
Decor: A festive, contemporary Mexican restaurant.
49 Seats.

 Katharine Kagel

Regional Southwestern

Grilled Salmon Burrito. Chorizo Burrito.
Famous Breakfasts.

"A lively, small and crowded breakfast and lunch
spot. The Mexican/New Mexican cuisine is
excellent, and it's worth the wait to get in!"

Pizza Etc.

151 Paseo de Peralta, in DeVargas Center
(enter across from the movies)
Santa Fe, NM 87501
(505) 986-1500 • Fax (505) 986-1035
Website www.pizzaetc.com
Lunch and Dinner 7 Days.
Decor: A canopied sidewalk trattoria inside a busy
shopping mall with black and white tile, and a
bold, urban mural. 46 Seats.

Roland Richter

Italian

Pizza Giovanni: Montrachet Goat Cheese,
Roasted Red Pepper, Roasted Garlic and Fresh
Oregano. Pizza Pontchartrain: Louisiana-Style
Andouille Sausage, Shrimp, Caramelized Onions
and Fresh Scallions. Pizza Amaro-Dolce: Rapini
Sautéed with Red Onion, Topped with Gorgonzola
"Dolce" and Accented with Crumbled Amaretti.

"I love the cepes (porcini) pizza!" "An adventure in
Pizza-dining!"

Tip: Always use fresh herbs, it will make the difference between good food and great food. **Gary Suarez, Cardwell's**

A Saudi harem of 20 women came in for lunch, drank straight cans of Coco Lopez, pulled the tablecloths off the tables and got down on their knees and prayed to Allah! *Haliimaile General Store*

Tip: A splash of strong coffee in a homemade barbecue sauce adds a good, secret authenticity to BBQ. **John Currence, City Grocery**

The Japanese make food look so real that I decided to give one of my customers a plastic shrimp sushi. He dipped it in his soy and tried to bite it. He was a good sport and started laughing and put the shrimp back down. His girlfriend didn't see this and was thinking what a nice guy her boyfriend was for leaving her a piece, so she picked up the same piece and the rest is history... All the regulars know about the infamous Shrimp Sushi.

Sansei Seafood Restaurant & Sushi Bar

Tip: Finish fresh legumes with lemon zest and a delicate vinaigrette to amplify flavors.
Ben Barker, Magnolia Grill

Bedford

La Cremaillère

46 Banksville Road, Bedford, NY 10506
(914) 234-9647 • Fax (914) 234-0736
Website www.cremaillere.com
Lunch Th.-Su. Dinner Tu.-Su.
Decor: Charming French country style decorated
with murals of French regional costumes, located in
Westchester horse country. 120 Seats.

 Matthew Tivy  Eric Chambry

French-Modern

Seared Duck Foie Gras with Cider Vinaigrette
and Julienned Apple Salad. Crisp Shrimp and
Scallop Dumplings with Lobster Passion Fruit
Coulis. Roasted Squab with Truffle Polenta,
Caramelized Garlic and Port Sauce.

"I love the interior: it has a sophistication and the
patina of age that you can't get with mere
decorations." "Matthew Tivy just keeps cooking
better and better."

$$$$

Brooklyn

Peter Luger

178 Broadway, Brooklyn, NY 11211
(718) 387-7400 • Fax (718) 387-3523
Lunch M.-Sa. Dinner 7 Days.
Decor: A German Tudor-style Restaurant.
150 Seats.

 Ortwin Windmuller

Ortwin Windmuller

Steakhouse

Porterhouse Steak. Salad of Beefsteak
Tomatoes and Onions with Peter Luger Sauce.
Jumbo Shrimp Cocktail.

"The best steak in NYC!" "Great service all the
time!" "I love the Black and Tan beer!"

 **$$**

NEW YORK

East Hampton

Nick & Toni's Restaurant

136 North Main Street
East Hampton, NY 11937
(516) 324-3550 • Fax (516) 324-7001
Lunch Su. Only. Dinner 7 Days.
Decor: A casually elegant, welcoming room.
100 Seats.

 Joseph Realmuto   Bonnie Munshin

Mediterranean

Whole Fish from the Wood-Burning Oven.
Penne alla Vecchia Bettola.

"A great spot in the Hamptons."

$$$

The Maidstone Arms
Inn & Restaurant

207 Main Street, East Hampton, NY 11937
(516) 324-5006 • Fax (516) 324-5037
Lunch and Dinner 7 Days, Sunday Brunch.
Decor: A cozy, romantic historic landmark with a
fireplace. 75 Seats.

William Valentine   Meredith Hazemann

American-Contemporary

Seared Atlantic Salmon in Miso with Organic
Spinach and Shiitake Mushrooms. Roasted Rack of
Colorado Lamb with Toasted Garlic Herb Orzo.

"An excellent casual restaurant on the East End of
Long Island."

$$$

NEW YORK

Lexington Square Café

510 Lexington Avenue, Mt. Kisco, NY 10549
(914) 244-3663 • Fax (914) 244-3665
Lunch M.-Sa. Dinner 7 Days. Sunday Brunch.
Decor: A bright, multi-leveled, rustic restaurant with cathedral ceilings, French doors and alfresco dining. 170 Seats, Dining Room. 50 Seats, Outside.

Dimitri Cruz

Craig Fiacco, Michael Grossberg and James Brown

American-Contemporary

Mussels du Jour. Grilled, Marinated Hangar Steak with Roasted Garlic Mashed Potatoes and Cabernet Reduction. Oven-Roasted Free Range Chicken with Grilled Corn Succotash and Black Pepper Jus.

"The chef has traveled and cooked all over Europe, and it shows: intelligent, creative and well-balanced food from an American kitchen."

$$

New York

An American Place

2 Park Avenue, New York, NY 10016
(212) 684-2122 • Fax (212) 684-3599
Lunch M.-F. Dinner M.-Sa.
Decor: A warm dining room with high ceilings, art deco fixtures and modern art. 100 Seats.

Larry Forgione and Richard d'Orazi

Kevin Dwyer

American-New

Cedar Plank Salmon. Adobo-Style Duck.

"Quintessential American cooking, with great service, to boot!" "The best of American ingredients, creatively prepared."

$$$

New York

Arizona 206

206 East 60th Street, New York, NY 10022
(212) 838-0440 • Fax (212) 988-3703
Dinner Only 7 Days.
Decor: An elegant adobe-style design. 50 Seats.

 Scott Linquist

Southwestern

Lobster Tamales. Petite Tuna Tacos with
Wasabi Tobiko. Lipstick Chile Relleno of Crab with
Carrot Ginger Butter.

"The most tantalizing flavors!" "Fun and laid-back,
but serious food." "I can honestly say it is one of
my favorite restaurants, consistently serving some of
the most exciting Southwestern food I've ever
tasted!"

$$$

Asia de Cuba

237 Madison Avenue, between 37th & 38th St.
New York, NY 10016
(212) 726-7755 • Fax (212) 726-7575
Lunch M.-F. Dinner 7 Days.
Decor: A chic, white and marble Philippe Starck-
designed restaurant with a communal dining table
on the main floor. 180 Seats.

Eric Basulto   Rolando Ramos

Fusion

Oxtail Spring Rolls. Cuban Coffee and Vanilla
Lacquered Duck Chow Chow. Chinese Five-Spice
Foie Gras.

"Cuban-Oriental fusion gone wild! Awesome,
intense flavors in an eclectic setting."

$$$

Aureole

34 East 61st Street, New York, NY 10021
(212) 319-1660 • Fax (212) 750-8613
Website www.aureolerestaurant.com
Lunch M.-F. Dinner M.-Sa.
Decor: An elegant and comfortable dining room
with towering flower arrangements and dramatically
lit sculptures. 96 Seats.

Charlie Palmer

Alex Gouras, Vincent Santoro

American-Progressive

Sea Scallop Sandwiches. Game Dishes.
Famous Desserts.

"Superb cuisine, classy room." "Consistently
creative and great-tasting food." "Words cannot
describe what Charlie plates every night. Dessert is
NEVER to be missed." "Great ambiance, unique
marriage of flavors, and exciting presentations make
this one of my favorites."

Babbo Restaurant & Enoteca

110 Waverly Place, New York, NY 10011
(212) 777-0303
Dinner Only Tu.-Su.
Decor: A comfortable room filled with golden,
twinkling lights and fragrant food. 100 Seats.

Mario Batali   Tom Piscitello

Italian

Sable Carpaccio. Beef Cheek Ravioli. Squab
"al Mattone."

"Delicious country-style Northern Italian fare with
a flair!" "Hearty and satisfying..."

NEW YORK

New York

Balthazar

80 Spring Street at B'way and Lafayette
New York, NY 10012
(212) 965-1414 • Fax (212) 966-2502
Lunch and Dinner 7 Days. Breakfast in the Bakery.
Decor: Traditional French brasserie-style room.
High ceilings and plenty of room to people-watch!
150 Seats.

Lee Hansen and Riad Nasr

French Bistro

Brandade of Cod. Balthazar Platter of Fresh
Chilled Seafood. Braised Short Ribs of Beef with
Mashed Potatoes.

"Finally, a true Parisian-style bistro in the US!"
"This place embodies why I am in the restaurant
business." "Fabulous atmosphere, the perfect place
for late night dining."

Barbetta

321 West 46th Street, New York, NY 10036
(212) 246-9171 • Fax (212) 246-1279
Website www.barbettarestaurant.com
Lunch and Dinner Tu.-Sa.
Decor: The spectacular main dining room is
decorated with 18th century Italian antiques and
opens onto a lush garden with century-old trees.
280 Seats.

Marius Pavlak   Robert Warren

Italian

Diver Scallops Capped with a Julienned
Potato Crust in an Intense Tomato Jus with Braised
Bok Choy. Roasted Rack of Venison with a Hudson
River Valley Apple and a Pear Potato Croquette.
Monte Bianco.

"Wonderful Modern Italian cuisine in the heart of
the Theater District!"

Blue Ribbon

97 Sullivan Street, New York, NY 10012
(212) 274-0404 • Fax (212) 274-8156
Dinner Only Tu.-Su.
Decor: Modern Bistro design, candlelight and
banquettes. 30 Seats, plus a happening bar.

 Eric and Bruce Bromberg

 Ellen Bromberg

 American-Eclectic

Blue Ribbon Royale: Caviar and Vodka. Raw
Bar with Fresh Daily Seafood. Very-late-night
dining. Rustic, hearty dining.

"Nothing beats a 1:00am fix of fried oysters, crispy,
briny, on a bed of spinach with a kick!" "This is the
place to go for heart-warming cuisine after theater,
or after working in the kitchen all night!"

$$$

Bouterin

420 East 59th Street, New York, NY 10022
(212) 758-0323 • Fax (212) 758-1312
Dinner Only 7 Days. Closed Su. in Summer.
Decor: A cozy dining room with fresh flowers,
antiques and a French Provençal atmosphere.
130 Seats.

Antoine Bouterin   Ellen Wolkonski

French-Modern

Lobster Cake with Herbs and Mild Spices.
Provençal Onion Tart with Black Olives and a
Garden Salad.

"Antoine is one of the most inventive chefs around.
But don't expect high prices, this stuff is authentic!"

$$$

NEW YORK

Café Boulud

80 East 76th Street, New York, NY 10021
(212) 772-2600 • Fax (212) 772-7755
Lunch and Dinner 7 Days.
Decor: A recreation of an elegant 1930's Parisian rendez-vous, Café Boulud is casual yet sophisticated, a place where you feel at home from the start. 85 Seats.

 Daniel Boulud

Eclectic

La Tradition: Braised Pork Breast with Lentils. La Saison: Roasted Venison Loin with Chestnut Crust and a Spiced Date Purée. Le Potager: Whole Sweet Onion Baked with a Fall Vegetable Stuffing. Le Voyage: Spanish Garlic Soup "Piperade" with a Bacalao Crouton.

"Daniel, the Master, brings us his elegant home-style cuisine in a lively, relaxed atmosphere. I could eat here every night!"

$$$

Carmine's

200 West 44th Street, New York, NY 10036
(212) 221-3800 • Fax (212) 221-0259
Lunch and Dinner 7 Days.
Decor: A large but homey, very Italian-style spot with old family photos. 300 Seats.

Ralph Scamardella

Hat Shet Sepshaw, India Hammer

Italian

Everything you'd expect, served family-style, to be shared.

"The best Southern Italian food in NYC!" "Family-style, and heavenly helpings!"

$$$

Carnegie Deli

854 7th Avenue, New York, NY 10019
(212) 757-2245 • Fax (212) 757-9889
Breakfast, Lunch and Dinner 7 Days.
Decor: Bright and brassy New York style.
170 Seats.

 Mike Ayala

 American

 Immense sandwiches! The Danny Rose:
Pastrami and Corned Beef. The Jeff Tatalan:
Corned Beef, Turkey, Swiss, Coleslaw and Russian
Dressing on Pumpernickel. Matzo Ball Soup.

"The perfect matzo ball soup, ridiculously tall
corned beef sandwiches, and the cheese cake will
make you fall in love!"

Cascabel

218 Lafayette, New York, NY 10012
(212) 431-1527 • Fax (212) 226-1398
Dinner Only M.-Sa.
Decor: Vivid red walls with geometric mirrors and
flamboyant upholstery. 80 Seats.

 Sam Hazen Stavros Aktipis

 Global

 Seared Diver Scallops with Polenta Croutons,
Roasted Tomatoes and Garlic Cream. Pan Roasted
Veal Chop with Butternut Squash Marmalade and
Honey Shallot Jus.

"A great place in a great location!" "Solid, consistent
cooking."

NEW YORK

New York

Cendrillon

45 Mercer Street, New York, NY 10013
(212) 343-9012 • Fax (212) 343-9670
EMail acbesa@aol.com
Lunch and Dinner Tu.-Su. Sa.& Su. Brunch.
Decor: A modern restaurant with Southeast Asian
influences, brick walls and an open kitchen.
60 Seats.

Romy Dorotan

Asian-Southeast

Black Rice Paella Cooked in a Clay Pot with
Seafood. Romy's Spare Ribs, Spice-Rubbed and
Slow-Smoked.

"Deliciously creative home cooking!"

$$$

China Grill

52 West 53rd Street, corner of 6th
New York, NY 10016
(212) 333-7788 • Fax (212) 956-7062
Lunch M.-F. Dinner 7 Days.
Decor: A bright, fun, modern Asian restaurant with
high ceilings. 180 Seats.

Owen Stewart   Michael McKimmey

Global

Grilled Dry-Aged Szechuan Beef. Pan-Seared
Spicy Tuna. Crackling Calamari Salad.

"Great fun, chic food and always good people-
watching!" "The portions are immense, and the
flavors are sublime!"

$$$

Corner Bistro

331 West 4th Street, New York, NY 10014
(212) 242-9502
Lunch and Dinner 7 Days.
Decor: A bohemian village saloon. 34 Seats.

■ Louis Rubio

■ Hamburger Joint ■

■ The Bistro Burger.

"My favorite hamburger in the city! Single malts and draft beers complete the crowded picture and local color."

$$ ■ ■

Daniel

60 East 65th Street, New York, NY 10021
(212) 288-0033 • Fax (212) 737-0612
Lunch Tu.-Sa. Dinner M.-Sa.
Decor: Three elegant dining rooms: Venetian Renaissance, "l'Orangerie" and for private functions, The Mayfair Room, providing the perfect atmosphere in which to have a culinary experience you won't soon forget. 120 Seats, Dining Rooms. 100 Seats, The Mayfair Room.

■ Daniel Boulud ■ Bruno Jamais

■ French ■ ■

■ Chilled Five-Pea Soup with a Rosemary-Infused Cream, Bacon and Crisp Croutons. Maine Sea Scallops Layered with Black Truffle in a Golden Puff Pastry. Morels with a Duck and Foie Gras Stuffing, Lamb's Quarter Greens and Truffle.

"A must-visit in New York, consistently great."
"Excellent food, outstanding service and ambiance." "Still the King of the Dégustation menu." "It is he who drives our passion as young chefs." "The premier dining establishment in NYC, and one of the greatest in the world."

$$$$ ■ ■ ■ ■ ■

NEW YORK

New York

Drovers Tap Room

9 Jones Street, New York, NY 10014
(212) 627-1233 • Fax (212) 627-1182
Dinner 7 Days. Sunday Brunch.
Decor: Comfortable Midwestern-tap-room style.
65 Seats.

David Page   Barbara Shinn

American

Skillet Macaroni and Cheese with Sliced
Tomatoes and Fresh Herbs. Slow-Cooked Pork Ribs
with Brown Ale Glaze and Baked Beans.

"Nice, simple food like Mama used to make!"

Elio's

1621 2nd Avenue at 84th Street
New York, NY 10028
(212) 772-2242 • Fax (212) 988-0514
Dinner Only 7 Days.
Decor: Features include wood-panelled walls,
hardwood floors, original Italian artwork, and fresh
flowers. 80 Seats.

Giuseppe Lentini

Giovanni Bertagnolli

Italian

Tuna Carpaccio. Farfolce with Grilled Green
Vegetables.

"My favorite neighborhood Italian restaurant!"
"A classic in the City!"

Felidia

243 East 58th Street, New York, NY 10022
(212) 758-1479 • Fax (212) 935-7687
Website www.lidiasitaly.com
Lunch M.-F. Dinner M.-Sa.
Decor: A converted brownstone dotted with wine bins and shelves of crystal decanters, elegant mahogany and terra cotta floors. 120 Seats.

 Lidia Matticchio Bastianich and Fortunato Nicotra

John Fanning

Italian-Northern

Osso Bucco with Barley Vegetable Risotto. Krafi: Istrian Wedding Pillows filled with Fontina, Asiago and Parmigiano with Citrus Rind, Pistachio, Rum and a Savory Sauce. Pala Chinke: Warm Crêpes filled with Orange Marmalade.

"Truly original, natural presentations. A great family feeling." "The pasta and seafood are simply superb. Lidia takes marvelous care of her guests."

$$$$

First

87 First Avenue at 5th Street
New York, NY 10003
(212) 674-3823 • Fax (212) 674-8010
Dinner 7 Days. Sunday Brunch.
Decor: An eclectic, industrial chic restaurant with good music. 80 Seats.

Sam De Marco   Steven Billings

Global

Tokyo Roast: Cooked Sushi Roll. Seafood Tacos.

"This chef is one to watch! He cooks pure excitement and is a fanatic for perfection." "It's always a party at First. Great Tiny Tinis, and the menu is oh-so-festive!"

$$

New York

Gertrude's

33 East 61st Street, New York, NY 10021
(212) 888-9127 • Fax (212) 751-9829
Lunch and Dinner 7 Days.
Decor: An elegant, country house feel. 120 Seats.

Laurent Manrique   Marion Maur

French

Trio of Foie Gras. Roasted Colorado Rack of Lamb. Terrine de Cassoulet.

"Tasty, yummy, delicious!" "A young French chef from Gascony renowned in New York for his great foie gras preparations." "Talent and finesse in the kitchen."

$$$

Gotham Bar and Grill

12 East 12th Street, New York, NY 10003
(212) 620-4020 • Fax (212) 627-7810
Website www.citysearch.com/nyc/gothambarngrill
Lunch M.-F. Dinner 7 Days.
Decor: A vast, comfortable room with high ceilings and seating that provides intimacy and a sense of watching without being watched. 153 Seats.

Alfred Portale   Laurie Tomasino

American-Modern

Mixed Seafood Salad. Chinese-Spiced Duck Breast.

"The only structurally perfect food that has the taste to live up to the presentation." "Consistently excellent year after year. Great menu variety."
"An old favorite that never disappoints." "The quintessential N.Y. restaurant: sharp, clean flavors and composition, brilliantly executed." "I love the room, the service and the food."

$$$$

Gramercy Tavern

42 East 20th Street, New York, NY 10003
(212) 477-0777 • Fax (212) 477-1160
Website www.kerrymenu.com/gramercy-tavern
Lunch M.-Sa. Dinner 7 Days.
Decor: Refined tavern style, decorated with
American antiques, artwork and fixtures.
150 Seats, Dining Room. 40 Seats, Tavern. 22
Seats, Private Dining.

Tom Colicchio   Nick Mautone

American-Contemporary

Saddle of Rabbit with Olives, Roasted Garlic,
Shallots and Rosemary. Crispy Sweetbreads with
Bacon, Honey-Glazed Onions, Pickled Jerusalem
Artichokes and Sherry Vinegar.

"Innovative food, outstanding combinations, great
wine list and a comfortable ambiance." "Haute
Grandma cuisine!" "Tom's food is always in season,
tasty and well-presented and the service is
impeccable." "What American dining in the 90's
should be." "Consistently great, especially the
desserts!"

Hangawi

12 East 32nd Street, New York, NY 10016
(212) 213-0077 • Fax (212) 689-0780
Lunch and Dinner 7 Days.
Decor: A very tranquil, traditional setting
reminiscent of a Buddhist temple with low tables
and Korean artwork. 65 Seats.

Madeline Lee   Andy Chun

Korean Vegetarian

Chef's Special Emperor's Meal with Steam
Boat. Grilled Mountain Root and Ginger Soy
Sauce. Fragrant Bamboo Rice.

"For the best example of sophisticated Korean
cuisine, try this restaurant!"

New York

Honmura An

170 Mercer Street, New York, NY 10011
(212) 334-5253 • Fax (212) 334-6162
Lunch W.-Sa. Dinner Tu.-Su.
Decor: A contemporary Japanese restaurant in a
Soho loft environment. 68 Seats.

 Akio Furukawa Koichi Kobari

Japanese

Handmade Soba Noodles. Tempura.

"Soba as religion."

$$$

Indigo

142 West 10th Street, New York, NY 10014
(212) 691-7757 • Fax (212) 691-4415
Website www.indigojazz.com
Dinner Only 7 Days.
Decor: A very subtle room with wood floors,
banquettes, muted colors and indigo blue votives
on the tables. 80 Seats.

 Scott Bryan & Guy Ferri

French-American

Wild Mushroom Strudel served with Wild
Mushroom Sauce and Baby Greens. Porcini-Dusted
Skate with Truffled Chive Potatoes, Spicy
Watercress and Balsamic Reduction. Grilled Hangar
Steak with Horseradish Mashed Potatoes, String
Beans, Glazed Shallots and Zinfandel Sauce.

"Hearty, soul-satisfying food at reasonable prices!"
"Scott Bryan is a chef to watch!"

$$$

Jean Georges

One Central Park West, New York, NY 10023
(212) 299-3900 • Fax (212) 299-3914
Breakfast, Lunch & Dinner 7 Days.
Decor: An Adam Tihany-designed, strikingly
simple restaurant in a palette of taupe, ecru and
silver. 60 Seats, Jean Georges. 70 Seats, Nougatine.

Jean-Georges Vongerichten

Alain Michel and Philippe Vongerichten

French-Modern

Young Garlic Soup with Sautéed Frogs Legs.
Porcini Tart and Herb Salad. Arctic Char with
Potatoes and Horseradish Cream.

"The most incredible meal of 1997; beautiful room
and professional service." "A chef at the top of his
form." "Delicious, very creative cuisine in an
unpretentious, elegant setting." "Pure inspiration."

JoJo

160 East 64th Street, (Lexington & Third)
New York, NY 10021
(212) 223-5656 • Fax (212) 755-9038
Lunch M.-F. Dinner M.-Sa.
Decor: Charming townhouse on two floors. Warm,
comfortable, Parisian-style rooms with plush, red
banquettes and cream walls. 90 Seats.

Jean-Georges Vongerichten

Lois Freedman

French-Modern

Twenty-Seven Vegetables Simmered in their
own Juice with Chive Oil. Lobster Roasted with
Artichokes, Garlic and Potatoes.

"This is still my favorite of his restaurants! The
food is soulful and perfect without being overkill."
"Innovative Bistro cuisine..."

NEW YORK

New York

Katz's Deli

205 East Houston Street
New York, NY 10002
(212) 254-2246 • Fax (212) 674-3270
Breakfast, Lunch and Dinner 7 Days.
Decor: An 110 year-old Jewish deli. 355 Seats.

 American

Pastrami Brisket. Voted "Best Hot Dogs in the US" for over 20 years.

"The best hand-carved Pastrami in the world!"

L'Absinthe Brasserie

227 East 67th Street, New York, NY 10021
(212) 794-4950 • Fax (212) 628-5089
Website www.newyorksidewalkl'absinthe.com
Lunch M.-F. Dinner 7 Days. Sa. and Su. Brunch.
Decor: A turn-of-the-century, art nouveau, Parisian brasserie, featuring an authentic zinc bar, lace curtains, and bronze-encased crystal tulip chandeliers. 120 Seats.

Jean-Michel Bergougnoux

Guillaume

French-Modern

Shellfish Tray. Broiled Halibut with Braised Baby Artichokes and Lime Vinaigrette. Beaujolais-Style Warm Poached Sausage with Potato and Lentil. Poached Free-Range Chicken in a Black Truffle Broth.

"True French bistro food comes to New York City. And it's creative!" "Jean-Michel is an extremely accomplished chef who cooks with finesse and respect for tradition..."

L'Ecole

462 Broadway at Grand, New York, NY 10013
(212) 219-3300 • Fax (212) 334-4866
Website www.frenchculinary.com
Lunch M.-F. Dinner M.-Sa.
Decor: An elegant room with high ceilings
decorated with impressive local works of art.
75 Seats.

 Alain Sailhac  Marc Mainville

 French-Modern

 Terrine of Roasted Eggplant and Red Pepper.
Crispy-Skin Roasted Salmon with Meunière
Endives. Rack of Lamb Poêlé with Provençal Herbs.

"Always fresh, simple, inexpensive fare." "It's hard
to imagine that students can cook this well!"

Le Bernardin

155 West 51st Street, New York, NY 10019
(212) 489-1515 • Fax (212) 265-1615
Website www.le-bernardin.com
Lunch M.-F. Dinner M.-Sa.
Decor: With its vaulted ceilings and elegant teak
wood decor, Le Bernardin harmonizes the spirit of
New York City with Old World charm. 150 Seats.

Eric Ripert

Ben Chekroun and Sally Sarmiento

Seafood

Thinly-Pounded Yellowfin Tuna, Shaved
Chives and Extra Virgin Olive Oil. Crispy Chinese-
Spiced Red Snapper with Cepes, Aged Port and
Jerez Vinegar.

"Excellent, inventive seafood in a shining setting."
"Impeccable taste and simplicity." "Outstanding,
the best in NYC!"

NEW YORK

New York

Le Cirque

455 Madison Avenue, New York, NY 10022
(212) 303-7788 • Fax (212) 303-7712
Lunch and Dinner 7 Days.
Decor: Italian Renaissance mansion, with a circus-motif interior designed by Adam Tihany. 155 Seats plus Cocktail Lounge.

Sottha Khunn   Mario Wainer

French

Black Tie Sea Scallops. Roasted Cod with Szechuan Peppers. Le Cirque Chocolate Stove.

"New location and decor, same excellent food."
"Sottha Khunn is one of the unsung masters of modern French cuisine. He has influenced countless young chefs all over the world." "People come here for the show, but they come back for the food..."

$$$$

Lespinasse

2 East 55th Street, New York, NY 10022
(212) 339-6719 • Fax (212) 350-8722
Lunch and Dinner Tu.-Sa.
Decor: Spacious, Louis XVI feel, accented with Maxfield Parish paintings. 88 Seats.

Christian Delouvrier

Pierre Tagournet

French-Modern

Foie Gras "Big Apple." Parmentier of Beef Cheeks with Black Truffles. Lobster with American Sauce.

"Regal atmosphere, seamless service, flawless integration of classical and modern French cuisine."
"The best meal I ever had." "Exciting combinations and great service."

$$$$

Lutèce

249 East 50th Street, New York, NY 10022
(212) 752-2225 • Fax (212) 225-9050
Website lutece@ix.netcom.com
Lunch Tu.-F. Dinner M.-Sa.
Decor: Elegant, cozy garden-like feel. 92 seats.

Eberhard Muller   Katherine Kapatos

French-Alsatian

Maine Crabmeat and Potato Salad with Black Truffle Vinaigrette. Sautéed Skate with Brown Butter and Capers.

"Fabulous culinary finesse and elegance" "I go there just for the soufflés!"

March

405 East 58th Street, New York, NY 10022
(212) 754-6272 • Fax (212) 838-5108
Dinner Only 7 Days.
Decor: A small, turn-of-the-century townhouse filled with French antiques and Persian carpets. 75 Seats.

Wayne Nish   Joseph Scalice

American-New

Sashimi of Hamachi with White Soy Sauce and Olive Oil. Beggar's Purse with Lobster and Black Truffles. Prince Edward Island Lobster with Muscat de Beaumes de Venise Sauce.

"Wayne Nish is a master." "A light touch, but no compromises on flavor!" "Clever, sensitive, innovative cuisine, and perfect 'white glove' service!"

New York

Montrachet

239 West Broadway, New York, NY 10013
(212) 219-2777 • Fax (212) 274-9508
Website www.gourmetmyriad.com
Lunch F. Only. Dinner M.-Sa.
Decor: An understated and intimate room
decorated with light pastels. 85 Seats.

 Chris Gesualdi   Eric Rota

French-Modern

Truffle-Crusted Salmon. Warm Oysters with
Champagne Sauce and Caviar.

"Great French cuisine, and a fabulous wine list!"
"I would say this place is now an institution."

$$$$

New World Grill

329 West 49th Street, New York, NY 10019
(212) 957-4745 • Fax (212) 957-4758
Lunch and Dinner 7 Days. Seasonal.
Decor: A bright atrium enclosed in glass with
exterior courtyard for drinks and dining in season.
35 Seats, Indoors. 150 Seats, Outdoors.

Katy Keck   Richard Barber

American

Grilled Salmon with Blood Orange Citrus
Sauce. Grilled Shrimp with Thai Noodles. Grilled
Pear Salad with Walnuts and Stilton Cheese.

"They do some really unique blending of global
foods." "You can tell there are professionals at work
here!"

$$$

Nobu

105 Hudson Street, New York, NY 10013
(212) 219-0500 • Fax (212) 219-1441
Lunch M.-F. Dinner 7 Days.
Decor: A highly-stylized Japanese look with a wall
of black pebbles and birch trees. 120 Seats.

 Nobu Matsuhisa   Richard Notar

Japanese

Omakase: Chefs' Tasting Menu. Black Cod
with Miso.

"Wonderful service and atmosphere and each
course is more delicious than the last!" "Very
innovative and exciting menu. I like to have the
chef pick my dishes for me." "Nobu's food is so
incredibly sophisticated in its simplicity, yet the
flavors are complex."

Oceana

55 East 54th Street, New York, NY 10022
(212) 759-5941 • Fax (212) 759-6076
Website www.oceanarestaurant.com
Lunch M.-F. Dinner M.-Sa.
Decor: An elegant townhouse with plush
banquettes, intimate tables and a dramatic bar on
the second floor. 120 Seats.

Rick Moonen   Paul McLaughlin

Seafood

Crabcakes with Chipotle Sauce. Blackfish
with Chive-Whipped Potatoes and Black Truffle
Vinaigrette. Lobster Ravioli with Tomato-Basil
Broth.

"An elegant venue for superbly cooked seafood."

NEW YORK

New York

Omen

113 Thompson Street, New York, NY 10012
(212) 925-8923 • Fax (212) 431-5638
Dinner Only 7 Days.
Decor: Old brick, very Soho-style design. 65 Seats.

🔪 Norio Shinohara 🍶 Mikio Shinagawa

🚬 Japanese 🍸 🍴

⭐ Tuna Steak with Ginger. Acorn Squash Stuffed with Vegetables.

"Low-key place, featuring authentic Japanese cooking."

$$$ AMERICAN EXPRESS 👔

Park Avenue Café

100 East 63rd Street, New York, NY 10021
(212) 644-1900 • Fax (212) 688-0373
Lunch and Dinner 7 Days.
Decor: American country-style room featuring interesting folk art. 180 Seats.

🔪 David Burke and Neil Murphy

🍶 Nick DeSeve

🚬 American 🍸 🍴

⭐ Swordfish Chop™ Pastrami Salmon™ Pastry Chef Richard Leach's Desserts.

"Fantastic." "Every chef questions his own ability when eating here. David takes cooking and creativity to a higher level every time." "Creative American with cool presentations."

$$$$ AMERICAN EXPRESS VISA MasterCard ⬦ 👔

Park Bistro

414 Park Avenue South, New York, NY 10016
(212) 689-1360 • Fax (212) 689-6437
Website www.microsoftsidewalk.com/ny
Lunch M.-F. Dinner 7 Days.
Decor: A small, very Parisian-style bistro with dim
lighting, long red banquettes, old photographs,
hardwood floors and an open kitchen. 65 Seats.

 Christopher Dillon  Max Bernard

 French Bistro

 "Pétatou" of Goat Cheese. Wild Mushroom
Ravioli with Aged Parmesan. Hangar Steak Au
Poivre with "Street Corner" Potatoes.

"As close to a Parisian Left Bank bistro as I can find
in New York! Jean-Michel Diot's Terrine de Foie
Gras is pure heaven!"

$$$

Patria

250 Park Avenue South, New York, NY 10003
(212) 777-6211 • Fax (212) 777-0786
Lunch M.-F. Dinner 7 Days.
Decor: A vibrant and airy, multi-tiered room,
decorated with whimsical original art. 120 Seats.

 Douglas Rodriguez

 Jorge Liloy and Ivan Ruiz

 Nuevo Latino

 Oysters Rodriguez. Black Lobster Empanada.
Patria Pork.

"The mecca for Nuevo Latino cuisine." "Douglas
opens the senses to a new world of food: his
presentations and flavors are dazzling." "Douglas
has single-handedly created an exciting, outrageous
cuisine." "The Cubano Ceviche would make Castro
defect!"

$$$$

NEW YORK

New York

Payard Patisserie and Bistro

1032 Lexington Avenue, New York, NY 10021
(212) 717-5252 x121 • Fax (212) 717-0986
Lunch, Tea and Dinner M.-Sa.
Decor: The David Rockwell-designed space is reminiscent of a long-established pastry shop and bistro on Paris' Left Bank. Don't forget to look at the moldings...120 Seats.

Philippe Bertineau and Francois Payard

Jean David Bordonero

French Bistro

Foie Gras Terrine. Bouillabaisse. Cassoulet. Patisserie.

"Francois is the most talented French pastry chef outside France, and Payard is a must in NYC."
"It's hard to wait until dessert, but the food here is just as exquisite! A great bistro!"

$$$

Picholine

35 West 64th Street, New York, NY 10023
(212) 724-8585 • Fax (212) 875-8979
Lunch Tu.-Sa. Dinner 7 Days.
Decor: A sophisticated, French country atmosphere, with beautiful fabrics and crystal chandeliers. 112 Seats.

Terrance Brennan   David Merves

Provençal

Carpaccio of Tuna. Wild Duck and Mushroom Risotto. Cheese Cart.

"The best cheese cart in the country! Terrance takes great care of his customers." "A well-balanced menu with great flavor combinations; comforting food."
"Some of the most exquisite cooking on both sides of the Atlantic!"

$$$$

228

Po

31 Cornelius Street, New York, NY 10014
(212) 645-2189
Lunch W.-Su. Dinner Tu.-Su.
Decor: A comfortable room filled with golden,
twinkling light and fragrant food. 34 Seats.

 Mario Batali   Steven Crane

Italian

Goat Cheese Truffle. White Bean Ravioli.
Quail with Pomegranate Molasses.

"Simple, great food and excellent prices."

$$$

Rosa Mexicano

1063 First Avenue, New York, NY 10022
(212) 753-7407 • Fax (212) 753-7433
Dinner only 7 Days.
Decor: Cool and airy, with a "Hacienda" feel. Open
kitchen with wood-fired grill. 100 Seats.

Josefina Howard and Ruperto Cantor

Cindy Hepner

Mexican

Tableside Guacamole. Huitlacoche-Stuffed
Chicken.

"The place for solid, modern Regional Mexican
cuisine and the best margaritas. Josefina is one of a
kind!" "For so many years, this place has been the
standard-bearer for true gourmet Mexican cuisine.
No restaurant does it fresher or better, not even in
Mexico!"

$$$

NEW YORK

New York

San Domenico

240 Central Park South
New York, NY 10019
(212) 265-5959 • Fax (212) 397-0844
Website www.food2go.com
Lunch M.-F. Dinner 7 Days.
Decor: This aristocratic, Italian villa-inspired
restaurant, designed by Italian architects, features
furnishings imported from Italy. 140 Seats.

Odette Fada

Angelo Amabile and Marisa May

Italian

Soft Egg Yolk-Filled Raviolo. Filet of Pork in a
Black Sesame Seed Crust over a Fennel Purée with
Aromatic Herb Oil. Chocolate Hazelnut and
Cornmeal Soufflé in a White Chocolate Sauce.

"Whenever people ask me for my favorite Italian
restaurant in New York, I always tell them about
this place. It's sort of a find, but the food is elegant
and exquisitely authentic."

$$$$

Sarabeth's

1295 Madison Avenue, New York, NY 10128
(212) 410-7335 • Fax (212) 423-0128
Breakfast, Lunch and Dinner 7 Days.
Decor: An American country restaurant. 75 Seats.

Terrence John

American-Eclectic

Smoked Trout with Warm Potato-Wild Rice
Waffle. Braised Lamb Shank with Corn Grits and
Portobello Mushroom.

"The quintessential breakfast and lunch spot in
New York!" "Everything is so delicate and refined,
as though you were in your grandmother's kitchen!"

$$$

New York

Savoy

70 Prince Street, New York, NY 10012
(212) 219-8570
Lunch M.-Sa. Dinner 7 Days.
Decor: Very "Soho-Style," on two floors with three
working fireplaces. 65 Seats.

 Peter Hoffman   John Tucker

Mediterranean

Salt-Crusted Duck with Local Sour Cherries.

"A little off the beaten path, but well worth the
effort. Peter is a big supporter of organic food, and
his is simple and tasty."

$$$

Spartina

355 Greenwich Street, New York, NY 10013
(212) 274-9310 • Fax (212) 941-4997
Lunch M.-F. Dinner 7 Days.
Decor: A stylish and sophisticated restaurant with
some Mission aspects, featuring major pieces of
contemporary art. 100 Seats.

Stephen Kalt   Cindy Smith

Mediterranean

Roasted Trout Basquaise. Roasted Tuna Belly
with Yukon Gold Potatoes, Black Truffles and Basil
Purée. Grilled Pizza.

"A great mix of the art, fashion and food worlds."
"Stephen's food is inspired by his passion for the
Mediterranean. An extremely comfortable place."

$$$

NEW YORK

Sushisay

38 East 51st Street, New York, NY 10022
(212) 755-1780 • Fax (212) 755-1788
Lunch M.-F. Dinner M.-Sa.
Decor: A simple, peaceful, very traditional Japanese
restaurant. 96 Seats.

M. Uehara

Japanese

Sushi and Sashimi Only.

"Very, very, very fresh fish, great management, and
friendly service." "We try to always make it here for
lunch when in New York..."

$$$

The Four Seasons Restaurant

99 East 52nd Street, New York, NY 10022
(212) 754-9494 • Fax (212) 754-1077
Website www.fourseasonsrestaurant.com
Lunch M.-F. Dinner M.-Sa.
Decor: An architectural landmark of classic
modernism. 500 Seats.

Christian Albin   Lorez Pretterhofer

American

Crisp Farmhouse Duck. Maryland Crabmeat
Cakes with Mustard Sauce. Steak Tartare.

"The best large restaurant in the USA." "I'm wild
about the sweetbreads in truffle sauce!"

$$$$

The Lobster Club

24 East 80th Street, New York, NY 10021
(212) 249-6500 • Fax (212) 396-0829
Lunch and Dinner 7 Days.
Decor: An elegant, comfortable living room with
stylishly eclectic elements in an East Side
townhouse. 80 Seats.

 Anne Rosenzweig

American-Eclectic

Crispy Rock Shrimp in Paper with Spicy
Tartar Sauce. Citrus Butter-Braised Maine Lobster
with Truffled Mashed Potatoes and Braised Greens.

"Fine comfort food."

$$$

The Sea Grill

19 West 49th Street, New York, NY 10019
(212) 332-7610 • Fax (212) 332-7676
Website www.seagrill.com
Lunch M.-F. Dinner M.-Sa.
Decor: A spacious dining room overlooking a
beautiful garden in the summer and the world's
largest Christmas Tree and the Rockefeller Plaza ice
rink in the winter. 135 Seats.

Edward Brown   Ken Gordon

Seafood

Seared Live Fluke with Vanilla Oil. Crab
Cakes. Lobster Salad with Couscous.

"Romantic ambiance and superb combinations."

$$$

New York

Tribeca Grill

375 Greenwich Street at Franklin
New York, NY 10013
(212) 941-3900 • Fax (212) 941-3915
Website www.cuisine.com
Lunch and Dinner 7 Days. Sunday Brunch.
Decor: This energetic restaurant is located in a
converted downtown warehouse with exposed brick
and oil paintings by Robert DeNiro, Sr. 180 Seats,
Dining Room. 200 Seats, Special Events Loft.

 Don Pintabona Marty Shapiro

American

Rare-Seared Tuna with Sesame Noodles. Crab-
Crusted Sea Bass with Red Wine Fumet.
Caramelized Banana Tart with Milk Chocolate Malt
Ice Cream.

"Don Pintabona is a very talented chef, who has
trained with the very best!" "A star-studded crowd,
but the food is still the main focus."

$$$

Trois Jean

154 East 79th Street, New York, NY 10021
(212) 988-4858 • Fax (212) 988-4719
Lunch M.-Sa. Dinner 7 Days. Sunday Brunch.
Decor: An authentic French bistro with art deco
lighting, dark wood, mirrors and large paintings.
Seasonal flowers abound in the outdoor café. 75
Seats.

 Jean-Louis Dumonet

Jean-Luc Andriot

French

Jean-Louis Dumonet Cassoulet. Foie Gras.
Chocolate Pyramid.

"What cooking is all about." "A simple and elegant
neighborhood bistro, serving the kind of food you
could eat every day."

$$$

Union Pacific

111 East 22nd Street, New York, NY 10011
(212) 995-8500 • Fax (212) 460-5881
Lunch M.-F. Dinner M.-Sa.
Decor: A warm, open room with a peaceful Asian feeling. 114 Seats.

Rocco DiSpirito

American-Contemporary

Taylor Bay Scallops with Uni and Mustard Oil. White Truffle Risotto with Gulf Shrimp Fondue. Sea Bass with Black Figs and Sunflower Seeds.

"Great food; simply unforgettable." "Technically-savvy, ingredient-driven cuisine with layers and layers of surprises and treats!" "Elegant food, great wine list and a beautiful decor." "This is a guy to watch; brilliantly executed food."

$$$$

Union Square Café

21 East 16th Street
New York, NY 10003
(212) 243-4020 • Fax (212) 627-2673
Website www.kerrymenu.com/union-square-café
Lunch M.-Sa. Dinner 7 Days.
Decor: Three separate, non-smoking dining areas. 125 Seats.

Michael Romano   Paul Bolles-Beaven

American-Contemporary

Grilled Marinated Filet Mignon of Tuna. Fried Calamari with Spicy Anchovy Mayonnaise. Lobster Shepherd's Pie.

"Warm, comfortable atmosphere, intelligent food, service and wine list, with many small, rare values." "Hospitality reigns supreme. Year after year the place gets it right." "Homey feeling, comfort cuisine."

$$$$

New York

Verbena Restaurant

54 Irving Place, New York, NY 10003
(212) 260-5454 • Fax (212) 260-3595
Dinner 7 Days. Sa. & Su. Brunch.
Decor: Serenity reigns here. 145 Seats.

Diane Forley   Marishka

American-New

Butternut Squash Ravioli with Roasted
Orange and Sage. Seared Tuna in Coriander Seed
with Minted Cucumbers and Red Pepper Romesco.

"Small, hidden; just the kind of place you'd expect
to find a treasure. This is it!"

$$$ AMERICAN EXPRESS   VISA   MasterCard

Vong

200 East 54th Street, New York, NY 10022
(212) 486-9592 • Fax (212) 980-3745
Lunch M.-F. Dinner 7 Days.
Decor: Designed by David Rockwell, this Asian-
inspired fantasy is done in gold leaf, Thai silk
fabrics and Chinese red lacquered paint.
Noteworthy elements are the private table for 12,
recessed, niche banquettes and an Asian-inspired
collection of plateware to suit each dish. 140 Seats.

Jean-Georges Vongerichten & Pierre Schutz

Philippe Gouze & Christian Carrere

Asian-French

Sautéed Foie Gras with Ginger and Mango.
Lobster with Thai Herbs. 27 Asian Vegetables
Simmered in Ginger with Shiitakes.

"Eclectic, creative, modern and elegant cuisine."
"Reserve early, it's still one of the hardest tables to
get in the world!"

$$$ AMERICAN EXPRESS   VISA   MasterCard

Zoe

90 Prince Street, New York, NY 10012
(212) 966-6722 • Fax (212) 966-6718
Lunch and Dinner 7 Days. Weekend Brunch.
Decor: A landmark building in the cast iron district
of Soho with a contemporary decor, original tiles
and columns. 130 Seats.

Kevin Reilly   Scott Lawrence

American-Contemporary

Crispy Calamari with Vietnamese Dipping
Sauce. Monkfish and Lobster Pan-Roast with
Carrot Risotto.

"Just really good food!"

$$$

Old Chatham
Sheepherding Co. Inn

99 Shaker Museum Road
Old Chatham, NY 12136
(518) 794-9774 • Fax (518) 794-9779
Website www.oldsheepinn.com
Dinner Only W.-M.
Decor: Country elegance on a working sheep farm
with rolling hills and beautiful gardens. 45 Seats.

Melissa Kelly   George Shattuck

Regional American

Fresh Sheep's Cheese Wrapped in Grape
Leaves, Marinated in Herbes de Provence, then
Grilled and Served with our Housemade Country
Bread.

"A very unique experience; I highly recommend this
place!" "What a way to spend the weekend!"

$$$

NEW YORK

Piermont

Xavier's at Piermont

506 Piermont Avenue, Piermont, NY 10968
(914) 359-7007 • Fax (914) 359-4021
Website www.nywedding.com
Lunch F. & Su. Dinner W.-Su.

Decor: An intimate restaurant with a profusion of fresh floral work, Versace china, Riedel stemware and Baccarat crystal. 40 Seats.

Peter Xavier Kelly   Daout Coleston

American-Contemporary

Lasagna of Grilled Quail. Asian Lobster Salad with Mango and Orange. Cappucino of Poached Oysters.

"An elegant, very romantic restaurant."

$$$

Rhinebeck

Calico Restaurant & Patisserie

9 Mill Street (Route 9)
Rhinebeck, NY 12572
(914) 876-2749
Lunch and Dinner W.-Su.

Decor: A tiny French left bank bistro. 17 Seats.

Tony Balassone

American-Eclectic

Bouillabaisse. Roasted Breast of Duck with Balsamic, Beurre Blanc and Fresh Berries.

"A nice café with great desserts, and inexpensive dining!"

$$

Mirabelle

404 North Country Road
St. James, NY 11780
(516) 584-5999 • Fax (516) 751-1089
Lunch Tu.-F. Dinner Tu.-Su.
Decor: A simple, elegant restaurant with peach walls and banquettes. 60 Seats.

Guy Reuge   Julie Pasquier

French

 Duck in Two Courses. Ginger Almond Tart.

"A very pleasant and welcoming place, and they're cooking fine food."

$$$ AMERICAN EXPRESS   VISA   MasterCard   ①   DISCOVER

*Tip: Refresh deep-frying oil
with ginger and scallion tops.*
Charles Powell, East of Suez

Dustin Hoffman was playing the piano
when Michael Bolton, who was passing by,
stopped to sing. This almost caused a riot in
the restaurant! **Seasons**

*Tip: Sprinkle powdered vitamin C
into pesto to make it a beautiful,
vibrant bright green. Also helps to
preserve the color.* **Paul Sale,
The Dining Room at the Hilton
at Short Hills**

NORTH CAROLINA

Magnolia Grill

1002 Ninth Street, Durham, NC 27705
(919) 286-3609 • Fax (919) 286-2691
Dinner Only Tu.-Sa.
Decor: A bright, spacious, lively bistro atmosphere.
105 Seats.

Ben and Karen Barker   Rik Meijer

Regional American

Green Tomato Soup with Crab and Country
Ham. Grilled Port Porterhouse Chop with Crawfish
Aioli and Low Country Risotto. Warm Lemon
Soufflé Pudding Cake with Seasonal Berries.

"Down-to-earth yet sophisticated use of regional
ingredients." "As a chef, I particularly appreciate
the variety of the cuisine..."

$$$ VISA   MasterCard

Nana's

2514 University Drive, Durham, NC 27707
(919) 493-8545 • Fax (919) 403-8487
Dinner Only M.-Sa.
Decor: Intimate and romantic, decorated with
modern art. 70 Seats.

Scott Howell   Michael Edwards

Regional American

Risotto with Sweet Caramelized Onions and
Nana's Duck Sausage, finished with a Roasted
Garlic Butter and Shaved Oregon Black Truffles.
Pan-Roasted American Red Snapper over Smoked
Bacon, Asparagus and Roasted Corn with Cipollini
Olives in a Blood Orange Sauce.

"Just good, personal cuisine." "American cooking
with no pretensions!"

$$$ AMERICAN EXPRESS   VISA   MasterCard   DINERS   DISCOVER

ANECDOTES & COOKING TIPS

Tip: Develop a relationship with a
local chef as an advisor to you when
executing recipes that require
assistance or special ingredients.
Craig Shelton, The Ryland Inn

Sometimes when he's especially happy,
Charlie does handstands in the dining room
for his guests! *Charlie Trotter's*

Tip: Timing is everything.
Matthew Yohalem, Bistro 315

Beachwood

Moxie Restaurant

3355 Richmond Road, Beachwood, OH 44122
(216) 831-5599 • Fax (216) 831-5992
Lunch M.-F. Dinner M.-Sa.
Decor: A New York-style warehouse with murals, an open kitchen and cigar bar. 200 Seats.

 Douglas Katz   Douglas Petkovic

American

Pan-Roasted Trout with Fresh Corn, Teardrop Tomatoes, Spinach and Bacon Vinaigrette. Filet Mignon with Grilled Peaches, Roasted Onions, Spinach, Blue Cheese and Zinfandel Sauce.

"American bistro-style restaurant with great duck confit and a nice game selection."

$$$ AMERICAN EXPRESS   VISA   MasterCard

Bexley

Bexley's Monk

2232 East Main Street, Bexley, OH 43209
(614) 239-6665 • Fax (614) 239-7861
Website www.bexleymonk.com
Lunch M.-F. Dinner 7 Days.
Decor: A comfortable, cozy restaurant featuring a wood-burning oven and nightly entertainment. 150 Seats.

Jack Cory   Steve Gifford

Eclectic

Wood Oven-Baked Red Snapper with Szechuan Vinaigrette. Tempura Soft-Shell Crabs (in season) with Mango Salsa. Blackened Porterhouse Steak.

"Fun and lively, and the food's delicious, too!"

$$$ AMERICAN EXPRESS   VISA   MasterCard   DINERS   DISCOVER

243

OHIO

Cincinnatti

Maisonette

114 East Sixth Street
Cincinnatti, OH 45202
(513) 287-7782 • Fax (513) 287-7785
Website www.maisonette.com
Lunch Tu.-F. Dinner M.- Sa.
Decor: Classical French dining room done in soft
coral tones, with circa-1900 paintings by former
local artists. 120 Seats.

Jean-Robert de Cavel   Richard Brown

French-Modern

Warm Duck Liver with Ohio Maple Syrup,
Corn Galette and Confit of Peach. John Dory with
Black Truffle, Artichoke and Celery. Venison with
Poivrade Sauce, Fall Vegetables and Fruit Compote.

"Updated classics, a wonderful treat." "This place
has been around a long time, but its new chef has
brought back the excitement!"

Cincinnati

The Palace Restaurant

The Cincinnatian Hotel, 601 Vine Street
Cincinnati, OH 45202
(513) 381-3000 • Fax (513) 381-2659
Website www.cincinnatianhotel.com
Breakfast, Lunch and Dinner 7 Days.
Decor: The Palace Restaurant has an elegant,
intimate ambiance in the heart of the city. 80 Seats.

Sean Kagy   Emerson Stambaugh

Regional American

Menu changes seasonally.

"A pretty room, great service and seasonal menus."

Parker's Restaurant & Bistro-Bar

2801 Bridge Avenue, Cleveland, OH 44113
(216) 771-7130 • Fax (216) 771-8130
Dinner 7 Days. Sunday Brunch.
Decor: A warm, casual restaurant and an upbeat
Bistro-Bar. 60 Seats.

Parker Bosley

Eclectic

Seasonal Vegetarian Entrées. Lamb. Lemon
Soufflé.

"Great food! I call it Ohio City New French."

$$$

Cena Copa Restaurant Bar

2206 Lee Road
Cleveland Heights, OH 44118
(216) 932-6995 • Fax (216) 932-6987
Dinner Only Tu.-Sa.
Decor: Located in Cleveland's historic East Side,
the restaurant has a contemporary design of natural
woods, industrial metals and artwork reminiscent of
Northern California or Manhattan, and features a
daily changing menu. 110 Seats.

Michael J. Herschman

Michael M. Hall

American-Contemporary

Sweet and Spicy Calamari with Carrot
Threads, Pepper and Scallion. Seared and Roasted
Asian Duck Breast with Cumin Black Beans,
Grilled Sweet Potato Queso and Corn Salsa. Tower
of Sashimis.

"Fusion with fantastic appetizers and a great,
sizzlin' catfish, from the former chef at Postrio."

$$$

OHIO

Columbus

K2U Bar and Grill

641 North High Street, Suite 101
Columbus, OH 43215
(614) 461-4766 • Fax (614) 461-1055
Lunch M.-F. Dinner M.-Sa.
Decor: A cozy, European-style bistro with eclectic, hand-painted murals and a great view of High Street. 80 Seats, Dining Room. 40 Seats, Bar.

Kent Rigsby   Tim Hawkins

Italian-American

Calamari Fritti with Tomato-Jalapeño Aioli. Spaghetti K2U with Sundried Tomatoes, Mushrooms, Olive Oil, Garlic and Shallots.

"Fun, creative cuisine from this chef-owner!"

L'Antibes

772 North High Street, Suite 106
Columbus, OH 43215
(614) 291-1666
Website www.users.aol.com/lantibes
Dinner Only Tu.-Sa.
Decor: An intimate, romantic French restaurant in Columbus' historic Arts District. 40 Seats.

Dale R. Gussett   Larry Williamson

French

Veal Sweetbreads Grenobloise. Beef Tenderloin with Roquefort Sauce. Pan-Seared Chilean Sea Bass with Mango Hollandaise.

"Creative bistro fare in this Midwestern college town..."

OHIO

Columbus

The Refectory Restaurant

1092 Bethel Road, Columbus, OH 43215
(614) 451-9774 • Fax (614) 451-4434
Website www.refectory.com
Dinner Only M.-Sa.
Decor: 125 Seats, Dining Room. 50 Seats, Banquet.

 Richard Blondin   Craig Bechler

French

Monkfish in a Wild Herb Crust and Smoked Bacon Sauce. Quenelles of Hare with a Mosaic of Vegetables in a Champagne Sauce. Chocolate Diamond.

"Exceptional, friendly service."

Dayton

The Pine Club

1926 Brown Street, Dayton, OH 45409
(937) 228-7463 • Fax (937) 228-5371
Dinner Only M.-Sa.
Decor: The pine-panelled dining room provides an informal, comfortable setting. The restaurant is conveniently located minutes from downtown Dayton and near the UD campus. 98 Seats.

David Hulme   Dan Nooe

Steakhouse

Steaks and Chops. Nantucket Cape Scallops.

"Great steaks and cocktails!"

ANECDOTES & COOKING TIPS

Tip: *Clean as you go.*
Zach Calkins,
Cowboy of Santa Fe

When Cindy Crawford came to eat dinner here the entire fire department from around the corner came in to stare! *Frontera Grill*

Tip: *The love and passion put into preparing a meal will always outshine fancy or exotic ingredients.*
Roland and Sheila Richter,
Pizza Etc.

OKLAHOMA

Misal of India

584 Buchanan Street, Norman, OK 73069
(405) 360-5888
Lunch M.-F. Dinner 7 Days.
Decor: Traditional East Indian exotica, with antique paintings and wall hangings. 40 Seats.

🚬 Indian 🍸 🍷

🦇 Tandoori Chicken. Vegetable Platter.

"I hold wonderfully sensuous memories of their Indian flavors. The prices are very reasonable, and the service is excellent!"

💲💲 AMERICAN EXPRESS VISA MasterCard 👔

Oklahoma City

Chelino's Mexican Restaurant

15 East California
Oklahoma City, OK 73104
(405) 235-3533 • Fax (405) 232-8513
Lunch and Dinner 7 Days.
Decor: Situated in an old, two-story warehouse with an enclosed patio. 500 Seats.

🧑 Mario Lares

🚬 Regional Tex-Mex 🍸 🍷

🦇 Fajitas. Carnequisada: Mexican Beef Stew.
"Big, but friendly and authentic!"

💲 AMERICAN EXPRESS VISA MasterCard DISCOVER 💳

OKLAHOMA

Oklahoma City

Iguana Lounge and Mango

6714 North Western
Oklahoma City, OK 73116
(405) 840-3474
Lunch M.-F. Dinner 7 Days.
Decor: A very festive restaurant filled with local and
Mexican folk art. 90 Seats.

 Alan Ferree

Robert Painter and Sheri Westover

Regional Tex-Mex

Chicken Campeche. Mixed Grill of Dijon-
Marinated Pork, Coconut-Marinated Shrimp and
Fruit-Marinated Chicken. Chocolate Chimichanga.

"Very original Tex-Mex food."

$$$

The Coach House

6437 Avendale Drive
Oklahoma City, OK 73116
(405) 842-1000 • Fax (405) 844-9777
Lunch M.-F. Dinner M.-Sa.
Decor: A very formal, candlelit dining room with
china and fresh flowers. 60 Seats.

Kurt Fleischfresser   Chris Lower

Continental

Dover Sole with Meunière Sauce. Roasted
Rack of Lamb with Ancho-Dried Cherry Sauce.
Grand Marnier Soufflé with Raspberry Sauce.

"Kurt is one of our finest chefs."

$$$$

OKLAHOMA

The Metro Wine Bar & Bistro

6418 North Western
Oklahoma City, OK 73116
(405) 840-9463 • Fax (405) 840-5963
Lunch M.-F. & Su. Dinner 7 Days.
Decor: A comfortable and relaxed atmosphere with
walls of wine and a cozy bar. 90 Seats.

 Chip Sears   Gary Sender

American French Brasserie

Chilled Avocado-Cucumber Soup. Crispy
Roasted Half-Chicken with Garlic and
Mediterranean Herbs. Seared Breast of Duck with
Confit Rice and Sauce Rouennaise.

"Some of the finest fare around."

$$$ AMERICAN EXPRESS   VISA   MasterCard   ◑   DISCOVER

Tip: Cook with love.
Emeril Lagasse, Emeril's

An eccentric neighborhood woman told us that her cats are particularly fond of the roasted duck carcasses that are thrown in the alley garbage can. **Le Bouchon**

Tip: Immerse onions in water when peeling, to keep from crying.
**Jean-Louis Palladin,
Napa at the Rio**

OREGON

Café Azul

112 Northwest 9th Street
Portland, OR 97209
(503) 525-4422 • Fax (503) 525-4421
Dinner Only Tu.-Sa.
Decor: A warm and lively café serving classical, regional dishes of Mexico, located in the heart of Portland's Pearl District. 50 Seats.

�,: Claire Archibald   ▮ Shawna Archibald

🚬 Mexican   🍸 🍷

💿 Mole Oaxaqueno. Quail with Wild Mushroom Empanadas. Prune Tequila Ice Cream.

"It is so great to taste true Mexican flavors... Claire's flavors astound!" "Excellent Latino cooking utilizing the bounty of the Northwest."

$$$ VISA MasterCard DISCOVER   👔

Couvron

1126 SW 18th Avenue, Portland, OR 97205
(503) 225-1844 • Fax (503) 244-9296
Dinner Only Tu.-Sa.
Decor: Reminiscent of the intimate European elegance found in a small French inn. 32 Seats.

▮ Anthony Demes   ▮ Maura Jarach

🚬 French-Modern   🍷

💿 Pan-Roasted Hudson Valley Foie Gras with Toasted Brioche, Crawfish Stew, Port Wine, and Lobster Sauce. Cherrywood-Smoked Oregon Quail Served with Pureed White Rose Potatoes, and Shallot Compote.

"Fine, inventive new cuisine By an up-and-coming star. And what a wine list!"

$$$ AMERICAN EXPRESS VISA MasterCard   🎩

OREGON

Portland

Dan & Lois' Oyster Bar

208 Southwest Ankeny Street
Portland, OR 97204
(503) 227-5906 • Fax (503) 227-0019
Lunch and Dinner 7 Days.
Decor: A nautical atmosphere that resembles the inside of a sailing ship. 200 Seats.

 Mienert Keoni Wachsmuch

Seafood

Oyster Stew (Since 1919). Pan-Fried Yaquina Oysters served with Shrimp Salad.

"It's been around for 90 years, and I hope it'll be here in another 90! It's a seafood museum and restaurant in one!"

$$

Genoa

2832 Southeast Belmont Street
Portland, OR 97214
(503) 238-1464 • Fax (503) 238-9786
Dinner Only M.-Sa.
Decor: An intimate dining room with only ten candlelit tables, antique sideboards and a 200-year-old Persian tapestry. 36 Seats.

Cathy Whims   Kerry DeBuse

Italian-Northern

Menu Changes Daily.

"Living-room comfort, welcoming staff and owner, great wine program and good value." "Beautiful Italian food and no fusion here, just the classics."

$$$

Heathman Restaurant

1001 Southwest Broadway in The Heathman Hotel
Portland, OR 97205
(503) 790-7752 • Fax (503) 790-7112
Website www.portlandcitysearch.com
Breakfast, Lunch and Dinner 7 Days.
Sa. & Su. Brunch.
Decor: Classic French bistro style. 94 Seats.

Philippe Boulot   Michelle Maida

French Bistro

Gigot of Lamb, Braised for 7 Hours. Veal
Breast with Wild Mushroom Stuffing. Herb-
Roasted, Farm-Raised Chicken with Natural Jus.

"Fun and cozy!" "Soul-satisfying food!"

$$$ AMERICAN EXPRESS   VISA   MasterCard

Higgins Restaurant & Bar

1239 Southwest Broadway
Portland, OR 97205
(503) 222-9070 • Fax (503) 222-1244
Website www.citysearch.compdx/higgins
Lunch M.-F. Dinner 7 Days.
Decor: Classic French bistro feel, creative blending
of new and old. Located in the center of Portland,
within walking distance of hotels, museums and
theaters. 130 Seats.

Greg Higgins   Paul Mallory

Regional Pacific Northwest

Menu changes nightly with a focus on local,
organic and sustainably-produced ingredients.

"Delicious food in a comfy ambiance!"

$$$ AMERICAN EXPRESS   VISA   MasterCard   ID   DISCOVER

OREGON

Portland

Original Pancake House

8601 Southwest 24th Street
Portland, OR 97219
(503) 246-9007 • Fax (503) 245-2396
Breakfast Only W.-Su.
Decor: A homey, traditional American restaurant with knotty pine walls. 76 Seats.

Craig Vondross

Breakfast

Apple Pancakes: Soufflé-Style Pancakes with Granny Smith Apples and a Cinnamon Sugar Glaze. German-Style Pancakes served with Butter, Powdered Sugar, Fresh Lemon and Syrup.

"The best breakfast house on the West Coast-Dutch Baby Pancakes to die for!"

Paley's Place Bistro and Bar

1204 Northwest 21st Avenue
Portland, OR 97209
(503) 243-2403 • Fax (503) 223-8041
Website www.citysearch.com/pdx/paleysplace
Lunch Tu.-F. Dinner Tu.-Sa.
Decor: A warm and charming Northwest bistro. 50 Seats, Dining Room. 12 Seats, Bar.

Vitaly Paley   Kimberly Paley

Regional Pacific Northwest

Oysters/Mussels with Hand-Cut Fries. Wild Salmon. Crème Brûlée.

"Precise but not too fussy." "The best new chef to come to Portland, this is a chef to watch!"

OREGON

Saucebox Café & Bar

214 Southwest Broadway
Portland, OR 97205
(503) 241-3393 • Fax (503) 243-3251
Website www.citysearch.com.portland.rest
Lunch M.-F.   Dinner M.-Sa.
Decor: A sleek, long, and narrow dining room.
"Frank Lloyd Wright meets Danish Modern."
50 Seats.

Jeff McMahon   Hector Sahagen

Asian-Pacific Rim

Roasted Javanese Salmon. Vegetarian Thai Red
Curry. Pork Tenderloin with Tamarind and Sweet
Soy.

"Deliciously exotic...Give your mouth a treat!"

Wildwood Restaurant

1221 Northwest 21st Avenue
Portland, OR 97210
(503) 248-9663 • Fax (503) 225-0030
Website www.citysearch.wildwoodpdx.com
Lunch and Dinner 7 Days.
Decor: An urban, casual restaurant with a
neighborhood feel. 120 Seats.

Cory Schreiber   Randy Goodman

Regional American

Wood-Roasted Mussels with Saffron, Tomato
and Garlic. Crispy Fried Oyster Salad with Pancetta
and Greens. Potato-Dungeness Crabcake with
Watercress, Oranges and Fennel.

"The definitive Portland restaurant. Great,
imaginative use of indigenous ingredients."

OREGON

Portland

Zefiro Restaurant & Bar

500 Northwest 21st Avenue
Portland, OR 97209
(503) 226-3394 • Fax (503) 226-4744
Website www.citysearch.compbx/zefiro
Lunch M.-F. Dinner M.-Sa.
Decor: A minimalist restaurant in an urban
neighborhood setting. 105 Seats.

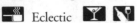 Christopher Israel Bruce Carey

Eclectic

 Caesar Salad. Roasted Chicken with 40 Cloves
of Garlic. Grilled Alaskan Halibut Wrapped in
Corn Husks with Tomatillo Salsa, Fried Potato
Cake and Grilled Baby Leeks.

"A fabulous range of food."

$$$ AMERICAN EXPRESS   VISA   MasterCard   ⬙

Tip: Use medium-grained, quick-cooking couscous instead of fine-grained instant, for better flavor and a texture that holds longer. **Charles Palmer, Aureole**

On opening night, the roof caught on fire. On our first anniversary we debuted our "Rooftop Smoked Porter." **The Glen Ellyn Brewing Company**

Tip: When making Bagna Cauda, there's no need to mash or purée anchovies, just simmer in olive oil (not extra virgin) for 20 minutes and they will fall apart into a purée. **Marius Pavlak, Barbetta**

Tip: Never use a wet towel to
pick up a hot pan!
**Nancy Silverton and Mark Peel,
Campanile**

We mistakenly thought a customer was
deceased. While offering condolences to his
wife, the guy walked in... *Equus*

Tip: When cooking pasta at home,
never rinse it. Return drained pasta
to the pot and mix well with half
of the sauce until all pasta is coated.
Put pasta on plates and spoon the
rest of the sauce on top.
**Lidia Matticchio Bastianich,
Felidia**

PENNSYLVANIA

Ruby's Diner

5 Coulter Avenue, Ardmore, PA 19003
(610) 896-7829 • Fax (610) 645-7930
Website www.rubys.com
Breakfast, Lunch and Dinner 7 Days.
Decor: 1940's style diner atmosphere with red
booths and counter seats. 74 Seats.

 Debbie Davenport

American

Hamburgers made with Angus Beef. Award-
Winning Milkshakes (Best of Philly '97 & '98).
Salads.

"We still go there weekly...the kids love it!"

The Old Guard House Inn

953 Youngsford Road, Gladwyne, PA 19035
(610) 649-9708 • Fax (610) 642-4859
Dinner Only M.-Sa.
Decor: A uniquely cozy, 1790's historical building
with an interior reminiscent of a medieval German
hunting lodge. 135 Seats.

Albert Breuers & Frank Miller

Gina Crisanti

Continental

Fresh Dover Sole with Lemon Butter Sauce.
Jumbo Lump Crabcakes with Red Curry Sauce.
Grilled Venison Medallions with Red Cabbage and
Spatzle.

"Chef-Owner Albert Breuers provides authentic
Bavarian fare in a beautiful and rustic setting."

261

PENNSYLVANIA

Gulph Mills

Savona

100 Old Gulph Mills Road
Gulph Mills, PA 19428
(610) 520-1200 • Fax (610) 520-2045
Lunch M.-F. Dinner 7 Days.
Decor: A warm, Mediterranean ambiance on three floors with fireplaces, carved Balinese panels, terra cotta tile and Casablanca fans. 125 Seats.

Dominique Filoni   Jeff Poli

Italian-Northern

Herb-Crusted Halibut, Yukon Gold Mashed Potatoes, Escarole and Truffle Beurre Blanc. Homemade Tagiatelle with Foie Gras and Shaved Black Truffles. Shaved Artichokes, Arugula, Reggiano Parmesan and Lemon Vinaigrette.

"Delicious, elegant cuisine!"

$$$$

Hershey

Circular Dining Room
at The Hotel Hershey

Hotel Road, Hershey, PA 17033
(717) 533-2171 • Fax (717) 533-8888
Breakfast, Lunch and Dinner 7 Days.
Decor: Charming, Old-World style with stained-glass windows overlooking formal gardens and romantic reflecting pools. 250 Seats.

Victor Bock

French-Country

Goose Foie Gras on Walnut Fig Bread with Warm Pear Vinaigrette. Garlic and Dijon-Crusted Rack of Lamb with White Beans and Goat Cheese. Chocolate Raspberry Gâteau Decorated with Hershey's Hugs and Kisses.

"A bit of France in a beautiful hotel." "An hommage to fine dining, especially the chocolate!"

$$$

PENNSYLVANIA

Arroyo Grille

One Leverington Avenue at Main Street
Manayunk, PA 19127
(215) 487-1400 • Fax (215) 487-1427
Website www.arroyogrille.com
Lunch M.-Sa. Dinner 7 Days. Sunday Brunch.
Decor: Authentic Southwestern decor with
amazing views of the blue sky and wide open
spaces. 400 Seats.

Christopher Todd   Molly Kelly

Regional Southwestern

Fried Oyster Nachos. Crabmeat Enchilada.
Achiote-Grilled Tuna with Tomatillo Jicama Salsa.

"Fun and lively, with creative cooking in the back!"

River City Diner

3720 Main Street at Ridge Avenue
Manayunk, PA 19127
(215) 483-7500 • Fax (215) 483-6425
Website www.rivercitydiner.com
Breakfast, Lunch and Dinner 7 Days.
Decor: Decorated in traditional diner fashion with
booths, counters, quilted aluminum, neon and a
juke box. 220 Seats, Diner. 60 Seats, Outdoors.

Matt Vesci   Steve Winkler

American

River City Diner Grilled Caesar Salad. Kansas
City Prime Meatloaf. Reuben Sandwich.

"For a tantalizing American food fix, this is the
place!"

PENNSYLVANIA

Manayunk

Sonoma

4411 Main Street, Manayunk, PA 19127
(215) 483-9400 • Fax (215) 483-1537
Website www.sonomarestaurant.com
Lunch M.-Sa. Dinner 7 Days. Sunday Brunch.
Decor: A contemporary restaurant serving
"Italifornia" cuisine, with three dining rooms,
two bars and steel and natural wood throughout.
160 Seats, Inside. 30 Seats, Outside.

Don Paone   Jennifer Bailer

American-Progressive

Grilled Tuna Achiote. Garlic Rib Steak.
Refried Risotto.

"The type of food you can eat every day and they
have a great bar with 165 brands of vodka!"

Philadelphia

BLT's Cobblefish

443 Shurs Lane, Philadelphia, PA 19128
(215) 483-5478 • Fax (215) 483-5479
Website www.cobblefish.com
Dinner Only Tu.-Su.
Decor: A classic seafood joint in a historic
cobblestone courtyard. 100 Seats.

Bill Shapiro

Seafood   BYOB

Whole Grilled Fish with Preserved Lemon
Sauce and Israeli Couscous. Rainbow Trout Stuffed
with Shiitake and Jumbo Lump Crab in a Wasabi-
Ginger Broth with Udon Noodles. Jumbo Lump
Crabcakes with Old-Fashioned Tartar Sauce.

"The only way to get fresher fish is to eat
underwater!"

PENNSYLVANIA

Brasserie Perrier

1619 Walnut Street
Philadelphia, PA 19103
(215) 568-3000 • Fax (215) 568-7855
Website www.brasserieperrier.com
Lunch M.-F. Dinner 7 Days.
Decor: A dramatic homage to modern French art,
the restaurant features art deco fabrics of plum ultra
suede and striped silk. Beautiful cracked glass
backdrop at the bar. 95 Seats, Dining Room.
65 Seats, Lounge. 95 Seats, Banquet.

Francesco Martorella   Roger Rice

Asian-French

Black Bass with Asian Sticky Rice in Ginger
Sauce. Handmade Cavatelli Pasta with Spicy
Sundried Tomato Coulis. Hoisin-Glazed Peking
Duck with Sweet Potato Purée and Star Anise Jus.

"A terrific addition to Philadelphia dining; great
Chocolate Soufflé Cake."

$$$

Cary Restaurant and Bar

211 South 15th Street
Philadelphia, PA 19102
(215) 735-9100 • Fax (215) 735-1733
Website www.caryrestaurant.com
Lunch M.-Th. Dinner M.-Sa.
Decor: Contemporary look with banquettes and a
copper bar. 80 Seats.

Cary Neff

Eclectic

Pepper-Crusted Tuna Seared Medium Rare
with Chili-Red Pepper Sauce. Crispy Calf's Liver
with Slab Bacon, Burnt Onions and a Balsamic
Splash.

"It's really, really cool!"

$$$

PENNSYLVANIA

Philadelphia

Dimitri's

795 South 3rd Street
Philadelphia, PA 19147
(215) 625-0556 • Fax (215) 731-1605
Dinner Only 7 Days.
Decor: Small, casual, and spare. 35 Seats.

Dimitri Chimes

Mediterranean **BYOB**

Grilled, Marinated Octopus. Bluefish
Greekfish.

"This is a hangout known mostly to locals."

$$

Dock Street Brewery and Restaurant

18th and Cherry Streets
Philadelphia, PA 19103
(215) 496-0413 • Fax (215) 496-0423
Website www.dockstreet.com
Lunch and Dinner 7 Days.
Decor: A grand restaurant with high ceilings,
cherry wood columns and marble bar. 180 Seats.

Olivier De Saint Martin

Philip Brown

French

Choucroute. Codfish with Caramelized
Onions. Chocolate Soufflé.

"Finally a true French restaurant with classic
cuisine."

$$

PENNSYLVANIA

Fountain Restaurant

Four Seasons Hotel, One Logan Square
Philadelphia, PA 19103
(215) 963-1500 • Fax (215) 963-9506
Website www.fourseasons.com
Breakfast, Lunch and Dinner 7 Days.
Sunday Brunch.
Decor: A warm, intimate room with rich wood
accents, lush flowers and a view of Alexander
Stirling Calder's swan fountain. 110 Seats.

Jean-Marie Lacroix

Ettore Ceraso

French-Modern

Braised Red Snapper Filet with Wild
Mushroom Risotto. Braised Jamison Farm Lamb
Shank and Roasted Lamb Rack with Minestrone
Vegetables, Shaved Locatelli Cheese and Thyme
Jus.

"Jean-Marie IS The Fountain!" "Innovative cuisine
with a long track record of success." "Still the most
classy, tasty and professional restaurant in town."

Hikaru Japanese Restaurant

4348 Main Street, Philadelphia, PA 19127
(215) 487-3500
Dinner Only 7 Days.
Decor: An exciting restaurant where the chef
prepares dinner tableside. Tatami room and Sushi
bar. 150 seats.

Taka Yuki Saito   Fuji Niimi

Japanese

Deluxe Nigiri: An Assortment of 10 Items.
All Traditional Japanese Cuisine.

"A simple Japanese restaurant with very good
sushi."

PENNSYLVANIA

Philadelphia

Kansas City Prime

4417 Main Street, Philadelphia, PA 19127
(215) 487-1700 • Fax (215) 487-7894
Website www.kansascityprime.com
Dinner Only 7 Days.
Decor: A warm room with gilt ceilings, peach walls and sycamore accents. Not your traditional steakhouse. 136 Seats.

Derek Davis and Michael Bell

Randal Mrazik

Steakhouse

Kobe Steak with Traditional Sauces. Jumbo Lobster (3 to 5.5 pound). Only the very best beef and seafood available.

"I'll never eat supermarket beef again!"

Le Bec-Fin

1523 Walnut Street
Philadelphia, PA 19102
(215) 567-1000 • Fax (215) 568-1151
Website www.lebecfin.com
Lunch M.-F. Dinner M.-Sa.
Decor: The elegant, Louis XVI-style dining room is distinguished by French period furniture, mantled fireplaces, brilliant mirrors and crystal chandeliers. 105 Seats.

Georges Perrier

French

Galette de Crabe Le Bec-Fin. Cailles Farcies au Foie Gras et Ris de Veau. Soufflé Glacé au Grand Marnier.

"Consistently the best meals; George is still on top." "For exquisite dining, there are few restaurants anywhere that can match the experience one has here!"

PENNSYLVANIA

London Grill

2301 Fairmount Avenue
Philadelphia, PA 19130
(215) 978-4545 • Fax (215) 978-4915
Lunch M.-F. Dinner 7 Days. Sunday Brunch.
Decor: A Victorian turn-of-the-century bar and five
dining rooms ranging from bright and sunny to
warm and cozy. 170 Seats.

👤 Michael McNally 👔 Terry Mc Nally

🍴 American-New 🍸 🍷

⭐ Grilled Duck Breast. Sautéed Calf's Liver.
Pan-Seared Sea Bass with a Rock Shrimp Stew and
Cilantro Peanut Pesto.

"This is a fun, unpretentious, American bistro. The
food is inventive, and the prices are reasonable."

$$$ 💳 VISA 💳 ⓪ DISCOVER 👔

Nicholas Nickolas, The Restaurant

210 West Rittenhouse Square
Philadelphia, PA 19103
(215) 546-8440 • Fax (215) 546-8489
Website www.harman-nickolas.com
Dinner Only M.-Sa.
Decor: Plush banquettes and a picturesque view of
Rittenhouse square. 180 Seats.

👤 Dany Chevalier 👔 Yanni Placonrakis

🍴 Continental 🍸 🍷

⭐ Lobster Thermidor. Cioppino Raymondo.
Nick's Classic Salad.

"Wonderful interpretations of the classics!"

$$$$ 💳 VISA 💳 ⓪ DISCOVER 🅰

PENNSYLVANIA

Philadelphia

Opus 251
Philadelphia Art Alliance

251 South 18th Street
Philadelphia, PA 19103
(215) 735-6787 • Fax (215) 735-6170
Lunch Tu.-Sa. Dinner Tu.-Su. Sunday Brunch.
Decor: A casually elegant restaurant in a turn-of-
the-century mansion on Rittenhouse Square. Lovely
gardens and private dining in the Art Alliance
galleries. 84 Seats, Dining Room. 40 Seats, Garden.

Alfonso Contrisciani Peter Coulson

Regional American

Black Sesame-Crusted Ahi Tuna. Truffled
Fettucine with Lobster Mushrooms, Diver Scallops
and Maine Lobster.

"Incredible presentations and amazing flavors from
a master chef."

Philadelphia Fish and Company

207 Chestnut Street
Philadelphia, PA 19106
(215) 625-8605 • Fax (215) 625-9529
Website www.philadelphiafishco.com
Lunch M.-Sa. Dinner 7 Days.
Decor: Newly renovated with a modern look in
Philly's hot new area, Olde City. The restaurant has
Zinfandel red walls, wrought-ironwork and
mahogany wood. 90 Seats.

Trish Morrissey Laurie Townesand

Seafood

Short Stack of Crab and Potato Pancakes with
Goat Cheese Crema and Red Pepper Coulis. BBQ
Shrimp with Cheddar Grits and Collard Greens.

"By far the best prepared seafood in Philadelphia. A
menu that is innovative and changes frequently
with moderate prices."

PENNSYLVANIA

Philippe at The Locust Club

1614 Locust Street
Philadelphia, PA 19103
(215) 735-7551 • Fax (215) 735-7609
Website www.locustclub.com
Dinner Only 7 Days.
Decor: A formal dining room and a hip,
chic bar. 140 Seats, Dining Room. 70 Seats, Bar.
400 Banquet.

Philippe Chin   Mark Trottnow

French-Asian

Six-Course Chef's Dégustation Menu.

"One of the best executions of Asian-influenced
French food. Playful presentations without
sacrificing quality."

$$$

Susanna Foo Chinese Cuisine

1512 Walnut Street
Philadelphia, PA 19102
(215) 545-2666 • Fax (215) 546-9106
Website www.susannafoo.com
Lunch M.-F. Dinner 7 Days.
Decor: The newly renovated restaurant combines
the magical setting of a fragrant Chinese garden
with Susanna's incredible Chinese/French Cuisine.
120 Seats, Dining Room. 150 Seats, Banquet.

Susanna Foo   Mike Dombkoski

Chinese

Hundred-Corner Crabcakes with Wasabi
Crème Fraîche and Pineapple Tomato Salsa. Grilled
Sea Bass with Shiitake Mushrooms and
Caramelized Balsamic Vinaigrette. Crispy Duck
with Star Anise Sauce and Green Apple-Kumquat
Chutney.

"Really creative, yet authentic flavors!" "Such a
treat, I wish I could eat here every night! Alas, I
don't live there, or I would!"

$$$

PENNSYLVANIA

Philadelphia

The Marker

City Line Avenue and Monument Road
Philadelphia, PA 19131
(215) 581-5010 • Fax (215) 581-5069
Website www.adamsmarkhotel.com
Lunch M.-F. Dinner 7 Days.
Decor: Reminiscent of a French country inn, the restaurant is elegant and has live piano music. 140 Seats.

Vince Alberici   Robert Moses

American-Contemporary

Sautéed Jumbo Lump Crabcakes, Old Bay Capellini and Chipotle Aioli. Asian Honey-Roasted Baby Chicken, Braised Lettuces and Thai Noodle Salad. Oven-Roasted Veal Chop, Goat Cheese Pierogies, Sautéed Vidalia Onion and Petite Arugula-Beet Salad.

"Creative American fusion cooking. Delicious combinations."

$$$ AMERICAN EXPRESS   VISA   MasterCard   ①   DISCOVER

Treetops
at The Rittenhouse Hotel

210 West Rittenhouse Square
Philadelphia, PA 19103
(215) 790-2533 • Fax (215) 546-9858
Breakfast, Lunch and Dinner 7 Days. Su. Brunch.
Decor: A casually elegant, airy, split-level restaurant with beautiful windows overlooking Rittenhouse Square. 98 Seats.

Jim Coleman   William Hoesch

American Bistro

Maine Lobster Spring Roll with Roasted Red Pepper-Ginger Sauce. Grilled Black Angus Filet atop Baby Potatoes and Grilled Vermouth-Scented Vegetable Kabobs.

"Great food, great prices and a great view."

$$$ AMERICAN EXPRESS   VISA   MasterCard   ①   DISCOVER

272

Vega Grill

4141 Main Street, Philadelphia, PA 19127
(215) 487-9600 • Fax (215) 508-2583
Website www.lisaorgreg@vegagrill.com
Dinner Only 7 Days.
Decor: A casual, unique 1930's tavern with a
1990's ambiance. 50 Seats, Dining Room.
40 Seats, Outdoor Patio. 20 Seats, Bar.

 Paul Trowbridge

Lisa Martenson-Pauwels

Nuevo Latino

 Mirin-Marinated Chilean Sea Bass with
Cilantro and Sundried Tomato Crust, Wild
Mushrooms and Tamarindo Sauce. Arepas con
Bacalau. Sweet and Spicy Cilantro Chicken with
Red Papaya Chutney.

"The chef is an artist!"

$$$

Tip: Before crushing a clove of garlic, sprinkle a bit of fine salt on top, so that you do not have to play volleyball. **Alain Sailhac, L'Ecole**

Daughter Lilly, age two, disrobed and streaked through the restaurant on opening night. *Lilly's*

Tip: When potatoes have been boiled, drain them and put the pot back over a low flame to steam out the moisture. This will yield fluffy potato dishes. **Douglas Rodriguez, Patria**

RHODE ISLAND

Haruki Japanese Restaurant

1210 Oaklawn Avenue, Cranston, RI 02920
(401) 463-6730 • Fax (401) 463-7699
Lunch M.-F. Dinner 7 Days.
Decor: Contemporary Japanese design with a
private tatami room. 70 Seats.

Haruki Kibe   Riley Sanders

Japanese

Famous for their sushi. Spider Roll. Rainbow
Roll.

"The finest sushi in the state. High quality, and
creative combinations."

$$$

East Greenwich

Raphael Bar-Risto

5600 Post Road, East Greenwich, RI 02818
(401) 884-4424 • Fax (401) 884-1874
Lunch F. only. Dinner Tu.-Su.
Decor: A quiet place with wood walls, murals by
Anthony Russo and Murano glass chandeliers.
100 Seats.

Sean Dutson   Carlo Slaughter

Italian-Northern

Lobster Fra Diavolo. Tagiatelle "Nero" Style
with Seared Scallops. Pan Seared Twin Red Snapper
Filets with a Strawberry-Balsamic Reduction Sauce.

"They know their business!" "Deliciously
satisfying!"

$$

RHODE ISLAND

Newport

Castle Hill Inn & Resort

Ocean Drive, Newport, RI 02840
(401) 849-3800 • Fax (401) 849-3838
Website www.castlehillinn.com
Lunch and Dinner M.-Sa. Sunday Brunch.
Decor: Victorian summer estate on a 40-acre
peninsula with a working lighthouse, old beech
trees, gardens, and ocean views all around. 90 Seats.

Wayne M. Gibson

Paul O'Reilly, Missy Gaffey and
Shawn Westhoven

Regional American

Truffled, Buttered Sauté of Lobster and
Mussels over Cornmeal Waffles. Seared Foie Gras
on Bourbon French Toast with Fresh Peach Jam.
Vanilla-Scented Lobster and Sweet Peas in a Toasted
Corn Popover.

"Wayne is super-talented! Newport's best
restaurant."

$$$$

White Horse Tavern

26 Marlborough Street, Newport, RI 02848
(401) 849-3600 • Fax (401) 849-7317
Website www.whitehorsetavern.com
Lunch Th.-Sa. Dinner 7 Days. Sunday Brunch.
Decor: An authentic colonial tavern over 300 years
old. 100 Seats.

Brian Conners

Jeff Korecky & Deborah Scott

American

Grilled New England Lobster. Rack of Lamb.
"Great wine list, perfect food."

$$$

RHODE ISLAND

Agora Restaurant

The Westin Hotel, One West Exchange Street
Providence, RI 02903
(401) 598-8011 • Fax (401) 598-8258
Dinner Only M.-Sa.
Decor: A warm, comfortable restaurant that exudes
charm, elegance and style. 75 Seats.

Casey Riley and Erick Salnave

Dana Des Roches

American-Eclectic

Spiced Yellowfin Tuna and Foie Gras with
Black Figs and Chanterelles. Maine Crab and
Avocado Ravioli with Pinenut-Orange Crackers and
Vine-Ripe Tomato-Basil Cream.

"A very creative and talented chef, a beautiful
dining room, and an extensive wine list. Makes for
a great evening."

Al Forno

577 South Main Street
Providence, RI 02903
(401) 272-8058 • Fax (401) 751-7803
Dinner Only Tu.-Sa.
Decor: The ambiance is reminiscent of a small
restaurant in the Tuscan countryside. 100 Seats.

Johanne Killeen & George Germon

Brian Kingsford

Italian-Northern

Dirty Steak. The Grilled Pizza.

"I've considered moving closer to Al Forno just for
the wood-grilled pizzas."

RHODE ISLAND

Providence

La Locanda del Coccio

265 Atwells Avenue, Providence, RI 02903
(401) 273-2652 • Fax (401) 273-6879
Website www.chefwalter.com
Dinner Only M.-Sa.
Decor: Elegant, Victorian interior. 120 Seats.

Walter Potenza   Luga Regoli

Regional Italian

Baked Strangozzi in Terracotta. Brustengo
Umbro. Stoccafisso Anconetano.

"Real Italian cooking, the best."

$$$ AMERICAN EXPRESS   VISA   MasterCard   ◐

New Japan

145 Washington Street
Providence, RI 02903
(401) 351-0300
Lunch Tu.-F. Dinner Tu.-Su.
Decor: A cozy hole in the wall! 30 Seats.

Yukio Hiyama

Japanese

Tempura. Fresh Sashimi.

"Sparklingly fresh sashimi, and extremely creative
new Japanese cooking. Go there on Sunday for
sushi (that's the only day they serve it.)"

$$ AMERICAN EXPRESS   VISA   MasterCard   ◐

RHODE ISLAND

Providence

XO Café

125 North Main Street
Providence, RI 02905
(401) 273-9090 • Fax (401) 861-2816
Website www.xocafe.com
Dinner Only 7 Days.
Decor: An artsy, eclectic and romantic restaurant.
66 Seats.

 John Elkhay Erin Henderson

Asian-New

Grilled Sushi-Grade Tuna with Lobster
Risotto and Pea Tendrils. Huge Pork Chop with
Potato Pyramid and Caramelized Onion, Andouille
Sausage Reduction.

"Very, very unique."

$$$ AMERICAN EXPRESS VISA MasterCard DISCOVER

Tip: Salt balances vinaigrettes that are too acidic... don't forget the salt!
Peter Hoffman, Savoy

"Night of the Blue Shrimp"- The boiled shrimp in our Rémoulade appetizer, for some reason, glowed blue in the dark and nobody would eat them. They were extremely fresh. We think they glowed blue because they were feeding on something phosphorescent. *Brigsten's*

Tip: Use toasted almonds, garlic and fried bread in the Spanish style (i.e. Romesco), as a thickener in sauces, soups, etc.
Stephen Kalt, Spartina

SOUTH CAROLINA

Anson

12 Anson Street, Charleston, SC 29401
(803) 577-0551 • Fax (803) 720-1955
Dinner Only 7 Days.
Decor: A Southern-plantation motif with an al fresco balcony. 225 Seats.

Eric Richards, Mike Lata, Mike Stevens

Rory Fosberry

Regional American

Low-Country Barbecued Black Grouper with Creamy Stone-Ground Grits. Crispy Flounder with Apricot Shallot Sauce.

"This people here are so nice and the food is great!"

$$$

Charleston Grill

The Charleston Place Hotel, 224 King Street
Charleston, SC 29401
(843) 577-4522 • Fax (843) 724-8405
Website www.charleston-place.com
Dinner Only 7 Days.
Decor: Panelled walls, herringbone floors, padded carver chairs and local folk art create the casually elegant ambiance. 130 Seats.

Bob Waggoner   Jeff Moquin

Regional Southern

Maine Lobster Tempura over Lemon Grits and Fried Mini Green Tomatoes in a Yellow Tomato, Tarragon Butter. Baby Lola Rosa Leaves with Chemson Blue Cheese, Marinated Shiitakes and Roasted Hazelnuts in a Sweet Port and Fresh Rosemary Sauce.

"Innovative French cooking with low-country influence."

$$$

SOUTH CAROLINA

Charleston

Magnolias Uptown /Down South

185 East Bay Street, Charleston, SC 29401
(803) 577-7771 • Fax (803) 722-0035
Website www.magnolias-blossom.com
Lunch and Dinner 7 Days.
Decor: Situated in an historic building decorated
with custom iron work and beautiful works of art.
170 Seats.

 Donald Barickman

Regional Southern

Grits. Creative Seafood and Meats.

"Excellent New Southern cuisine." "I go here just
for the grits!"

Peninsula Grill

112 North Market Street
Charleston, SC 29401
(843) 723-0700 • Fax (843) 577-2125
Website www.plantersinn.com/grill
Dinner Only 7 Days.
Decor: Evocative of the Low Country, with
its velvet walls, 19th-Century landscapes and
courtyard dining, located in the historic Planter's
Inn. 100 Seats.

Robert Carter   Andrew Fallen

Regional Southern

Wild Mushroom Grits with Low Country
Oyster Stew. Jumbo Lump Crab, Tomato and
Spinach Salad with Fried Green Tomatoes. Benne
Seed-Crusted Rack of Lamb with Coconut-Mint
Pesto.

"Very consistent food and good service."

SOUTH CAROLINA

Robert's of Charleston

182 East Bay Street, Charleston, SC 29401
(843) 577-7565 • Fax (843) 723-0580
Website www.robertsofcharleston.com
Four-Course Prix-Fixe Dinner W.- Sa. Only.
Decor: A small, intimate dining room done in the
warm, earth tones of Tuscany with original art,
piano music and live singing. 45 Seats.

🔪 Robert Dickson 🍴 Lesa Gregory

🚬 Continental 🍷

🥢 Scallop Mousse with Lobster Sauce. Oriental
Duckling Salad. Chateaubriand, Sauce Béarnaise.

"The 'singing chef' of Charleston opened this new
rendition of one of my old favorite spots."

$$$$ 💳 VISA 💳 MasterCard 🛋️

St. John's Island

Rosebank Farms Café

1886 Andel Bluff Boulevard
St. John's Island, SC 29455
(803) 768-1807 • Fax (803) 768-1371
Lunch and Dinner 7 Days.
Decor: An ecclectic Southern bistro overlooking
Bohicket Marina and the surrounding South
Carolina coastal wetlands. 80 Seats.

🔪 Andrew Casey Taylor 🍴 Rebecca Davis

🚬 Regional Southern 🍸 🍷

🥢 Honey-Buttermilk Fried Chicken with Braised
Cabbage and Roasted Garlic Mashed Potatoes.
Whole Fried Catfish with Firecracker Creole and
Stoneground Grits. Grilled Thick-Cut Pork Chops
over Cheddar Grits with Mushroom Jus, Pepper
Jelly and Tobacco Fried Onions.

"Produce grown on the premises enhances the
incredible down-home cookin'."

$$$ 💳 AMERICAN EXPRESS 💳 VISA 💳 MasterCard 🛋️

SOUTH CAROLINA

Summerville

Dining Room at The Woodlands

125 Parsons Road, Summerville, SC 29483
(803) 875-2600 • Fax (803) 875-2603
Website www.woodlandsinn.com
Lunch 7 Days. Dinner M.-Sa.
Decor: A formal, very elegant restaurant with a fresco of clouds on the ceiling, baroque chairs and crystal. 85 Seats.

 Kenneth Vedrinski Reno Brown

 American-Contemporary

 Golden Tomato Gazpacho with Black Radishes and 50-Year-Old Sherry Vinegar. Crispy Filet of Black Bass with Honski Meji Mushrooms and Chinese Black Bean Sauce. Muscovy Duck Breast with Whole Wheat Couscous and Pomegranate Juice.

"Five-star cuisine, worth the drive." "The total experience!"

$$$$ AMERICAN EXPRESS   VISA   MasterCard   ①   DISCOVER   ∧∥

Tip: *My advice is to continually taste your food at every stage of the cooking process. With every new ingredient and every temperature change, the flavor is altered. Constant tasting ensures a correct level of seasoning when the dish is plated.*
Rocco DiSpirito, Union Pacific

The staff put salt on one crème brûlée, the last of 350 served. When the chef couldn't get it to caramelize, he tasted it and panicked thinking they were all salted. The staff laughed and applauded! *Windsor Court*

ANECDOTES & COOKING TIPS

Tip: A tip from Madame E.: when working with hot peppers, rub your hands with salt first to prevent the oils from getting on your skin.
Lydia Shire, Biba

The Louisiana Wildlife and Fisheries Department elected to create new recipes featuring nuisance animals in the swamplands. The nutria was selected and Chef Folse was contacted to prepare a recipe. CNN picked up on the story and came to Lafitte's Landing to tape a Headline News segment of Chef Folse preparing a Crawfish-Stuffed Leg of Nutria. This segment ran on Headline News to viewers worldwide. *Lafitte's Landing*

Tip: Use dental floss for cutting soft cheese. **Dale Gussett, L'Antibes**

TENNESSEE

Chez Philippe
at the Peabody Hotel

149 Union Avenue, Memphis, TN 38103
(901) 529-4188 • Fax (901) 529-9600
Website www.peabodyhotel.com
Dinner Only M.-Sa.
Decor: Lush, Louis XVI antiques and fabrics.
85 Seats.

Jose Gutierrez   Nancy Askew-Regador

French-Modern

Hush Puppies Stuffed with Shrimp Provençal.
Grits Pudding with Peaches and Honey.

"A five-star restaurant serving great French-
Southern cuisine." "Delicious and delightfully
elegant, yet down-home!"

$$$

Cielo

679 Adams, Memphis, TN 38105
(901) 524-1886 • Fax (901) 526-3635
Lunch Tu.-F. Dinner Tu.-Sa.
Decor: A restored 1886 Victorian mansion turned
eclectic with gold-leaf ceilings and silk banquettes.
65 Seats.

Karen Blockman-Carrier & Don Fox

John Robilio   Fusion

Roasted Beef Tenderloin Au Poivre with
Mustard-Horseradish Oil, Port Wine Reduction
and Porcini-Mushroom Butter. Whole Roasted Fish
with Moroccan Olives, Tomatoes, Garlic-Lemon
Bread Crumbs and Yukon Gold Potatoes.

"A beautiful mix of Caribbean and American
cuisines."

$$$

TENNESSEE

Memphis

dux

The Peabody Hotel, 149 Union Street
Memphis, TN 38103
(901) 529-4199 • Fax (901) 529-3629
Website www.peabodymemphis.com
Breakfast, Lunch and Dinner 7 Days.
Decor: Cozy banquettes and white-linened tables
with windows overlooking the opulent lobby.
140 Seats.

 Scott Lenhart   Paula Hodges

Regional American

Chocolate Apricot Torte.

"Delicious American fare!"

$$$

Erling Jensen, The Restaurant

1044 South Yates Road, Memphis, TN 38119
(901) 763-3700 • Fax (901) 763-3800
Dinner Only 7 Days.
Decor: A converted home that is warm,
comfortable, elegant and conveniently located in
East Memphis, 15 minutes from anywhere in the
city. 100 Seats.

Erling Jensen   Andrew Khalilian

Global

Jumbo Lump Crabcakes with Smoked Red
Bell Pepper Sauce. Rack of Lamb with Pecan,
Mustard, Garlic and Molasses Crust. Fresh Fruit
Tart with Homemade Cinnamon Ice Cream and
Caramel Sauce.

"Wonderful food and a nice wine list."

$$$

TENNESSEE

LuLu Grille

565 Erin Drive, Memphis, TN 38117
(901) 763-3677 • Fax (901) 763-0338
Website www.lulugrille.com
Lunch and Dinner M.-Sa.
Decor: Warm and friendly, neighborhood
atmosphere with hand-painted murals. 145 Seats.

 Scott DeLarme

Don and Leigh McLean

American French Brasserie

Grilled Portobello Mushroom with House-
Smoked Salmon, Caramelized Onion and Dill
Havarti. Homemade Coconut Cake.

"Homey feeling, serving the kind of food you could
eat every night..."

Payne's BBQ

Elvis Presley Boulevard
Memphis, TN 38114
(901) 942-7433
Lunch and Dinner M.-Sa.
Decor: A renovated old service station. 16 Seats.

Emily Payne

Barbecue

Smoked Sausage. Barbecue-Baked Beans.

"Simply some of the best pork barbecue, beans and
sweet mustard slaw I'd ever imagined. You have to
love a place where you still have to buy your drink
from a Coke machine."

TENNESSEE

Nashville

Belle Meade Brasserie

101 Page Road, Nashville, TN 37205
(615) 356-5450 • Fax (615) 356-5456
Website www.bellemeadebrasserie.com
Dinner Only M.-Sa.
Decor: A sophisticated, romantic bistro tucked
away in the posh Belle Meade section of Nashville.
85 Seats, Dining Room. 24 Seats, Outdoor Deck.

Robert Siegel

Lisa Carrie and Mark Rubin

American-Contemporary

Mahogany Duckling with Spiced Peaches.
Skillet-Roasted Salmon with Potato Pancakes and
Fresh Spinach Sauté. Double-Thick, Thai Barbecue
Pork Chop.

"Always a great meal, great service and great
atmosphere—what a wine list!"

The Wild Boar

2014 Broadway, Nashville, TN 27203
(615) 329-1313 • Fax (615) 329-4930
Website www.citysearch.com/nas/wildboar
Dinner Only M.-Sa.
Decor: An elegant, old European hunting lodge.
120 Seats.

Guillaume Berlion

Abby Benrahmoun

French-Modern

Maine Lobster and Diver Sea Scallops with
Saffron Whipped Potatoes and Sundried Tomato Jus
de Viande. Pan-Seared Australian Lamb Tenderloin
over Wild Mushroom Tart with Truffle Infused Jus
and A Light Garlic Cream.

"Impeccable service, great atmosphere, a superb
wine list and, the food's good too!"

290

Anecdotes & Cooking Tips

Tip: When seeding a pomegranate, slice it in half and hit the side with a kitchen spoon until all the seeds fall out. **Douglas Katz, Moxie**

Chef Susan Regis gave Lydia Shire a real, live piglet for her birthday. He came squeeking into the kitchen with balloons tied around his little neck, and Lydia shrieked and dropped her mixing bowl full of beans! He ended up sleeping in the pantry for the night, and no, he wasn't dinner... **Biba**

Tip: The most important tools in your kitchen are your knives. So invest in good ones and make sure they are properly cared for.
Chip Sears, The Metro Wine Bar

Tip: Cook food as little as possible. When you're cooking Italian, limit each dish to two to three main ingredients, and you'll be on your way to what's really Italian.
Paul Bartolotta, Spiaggia

When the chef greeted Jacques Pepin in drag...Pepin didn't even flinch. **Pignoli**

Tip: Refrigerate onions before cutting to keep the tears down.
Philippe Boulot, Heathman

TEXAS

Castle Hill Café

1101 West 5th Street, Austin, TX 78703
(512) 476-0728 • Fax (512) 476-0055
Lunch M.-F. Dinner M.-Sa.
Decor: A very Southwestern look. 100 Seats.

David Dailey

Eclectic

Curried Lamb Empanadas. Smoked Pork Tenderloin Medallions in Chipotle, Chile-Apple Butter Sauce with Spiced Chutney and Pumpkin-Sage Tamale.

"Both the place and the food are lively!" "Cool combinations!"

Jeffrey's Restaurant

1204 West Lynn, Austin, TX 78703
(512) 477-5584 • Fax (512) 474-7279
Website www.citysearch.com\aus\jeffreys
Dinner Only M.-Sa.
Decor: Austin's special-occasion restaurant for 23 years, very warm and romantic. 120 Seats.

David Garrido   Jim Laine

Regional American

Duck and Shrimp with Black Bean Ravioli and Porcini Mushrooms. Crispy Oysters with Yuca Root and Habanero-Honey Aioli.

"We celebrate all our special occasions here."

TEXAS

Dallas

Anzu

4620 McKennie Avenue, Dallas, TX 75205
(214) 526-7398 • Fax (214) 521-3798
Lunch M.-F. Dinner 7 Days.
Decor: A modern-looking restaurant with granite floor, cement tables and walls and 10,000 origami birds fluttering across the ceiling. 96 Seats.

 Lawrence Doyle  Phina Nakamoto

 Asian-Pacific Rim

 Saki-Kasu-Marinated, Broiled Black Cod on Field Greens with Grapefruit and Chinese Black Vinegar. Tea-Grilled Lambchops with Eggplant Caponata.

"Easily the prettiest restaurant in Dallas, and often some of the best Pan Asian cuisine around."

Aquaknox

3214 Knox Street, Dallas, TX 75205
(214) 219-2782 • Fax (214) 219-0022
Website www.aquaknox.com
Dinner Only 7 Days.
Decor: A contemporary, minimalistic restaurant with Asian influences and water themes. 130 Seats.

 Stephan Pyles  George Majdalani

 Global

 Sugar-Cane-Skewered Tuna with Black Beans, Couscous and Pineapple-Banana Chutney. Canela-Scented Oak Roasted Lobster with Pumpkin-White Truffle Risotto.

"Very creative, delicious seafood by the master responsible for Star Canyon."

Daddy Jack's Lobster House

1916 Greenville Avenue, Dallas, TX 75206
(214) 826-4910 • Fax (214) 827-3330
Dinner Only 7 Days.
Decor: A casual, homey lobster and chowder house
with checkered tablecloths and memorabilia from
New England. 60 Seats.

 Jack Chaplin   Cary Ray

Seafood

Lobster Potato Cake with Lobster Brandy
Cream Sauce. Shellfish Fra Diavolo. New England
Dinner: 1 Pound each of Lobster and Crablegs with
Corn on the Cob and Baked Potato.

"I think this is the best seafood in Dallas."

Star Canyon

3102 Oak Lawn #144, Dallas, TX 75219
(214) 520-7827 • Fax (214) 520-2667
Website www.starcanyon.com
Dinner Only 7 Days.
Decor: A sophisticated, Texas ranch look with
contemporary Western elements. 165 Seats.

Stephan Pyles   Jesse Hernandez

Regional Southwestern

Bone-In Cowboy Ribeye with Pinto Bean-
Wild Mushroom Ragout and Red Chile Onion
Rings. Seared Duck Breast and Confit of Duck Leg
with Pepita-Herb Bread Pudding, Tart Cherry
Sauce and Creamed Swiss Chard.

"Looks great, tastes even better! Lots of fun and
priced right." "Exciting, creative, delicious!"

TEXAS

Dallas

The Mansion on Turtle Creek

2821 Turtle Creek Boulevard
Dallas, TX 75219
(214) 559-2100 • Fax (214) 520-5896
Website www.rosewood-hotels.com
Lunch M.-F. Dinner 7 Days. Sunday Brunch.
Decor: The residential-feeling restaurant is housed within the Sheppard King Mansion and features fireplaces, antiques, wood panelling, carved ceilings and leaded glass windows. 120 Seats.

 Dean Fearing Alex Jureeratana

 Regional Southwestern

 Warm Lobster Taco with Yellow Tomato Salsa and Jicama Salad. Tortilla Soup.

"The tasty tortilla soup lives up to its reputation; great service and atmosphere." "Dean knows how to marry flavors together for an explosion of tastes in your mouth!" "Rustic elegance..."

$$$$

Houston

Americas

1800 Post Oak Boulevard
Houston, TX 77056
(713) 961-1492 • Fax (713) 626-2701
Lunch M.-F. Dinner M.-Sa.
Decor: "A combination of The Jetsons and The Flinstones," a multicultural, pan-generational decor. 210 Seats.

 Michael Cordua Frank Ramirez

 Global

 Churrascos. Tres Leches. Cuisine of the American continent.

"Authentic pan-Continental creativity."

$$$

Anthony's

4007 Westheimer, Houston, TX 77027
(713) 961-0552 • Fax (713) 621-7826
Lunch M.-F. Dinner M.-Sa.
Decor: An elegant, continental bistro. 150 Seats.

Russell Cody   Maeve O'Gorman

Continental

Duckling Osso Bucco. Black Angus
Tenderloin. Chateaubriand of Swordfish.

"Some of the most exciting food around."

$$$

Brasil

2604 Dunlavy, Houston, TX 77006
(713) 528-1993 • Fax (713) 528-1993
Breakfast, Lunch and Dinner 7 Days.
Decor: A combination of old and new with
industrial windows adding extra light to this rustic,
warm interior. 80 Seats.

Magda Sayeg

American-Eclectic

Green Eggs & Ham: Focaccia Topped with
Sautéed Spinach, Prosciutto, Asiago and Poached
Egg. Pizza Verde.

"Casual and delicious. Fun and inventive!"

$

TEXAS

Houston

Café Annie

1728 Post Oak Boulevard
Houston, TX 77056
(713) 840-1111 • Fax (713) 840-1558
Lunch M.-F. Dinner M.-Sa.
Decor: A posh restaurant with mahogany, Italian marble, white tablecloths and a fabulous bar.
125 Seats.

Robert Del Grande   Victor Ventura

American-New

Crab Meat Tostado with Avocado Relish. Mussel Soup with Cilantro and Serrano Chile. Coffee-Roasted Filet of Beef with Sage Aioli, Rustic Mashed Potatoes, Fennel and Mushrooms.

"Wonderful cuisine and hospitality!" "We think the food is excellent, full of flavor, and the service is unsurpassed!"

Daily Review Café

3412 West Lamar, Houston, TX 77019
(713) 520-9217 • Fax (713) 520-1916
Lunch and Dinner Tu.-Sa. Sunday Brunch.
Decor: Located in a late 1800's building. Concrete, wood and exposed beams contribute to the industrial aesthetic, softened by the patio, garden and private dining room. 85 Seats.

Claire Smith   Janice Beeson

Global

Lamb Stew. Chicken Pot Pie with Fennel.

"Good, hearty, honest cooking."

Monica Pope's Boulevard Bistrot

4319 Montrose Boulevard
Houston, TX 77006
(713) 524-6922 • Fax (713) 524-9728
Lunch and Dinner Tu.-Su. Brunch Sa. & Su.
Decor: An eclectic bistro with great outdoor dining along the Boulevard or on the garden patio. 70 Seats, Dining Room. 60 Seats, Outside. 60 Seats, Private Functions.

Monica Pope   Andrea Lazar

Eclectic

Pistachio-Crusted Salmon with Warm Spinach Salad and Mandarin-Orange Sauce. Mushroom Pâté with Vanilla Bean Vinaigrette and Toasted Hazelnuts.

"Fine food and interesting flavors!"

Nit Noi Thai Restaurant

2462 Bolsover and 5211 Kelvin
Houston, TX 77056
(713) 524-8114 • Fax (713) 789-1989
Lunch M.-Sa. Dinner 7 Days.
Decor: Elegant Thai murals.
48 Seats.

Alice Vonguisith

Doi and Malisa Heckler

Thai

Soft Spring Roll. Putt Thai Korat. Crispy Red Snapper.

"The best Thai food in the United States, bar none!"

Tip: Use sea salt with ocean fish, it's where they come from!
Bill Shapiro, BLT's Cobblefish

I asked a dishwasher to drain the stock pot, so he did, throwing away the stock and saving the bones. *Five Lakes Grill*

Tip: When cooking black bass, put it in the hot pan skin side down, then place another, cold stainless steel sauté pan on top of the fish for even cooking and crispiness.
Francesco Martorella, Brasserie Perrier

The Tree Room

Sundance Resort, Provo Canyon
Sundance, UT 84604
(801) 223-4200 • Fax (801) 223-4213
Website www.sundance-utah.com
Dinner Only 7 Days.
Decor: Nestled in the Wasatch Mountains, elegant candlelit dining in a setting graced by Native American art and memorabilia from Robert Redford's personal collection. 86 Seats.

 Trey Foshee   Kendall Wimmer

Regional American

Black Bass with Morels, Spring Pea Purée and Truffled Onion Sauce. Chilled Tomato-Basil Soup with Fresh Peekytoe Crab Meat and Avocado. Seasonal Chef's Tasting Menu.

"A very talented young chef to watch!"

Tip: *Our favorite trick is taking half of the oil out of vinaigrettes and replacing with chicken stock. It makes it lighter and healthier.*
Trish Morrissey,
Philadelphia Fish

A collection of Madonna's bustiers, Danny DeVito and Bette Midler's shoes, Tim Allen's tool belt and other Hollywood memorabilia on display in an Asian restaurant! **Mon Jin Lau**

Tip: *When cleaning chanterelle mushrooms, peel down along the stem. You can then sauté them in advance until the stem is tender, and keep until ready to use.*
Vince Alberici, The Marker

VERMONT

Hemingway's

U.S. Route 4, Killington, VT 05751
(802) 422-3886 • Fax (802) 422-3468
Website www.hemingwaysrestaurant.com
Dinner Only W.-Su. Seasonal.
Decor: Eclectic design in a restored 1860
stagecoach stop. 60 Seats.

🍴 Ted Fondulas   🍽 Linda Fondulas

🚬 American-New   🍸 🍷

⭐ Local Trout and Venison. Game Birds. Hand-
Rolled Pasta.

"Imaginative, excellent food and decor."

$$$ AMERICAN EXPRESS   VISA   MasterCard   👔

The Norwich Inn Dining Room

325 Main Street, Norwich, VT 05055
(802) 649-1143
Breakfast, Lunch and Dinner Tu.-Su.
Decor: A formal, Victorian dining room and a more
casual Victorian brew pub, as well. 60 Seats.

🍴 Terrence Webb   🍽 Sally Wilson

🚬 Continental   🍸 🍷

⭐ Fresh Maine Crabcakes. Center-Cut Veal
Chop with Wild Mushrooms. Asian Duckling with
Wild Rice Stir-Fry.

"Excellent and creative hand-crafted food and
awesome beer that is made on the premises."

$$$ AMERICAN EXPRESS   VISA   MasterCard   ①   DISCOVER   👔

VERMONT

Richmond

Blue Seal

Bridge Street, P.O. Box 625
Richmond, VT 05477
(802) 434-5949
Lunch Sa. Only. Dinner Tu.-Sa.
Decor: A tiny, country-chic restaurant in a historic building. 34 Seats.

👤 Debra Weinstein

🚬 American-Modern **🍴**

⭐ Chili-Rubbed New York Strip Steak with Blue Seal Sauce, Grilled Red Onions, Smoked Chili Fries, Crumbled Blue Cheese and Smoked Ketchup. Marinated Portobello Mushroom with Grilled New Potatoes, Sautéed Spinach, Roasted Tomato and Goat Cheese with a Lemon Thyme Vinaigrette.

"Creative casual dining out in the sticks."
"Surprise: there's a practiced hand in the kitchen."

West Dover

The Inn at Sawmill Farms

Route 100 and Crosstown Road
West Dover, VT 05356
(802) 464-8131 • Fax (802) 464-1130
Dinner Only 7 Days.
Decor: The rustic yet elegant restaurant is located in a renovated old barn with exposed beams. Tables are set with china and crystal. 60 Seats.

👤 Brill Williams

🍷 Bobbie Dee Molitor and Wes Haight

🚬 Continental **🍸** **🍴**

⭐ Menu changes seasonally.

"A non-compromising, long-established restaurant with high-quality food and an excellent wine list."

VERMONT

Windham Hill Inn

311 Lawrence Drive
West Townshend, VT 05359
(802) 874-4080 • Fax (802) 874-4702
Website www.windhamhill.com
Breakfast 7 Days. Dinner Th.-Tu.
Decor: An elegant, romantic country inn nestled
into the green mountains of Vermont featuring
candlelit dining overlooking "Frog Pond." 24 Seats.

Cameron Howard

Grigs and Pat Markham

American-Contemporary

Wild Mushroom in Herbed Phyllo with
Madeira Tarragon Sauce. Vermont Maple
Decadence Dessert. Small Tiramisu.

"Simple, heart-warming cuisine." "Cameron has
trained with some great chefs, and it shows!"

Jackson House Inn

37 Route 4 West, Woodstock, VT 05091
(802) 457-2065 • Fax (802) 457-9290
Website www.jacksonhouse.com
Dinner Only Th.-M.
Decor: Elegantly nestled amidst English gardens
and the green mountains of Vermont. 45 Seats.

Brendan Nolan   David Madison

American-New

Pan-Seared Foie Gras with Black Mission Figs
and Gingerbread Brioche. Cider-Poached Salmon
with Toasted Almond Couscous and Braised Chard.

"A great place to escape the city."

Tip: Cucumbers are peeled from the middle to the ends, otherwise they turn bitter. Used coffee grounds are good for your flowers and your vegetable garden. **Albert Breuers, the Old Guard House Inn**

One of our waiters was standing in front of the restaurant, in full view of the dining room, getting soaked by a water cannon from a passing car of teenagers. **City Grocery**

Tip: When cooking legumes, don't salt the water until after the beans have softened. Salt causes a chemical reaction with the skin of the bean and prevents it from softening. **Johanne Killeen and George Germon, Al Forno**

VIRGINIA

Mamma Zu

501 South Pine Street, Richmond, VA 23220
(804) 788-4205 • Fax (804) 788-4225
Lunch M.-F. Dinner M.-Sa.
Decor: A corner storefront dive with a fire hydrant in front that sprays all summer long. 60 Seats.

Ed Vasaio

Italian

Risotto with Veal Heart. Veal Sweetbreads. Osso Bucco.

"Food with passion."

$$$

The Frog and The Redneck

1423 East Cary Street, Richmond, VA 23219
(804) 648-3764 • Fax (804) 782-0910
Website www.frogandredneck.com
Dinner Only M.-Sa.
Decor: An upscale bistro with neon, cartoon murals by Happy The Artist and fun, lively music. 150 Seats.

Jimmy Sneed   Adam Steely

American-Modern

Sweet Red Pepper Soup with Crabmeat. Sautéed Local "Velvet" Soft-Shell Crabs. "Redneck Risotto" with Local Smoked Sausage, Sautéed Mushrooms and Aged Parmesan.

"The best music and fantastic soft shell crabs!"
"This is one of our favorites on the funky side!"

$$$

VIRGINIA

Upper Arlington

Bistro Roti

1693 West Lane Avenue
Upper Arlington, VA 43221
(614) 481-7684
Lunch and Dinner M.-Sa.
Decor: A casually elegant, upscale bistro look.
White tablecloths. 180 Seats.

Jack Cory   Ed Miller

American Bistro

Blackened Rare Tuna with Garlic Whipped
Potatoes and Beurre Blanc. Smoked BBQ Pork
Chop with Bacon Cheddar Whips and Jack Daniels
Peppercorn Demi Glace. Horseradish Crusted Sea
Scallops with Dijon Wine Sauce.

Virginia Beach

Coastal Grill

1427 North Great Neck Road
Virginia Beach, VA 23454
(757) 496-3348
Dinnery Only 7 Days.
Decor: A simple, Country-French-style room with
dark wood and white lace curtains. 66 Seats.

Jerry Bryan

Regional American

Pan-Seared Tuna with Lemon Thyme Butter.
Roasted Chicken.

"Simple, fresh, and consistent cuisine."

VIRGINIA

The Inn at Little Washington

Middle & Main Streets
Washington, VA 22747
(540) 675-3800 • Fax (540) 675-3100
Dinner Only W.-Su.
Dinner 7 Days in May and Oct.
Decor: A Victorian ambiance with fine antiques.
80 Seats.

🐾 Patrick O'Connell

🚬 French Eclectic 🍸

⭐ Barbecue Baby Back Rack of Lamb in a Pecan
Crust. Charcoal-Grilled Poussin Marinated in
Blackberry Vinegar. Medallions of Veal Loin with
English Peas, Virginia Ham and Fettucine.

"One of America's biggest success stories." "I love
Patrick's delicious dishes and tongue-in-cheek menu
descriptions." "Maybe the best creator of eclectic
food, well worth the trip."

$$$$ 💳 VISA 💳 MasterCard 👔

The Trellis Restaurant

403 Duke of Gloucester Street
Williamsburg, VA 23185
(757) 229-8610 • Fax (757) 221-0450
Lunch and Dinner 7 Days.
Decor: A contemporary look with a patio on
historic Duke of Gloucester Street. 197 Seats.

🐾 Marcel Desaulniers   🍽 John Curtis

🚬 Regional American   🍸 🍷

⭐ Curried Apple and Onion Soup. Grilled Farm-
Raised Catfish with Gulf Shrimp and Fire-Roasted
Corn and Red Pepper Purée. The Original Death
By Chocolate.

"Innovative cuisine served in a contemporary
restaurant." "Desserts by Marcel are legendary and
exquisite!" "The Chocolate Master!"

$$$ 💳 AMERICAN EXPRESS 💳 VISA 💳 MasterCard 👔

Tip: We use dried corn cobbs for all of our smoking. They give a light yet distinctive flavor.
Wayne Gibson, Castle Hill Inn

A guest, after completing a first course of Duck Confit on Warm Green Lentils, commented, "Those were the best capers I've ever eaten!" *Magnolia Grill*

Tip: To preserve freshness and flavor, keep black or white truffles in rice, in a jar, covered and sealed. The rice will also become wonderfully aromatic.
**Walter Potenza,
La Locanda del Coccio**

WASHINGTON

Fall City

The Herb Farm

32804 Issaquah Fall City Road
Fall City, WA 98024
(206) 284-5667 • Fax (206) 789-2279
Website www.theherbfarm.com
Dinner Only Th.-Sa. at 7pm sharp.
Decor: A casually elegant restaurant with fresh
flowers and beautiful crystal. 49 Seats.

 Jerry Traunfeld

 Regional American

 Nine-Course Dégustation Menu Only.
Zucchini Squash Blossom Stuffed with Copper
River King Salmon on a Bed of Fresh Tomato
Coulis. Herb-Marinated Rack of Ellensburg Lamb
with Wild Huckleberry Sauce and Coriander
Potatoes.

"Ron and Carrie Zimmerman are the tops! The
food, centered around fresh vegetables and herbs, is
exquisite!" "Traunfeld is a master!"

$$$$

Seattle

Campagne

86 Pine Street, Seattle, WA 98101
(206) 728-2800 • Fax (206) 448-7740
Dinner Only 7 Days.
Decor: A sophisticated, urban setting in the heart
of downtown Seattle with windows overlooking the
historic Pike Place Farmer's Market. 70 Seats.

James Drohman Peter Lewis

French-Country

Veal Chop Stuffed with Ham, Watercress and
Cantal Cheese on Stewed Pearl Barley. House-
Cured Sturgeon Gravlax served with Blinis, Crème
Fraîche and Osetra Caviar. Traditional Cassoulet.

"A good, country French restaurant with a
Northwest twist." "A find!"

$$$

WASHINGTON

Seattle

Flying Fish

2234 1st Avenue, Seattle, WA 98121
(206) 728-8595 • Fax (206) 728-1551
Dinner Only 7 Days.
Decor: A colorful, casual restaurant featuring two large paintings by local artist, Bryan Yeck. 120 Seats.

Christine Keff

Seafood

Thai Crabcake with Lemongrass Mayonnaise. Salt and Pepper Dungeness Crab with Wheat Soba Noodles and Carrot-Daikon Salad.

"Both the food and the staff are wonderful!" "Creatively-prepared seafood in an upbeat atmosphere!" "I think this restaurant is a great example of excellent Pacific Rim cuisine!"

$$$

Fullers
at The Sheraton Seattle Hotel Towers

1400 Sixth Avenue, Seattle, WA 98101
(206) 447-5544 • Fax (206) 287-5508
Lunch M.-F. Dinner M.-Sa.
Decor: An elegant dining room with a fountain in the center. 134 Seats.

Monique Andrée Barbeau

Bonny Hawley

Regional American

Roasted Beet and Shallot Vinaigrette Tossed with Field Greens. Saffron and Sumac-Dusted Rack of Lamb with Barley, Black-eyed Peas, Port and Mango.

"A wonderful Asian/Mediterranean slant on contemporary French food, with the service details of an excellent restaurant in France."

$$$

WASHINGTON

Palace Kitchen

2030 5th Ave., Seattle, WA 98121
(206) 448-2001 • Fax (206) 448-1979
Website www.tomdouglas.com
Lunch and Dinner 7 Days.
Decor: Techno-industrial, urban bar feel. Italian chandeliers, a huge U-shaped bar, 20-foot ceilings, and an open kitchen. 85 Seats.

 Tom Douglas and Matt Costello

 Pam Leydon

 American Bistro

 Applewood-fired rotisserie. Nightly specials include: Leg of Lamb, Roasted Chicken. Featuring American farmstead cheeses and handmade pastas.

"A great place to take my kids for good bistro food." "Hearty and heart-warming 'real food'."

Rover's

2808 East Madison Street
Seattle, WA 98112
(206) 325-7442 • Fax (206) 325-1092
Website www.rovers-seattle.com
Dinner Only Tu.-Sa.
Decor: A cozy, romantic house turned into a restaurant. 49 Seats.

 Thierry Rautureau Cyril Frechier

 French-Modern

 Five-Course Dégustation Menu. Five-Course Vegetarian Menu. Eight-Course Grand Menu.

"Thierry is one of the best chefs in the Pacific Northwest, his cuisine is truly art." "Innovative, delicious, and unerring in his tantalizing combinations." "Very well-chosen wine program."

WASHINGTON

Seattle

Wild Ginger

1400 Western Avenue, Seattle, WA 98101
(206) 623-4450 • Fax (206) 623-8265
Lunch M.-Sa. Dinner 7 Days.
Decor: A casually elegant, intimate restaurant with
soft lighting. 120 Seats.

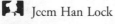 Jccm Han Lock

 Asian-Southeast

 Fragrant and Crispy Duck with Plum Sauce.
Black Pepper Scallops, Wok-Fried with a Touch of
Soy. Satay Bar.

"Great American-Asian cooking; clean and lean
cuisine." "Fanciful flavors in a peacefully vibrant
setting."

$$$ AMERICAN EXPRESS VISA MasterCard ◐ DISCOVER

Tip: Use a few beets when cooking red wine sauce to keep a deep red color. **Ken Vedrinski, The Dining Room at The Woodlands**

A harried waiter rushes into the kitchen and calls out, "One alphabet soup, hold the alphabet!" **East of Suez**

Tip: Try roasting your vegetables or mirepoix before making a soup or stock for a more robust undertone to the flavor. **Andrew Casey Taylor, Rosebank Farms Café**

I asked the new dishwasher to wash and cut some potatoes. He put them on a rack and ran them through the dishwasher!
The Creamery

Tip: To make perfect al dente pasta, do not rinse it in cold water after cooking. Instead, drain off the water in a colander, toss with a touch of olive oil and salt and spread pasta on a baking sheet. Allow to air-dry. **Robert Siegel, Belle Meade Brasserie**

WISCONSIN

Mangia

5717 Sheridan Road, Kenosha, WI 53140
(414) 652-4285 • Fax (414) 652-9313
Lunch M.-F. Dinner 7 Days.
Decor: An authentic Italian trattoria atmosphere.
120 Seats.

 Laura Piper

Italian

Farfalle with Cream Sauce, Shrimp and Broccoli. Osso Bucco, A Traditional Rendition with Risotto Milanese.

"Well-executed and satisfying, elegant Italian cooking."

The Clubhouse on Madeline Island

Old Fort Road, Lapointe, WI 54850
(715) 747-2612 • Fax (715) 779-3117
Dinner Only W.-Su. Seasonal.
Decor: After a relaxing ferry ride from Bayfield to Madeline Island you will enjoy the spectacular, panoramic view of the Madeline Island Golf Course and Marina overlooking Lake Superior. 85 Seats.

Jim Webster   Randy Anderson

Regional American

Wisconsin Chèvre-Stuffed Crispy Potatoes. Home-Smoked Lake Superior Trout and Whitefish with Locally-Grown Baby Greens.

"Great food and a wonderful wine list, not a bad island to be marooned on!"

WISCONSIN

Madison

L'Etoile

25 North Pinckney Street
Madison, WI 53703
(608) 251-0500 • Fax (608) 251-7577
Dinner Only M.-Sa.
Decor: Casual elegance with brass fixtures, white linen and fresh roses. 60 Seats.

Odessa Piper　　Kamille Adamany

Regional American

Seared Foie Gras with Cranberry Gastrique. Rack of Crawford Farm Lamb. Hickory Nut Caramel Pastry Purse.

"You can find excellent food, intelligent service, and an interesting wine list here. Try it!"

$$$　VISA　MasterCard　DISCOVER

Milwaukee

Sanford

1547 North Jackson Street
Milwaukee, WI 53202
(414) 276-9608 • Fax (414) 278-8509
Dinner Only M.-Sa.
Decor: A small, storefront restaurant in a historic Italian neighborhood with a warm and comfortable dining room. 50 Seats.

Sanford D'Amato　　Angela D'Amato

American-Modern

Grilled, Rare, Marinated Tuna with Cumin Wafers and Cilantro Dressing. Seared Red Snapper on Crab Hash with Red Onion and Pancetta Vinaigrette.

"Elegant, refined, delicious."

$$$　AMERICAN EXPRESS　VISA　MasterCard　◑

WISCONSIN

Wauwatosa

Ristorante Bartolotta

7616 West State Street
Wauwatosa, WI 53213
(414) 771-7910 • Fax (414) 771-1589
Lunch M.-F. Dinner 7 Days.
Decor: A charmingly quaint, rustic room with lace curtains, hardwood floors and old family photographs, literally a trip into Tuscany. 60 Seats.

 John Korycki and Paul Bartolotta

 John Halvorson

 Italian-Northern

 Pappardelle with a Rich Duck Ragu. Roasted Cornish Hen with Rosemary, Lemon and Caramelized Brussel Sprouts.

"Consistently tasty Italian food in a homey and comfortable setting."

INDEX TO RESTAURANTS

INDEX TO CUISINE

329

DINING JOURNAL

DINING JOURNAL